The Great European Stage Directors

Volume 8

The Great European Stage Directors

Volume 8

Bausch, Castellucci, Fabre

Edited by Luk Van den Dries and Timmy De Laet
Series Editor: Simon Shepherd

methuen | drama

LONDON • NEW YORK • OXFORD • NEW DELHI • SYDNEY

METHUEN DRAMA
Bloomsbury Publishing Plc
50 Bedford Square, London, WC1B 3DP, UK
1385 Broadway, New York, NY 10018, USA
29 Earlsfort Terrace, Dublin 2, Ireland

BLOOMSBURY, METHUEN DRAMA and the Methuen Drama logo are trademarks of
Bloomsbury Publishing Plc

First published in hardback in Great Britain 2019
This paperback edition published 2024

Cover design by Adriana Brioso
Cover image: *Tragedia Endogonidia: B.#03*. Processed by the Project ARCH:
Archival Research and Cultural Heritage: The Theatre Archive of Societas Raffaello Sanzio
www.arch-srs.com. (© Luca Del Pia / Societas Raffaello Sanzio)

A catalogue record for this book is available from the British Library.

A catalog record for this book is available from the Library of Congress.

ISBN: HB: 978-1-4742-5410-6
       HB Pack: 978-1-4742-5416-8
           PB: 978-1-3504-4584-0
       PB Set: 978-1-3504-4599-4
         ePDF: 978-1-4742-5996-5
        eBook: 978-1-3504-6194-9

Series: Great Stage Directors

Typeset by Integra Software Services Pvt. Ltd.
Printed and bound in Great Britain

CONTENTS

Jan Fabre 145

LIST OF FIGURES

NOTES ON CONTRIBUTORS

Thomas Crombez is a Lecturer in Philosophy of Art and History of Graphic Design at the Royal Academy of Fine Arts (Antwerp). He is a member of the research group ArchiVolt, which specializes in archives and the avant-garde. Further research interests are the history of aesthetics; avant-garde theatre and typography; mass theatre; and new methodologies for the humanities, such as digital text collections and data visualization. Recent books include the monograph *De moord op de kunst: Een historische inleiding tot de kunstfilosofie* (The Murder of Art: An Historical Introduction to Aesthetics; 2014) as well as the co-edited volumes *The Locus of Tragedy* (2008) and *Mass Theatre in Interwar Europe* (2014). In 2016, Crombez founded Letterwerk, an Antwerp-based publishing house and design studio.

Timmy De Laet is an Associate Professor of Theatre and Dance Studies at the University of Antwerp and a Lecturer at the BA and MA Dance program of the Royal Conservatoire Antwerp. His research interests include the reiterative nature of live performance in relation to archivization, documentation and historiography. He has published on these topics in journals as *Performance Research, Tanz* and *Muséologies*, as well as in the edited collections *Performing Memory in Art and Popular Culture* (2013), *Moments: A History of Performance in 10 Acts* (2013) and *The Oxford Handbook of Dance and Reenactment* (2017). His research has been supported by the Research Foundations Flanders, the Fulbright Commission and the Belgian American Educational Foundation (BAEF).

Mariama Diagne is a dance scholar at the Freie Universität Berlin, CRC 1512, Intervening Arts. After training as a dancer at the Dance Theatre Harlem (New York City), she studied Media, Theatre and Music (Bayreuth) as well as Dance Theory (Berlin). In her book *Schweres Schweben* (2019), she examines the specific stagings of antic myths (Orpheus) in Pina Bausch's Tanztheater. Further research interests are re-reading dance history by re-writing its aesthetic and ethic threads from the colonial period until today. As a researcher, she worked on several projects at the Pina Bausch Foundation.

Hans-Thies Lehmann was Professor Emeritus in Theatre Studies at the Johann Wolfgang Goethe-Universität Frankfurt am Main (Germany). He was also a Visiting Professor at the University of Amsterdam and at the Institut für Angewandte Theaterwissenschaft (Giessen). His most important book publications include *Bertolt Brecht's 'Hauspostille': Text und kollektives Lesen* (Bertolt Brecht's 'Manual of Piety': Text and Collective Readings; with Helmuth Lethen, 1978), *Theater und Mythos. Die Konstitution des Subjekts im Diskurs der antiken Tragödie* (Theatre and Myth: The Constitution of the Subject in the Discourse of Antique Tragedy; 1991), *Postdramatisches Theater* (1999), *Heiner Müller Handbuch* (Heiner Müller Handbook; 2003) and *Tragödie und Dramatisches Theater* (Tragedy and Dramatic Theatre; 2013).

Eleni Papalexiou is an Associate Professor at the Department of Theatre Studies, University of the Peloponnese, specializing in Theatre Genetics, Performance Analysis, as well as Digital Humanities and Arts. Her books include *La tragédie grecque sur la scène contemporaine* (The Greek Tragedy on the Contemporary Stage; ANRT-Université de Lille 3, 2005), *Όταν ο λόγος μετατρέπεται σε ύλη: Romeo Castellucci/Socìetas Raffaello Sanzio* (When the words turn into matter; 2009) and the forthcoming *Origins: The Archive of Socìetas Raffaello Sanzio* (co-edited with Avra Xepapadakou). She worked at the archive of Socìetas Raffaello Sanzio as a principal investigator in two European-funded research projects: 'Archivio' (2012–13) and 'Arch: Archival Research and Cultural Heritage-Aristeia II' (2014–15). She is currently the academic consultant and curator of the archive of Socìetas Raffaello Sanzio.

Luk Van den Dries is Professor Emeritus at the University of Antwerp (Belgium). His research deals with contemporary theatre, with a specific focus on post-dramatic aesthetics; representations of the body in contemporary performing arts; creative processes in the arts. His latest book publications include *Jan Fabre: Esthétique du paradoxe* (Jan Fabre: Aesthetics of the Paradox; co-edited with Marianne Beauviche, 2013); *Mass Theatre in Interwar Europe* (co-edited with Thomas Crombez, 2014); *Het geopende lichaam: Verzamelde opstellen over Jan Fabre* (The Opened Body: Collected Essays on Jan Fabre; 2014); *Theater: Een Westerse geschiedenis* (Theatre: A Western History, co-edited with Thomas Crombez, Jelle Koopmans, Frank Peeters and Karel Van Haesebrouck, 2015).

Royd Climenhaga Word is on the Arts Faculty at Eugene Lang College/The New School University in New York City, teaching in Integrated Arts and Theatre. He writes on the intersections between dance and theatre, including the books *Pina Bausch* (2009) and *The Pina Bausch Sourcebook: The Making of Tanztheater* (2013). Royd is currently working on a book on twentieth-century performance and culture which draws connections between popular performance traditions and the avant-garde in their cultural context. He also works as a grant writer and development consultant for several NYC arts organizations.

ACKNOWLEDGEMENTS

The editors of this book are grateful to Simon Shepherd, series editor of *The Great European Stage Directors*, for his invitation to compose a volume on three directors who have left an indelible mark on post-war European theatre. His guidance and encouragements ensured the successful completion of this project. We also want to thank all contributing authors for their continued cooperation and their patient responsiveness to all our queries.

We also wish to express our gratitude to the following companies and institutions for the use of copyright material: the Pina Bausch Foundation, the Socìetas Raffaello Sanzio and Troubleyn/Jan Fabre. Special thanks are due to the individual photographers for their generous approval to reprint their images: Bettina Stoess, Patrick T. Sellitto, Wonge Bergmann, Filip Van Roe and Jean Pierre Stoop.

Every effort has been made to trace copyright holders and to obtain their permission for the use of copyright material. The publisher apologizes for any errors or omissions in the above list and would be grateful if notified of any corrections that should be incorporated in future reprints or editions of this book.

Introduction to the Series

Simon Shepherd

The beginnings of directing

Directors have become some of the celebrities of contemporary theatre. Yet for most of its life, and across a range of practices, theatre has managed perfectly well without directors, celebrated or otherwise.

This is not to say that it has lacked direction, so to speak. Some form of directing, by actors, prompters, stage managers, designers, has always featured as an activity within theatre's processes. What was new was the concept that directing should be done by a role specifically dedicated to that purpose. Emerging around the 1890s after many centuries of theatre, it was both a historical novelty and geographically limited, to Europe and North America.

What these cultures had in common, at the start of the twentieth century, were the ideas and practices which we now call Modernism. In the arts it is associated with particular sorts of innovation made by short-lived movements such as Constructivism, Dada, Expressionism and Surrealism. But modernist thinking also influenced industrial innovation. This is seen in the creation of what F.W. Taylor called 'scientific' management, the systematization and hence separation of the role of a manager who bears responsibility for planning and oversight of the production process. As I have argued before,[1] the concept of director comes to be formulated at the same time as a managerial class is becoming defined. The value put upon the activity of management might be said to create the conditions for, and justify, the creation of a separable role of director.

This was apparent to Barker in 1911 when he observed that in Germany it was precisely the proliferation of management duties that made it impossible to combine the role of manager with that of actor. But German practice was perhaps in advance of the rest of Europe. Many of those now regarded as the founders of directing appeared to work in very similar ways to those who are not categorized as directors. Antoine ran his own company, selected the repertoire, took acting roles and directed plays, as did Stanislavski and Copeau. In this respect their practice differed little from, say, Henry Irving or Herbert Beerbohm Tree, both regarded as actor-managers.

Where the practice of the early directors seems consistently distinct throughout Europe is in its cultural, and sometimes political, positioning. Antoine, Copeau, Barker, Piscator, among others, positioned themselves against a dominant theatrical culture which they aimed to challenge and change. This positioning was an ideological project and hence brought with it an assumption of, or claim to, enlightened vision, artistic mission, the spirit of innovation. Adopting this rhetoric Antoine declared that directors had never existed before – that he was the first of a kind. When P.P. Howe wrote his 1910 book on that new organizational phenomenon the repertory theatre he distinguished the new director from the old stage manager on the grounds that, while the stage manager was adept at controlling the 'mechanical' aspects of the stage, the director was the guardian of the 'vision'.[2] This aesthetic formulation is, though, wholly cognate with management as industrially understood, as Alexander Dean makes clear. In 1926 he recommended that each company should have one person in the role of overall director because the director is not only responsible for each production but also, crucially, is 'the great connecting link between all parts of the organization'. Furthermore: 'Every organization needs a leader who has a vision; who sees a great achievement ahead.'[3] The non-mechanical visionary is also the Taylorist planner.

But some, it seems, were more visionary than others. You will have noted that none of the directors so far mentioned is North American. Yet while Antoine, Copeau and others were founding their theatres outside the mainstream, the same was happening in the United States. The Little Theatres of Chicago and New York started in 1912, the Neighbourhood Playhouse (New York), Portmanteau Theatre and Washington Square Players followed in 1915–16. Contemporary commentators such as Constance D'Arcy Mackay (1917) saw both the European and the American experiments as part of the same 'little theatre' movement.[4] Their practices look similar: founding theatres, against the dominant; culturally selecting audiences, possibly by a membership scheme; working with amateurs; performing explicitly naturalist dramatists, such as Ibsen. But while Antoine and Copeau have entered the canon of great directors, Winthrop Ames and Alice and Irene Lewisohn have not.

Reflecting on the contrast between North American and European practices, William Lyon Phelps suggested in 1920 that the United States lacked a public discourse that would take theatre as seriously as cars. His argument built on Moderwell (1914) and was taken up by Dean (1926).[5] Both saw little theatres as the mechanism for developing a larger theatre-going public, and hence were primarily interested in their success as organizational and economic entities, being much less interested in directors as artists. In Britain similar arguments proposed repertory theatre and the amateur movement as the mechanisms for building both democracy and a dramatic renaissance. Theatre, Barker argued in 1910, is a 'sociable' art. Thus North American and British discussions proposed that theatre could develop the cultural accomplishments of civil society. European discourses, meanwhile, were more interested in, and driven by, avant-gardist movements and experiment. For instance, Antoine positioned himself within an already existing public discourse about art, allying himself with the naturalist, and anti-racist, Zola; staging censored playwrights; distributing Strindberg's polemical preface to *Fröken Julie* (*Miss Julie*) – and making sure to invite reviewers to his theatre. For Piscator and Brecht the energizing link was to activists and ideas within both the political and the artistic avant-garde. The European director thus acquired the status of artistic activist, linked to and recognizable by existing networks of activists and makers, with their own mechanisms for dissemination and publicity. The European avant-garde, long celebrated as the supposed origins of performance art, was perhaps more clearly the originating moment of the theatre director.

The discursive position of European directors was consolidated by their own pronouncements and publications. Each of the early directors was adept in an established theatre craft, as were actor-managers. But when Barker, Meyerhold or Saint-Denis lectured on and wrote about the crafts of theatre, and even more when directors established regimes of training, they were showing themselves to be not just practitioners but theorists of a craft, not so much mechanics as visionaries. The early directors, and indeed directors since, claimed to understand how theatre works as an art form, and to have proposals for its future developments. In this sense they show themselves to be not only guardians of the vision of the play but also guardians of a vision of how theatre itself can and should work. The success of the claim to be visionary is evidence that what the director manages is not just the company or production but also the discourse about them.

Taken together new ideas about management, avant-garde practices and theories of theatre enabled the formulation of, and justified, a separated role of director. The role could then be seen as providing a specialism, missing hitherto, which is necessary to ensure the artistic seriousness and importance of theatre.

While the mechanism that formulated the role of director may have been discursive, its consequences were much more than that. Properly to carry out the guardianship of the vision meant taking responsibility for ensuring the aims and coherence of the processes of theatre-making. The artistic visionary slides into place as Dean's industrial manager. The discursive formulation results in actual power over other theatre workers. The director's control can determine not just that which is staged but also the hiring, if not firing, of those who stage it.

With the invention of directors a new power structure emerges. Yet it had been, and is, perfectly possible to make theatre without that role and its power structure. So there is a potential tension between the effectiveness and productivity of the crafts necessary for theatre and the new, but not demonstrably necessary, power structure that came to claim organizational authority over those crafts. This tension has made the role of director important and yet unstable, treated as celebrity and yet, after only a century, subject to questions as to whether it is actually necessary.

Those questions have been asked not least by directors themselves. Tangled up with the other issues summarized above they run through the volumes of this series. For the directors here have been selected not only because they are generally taken to be important, indeed 'great', but also because they reflect in interesting ways on the role of directing itself. Of course there are other important names, and interesting reflections, which have not made it into the selection list. Decisions such as these are usually difficult and almost always never satisfactory to everybody. But more stories are told than those of big names. The featured directors are not important because they possess some solitary essence of greatness but because they offer ways into, and are symptomatic of, a range of different practices and ideas. The discussion of each featured director frequently involves other directors, as well as designers, writers and actors with whom they worked and by whom they were influenced. For example, the authors of Volume 3 insist that we move our focus outwards from the featured male directors to attend to the women with whom they collaborated and on whom they depended.

The series begins with some of the earliest examples of the practice, but the only other chronological principle governing the distribution of directors is the decision to create two groups of volumes falling roughly either side of the midpoint of the twentieth century. What this arrangement highlights is the extent to which the practice of directing generates a system of self-reference as it rapidly developed an extensive discourse of its own very new art. Thus, for example, Volume 6 features directors who engage with, and perpetuate, the practices and legacy of Brecht.

Rather than suggesting a chronologically seamless evolution of practices the distribution of the directors across the series seeks to call attention to debate. Volume 1 deals with Naturalism, Volume 2 with critiques of Naturalism. The aim is to provoke thinking not so much about the director as an individual as about the art of directing in its different approaches and concerns. The vision of which the director is guardian and the assumptions as to what constitutes the art of directing are revealed as diverse and provisional. For some directors their creative work mainly involves the staging of their ideas about the world, for others creativity comes in the design of processes and the management of people, for yet others creativity has to do with the design and management of theatres. While Brook's philosophy of life may have constructed powerful and influential stagings, Guthrie's philosophy of life more or less invented the equally powerful, and perhaps more influential, concept of the role of artistic director.

If Volumes 1 and 2 display contrasted aesthetic approaches, Volume 3 has us focus on directors as founders and managers of companies and theatres. That topic of company formation and management returns again, in the context of the latter part of the twentieth century, in Volume 7. In a similar way Volume 4 brings together directors who may be seen as auteurs working within a modernist climate while Volume 5 gives us auteurs emerging from a post-Second World War Europe. In Volume 8, the directors are also auteurs, perhaps most powerfully so in that there is often no dramatist's text. But at the same time here the role of director begins to wobble, blurring into that of choreographer or visual artist.

In exploring the various directors, it becomes clear that, as noted above, some directors are major contributors to the discourses about directing, both reflecting on practices in general and foregrounding their own work in particular. This has an effect on their apparent status within the field. The existence of texts authored by directors often facilitates the study of those directors by others, which in turn generates more texts and elevates their apparent status, as a sort of greatness-construction machine. But there are other directors who are less textually established, perhaps because the director actively refuses to document their work, as did Planchon, or perhaps because there are cultural or geographical boundaries that English-speaking academics tend not to cross, as is the case of Strehler. Or it may be that directors have simply fallen out of theatrical or academic fashion, as, say, for Saint-Denis. That they are no longer, or ever were, serviced by the contemporary greatness-construction machine does not make these directors any less significant. Celebrity is not in itself necessarily relevant to being important.

Introduction to Volume 8

Luk Van den Dries and Timmy De Laet

> *The obscurest epoch is today;*
> *and that for a thousand reasons of inchoate tendency, conflicting report,*
> *and sheer mass and multiplicity of experience;*
> *but chiefly, perhaps, by reason of an insidious shifting of landmarks.*
>
> ROBERT LOUIS STEVENSON, 'THE DAY AFTER TOMORROW' (1887)

Writing at the end of the nineteenth century, in the heyday of modernity, the Scottish novelist Robert Louis Stevenson found himself amidst a continuously changing society, clearly impelling him to give expression to the difficulty of coming to terms with a reality that could not even be termed yet. Stevenson's observation that the attempt to get a grip on our own contemporaneity might be obscured by the abundance of fluctuating tendencies that are still in the process of manifesting themselves captures the challenge that composing this book immediately poses. With this eighth and last volume in the *Great European Stage Directors* series, we enter a period of time that is closest to our own, a time still driven by the 'insidious shifting of landmarks' that not only steers everyday life, but also continues to direct and redirect the theatre scene. Giving *re*-direction to what is known as director's theatre might indeed be the major shift this book intends to chart. Its three protagonists – Pina Bausch, Romeo Castellucci and Jan Fabre – stand as emblematic figures of the radical innovations that have reshaped the theatre during the past five decades, prolonging but also perturbing a longer lineage of artistic experimentation that – as this series demonstrates – runs through the entire history of twentieth-century theatre.[1]

Perhaps the greatest hindrance in wanting to chronicle the most recent part of this lineage is that history has not yet had the time to process and register its impact, or to measure the breadth of an oeuvre's afterlife. For Pina Bausch, who unexpectedly passed away in 2009 only five days after she was diagnosed with cancer, the extent of her influence – not only on the dancers at Tanztheater Wuppertal, but also on other generations of theatre artists – has become increasingly articulate, as time begins to unveil its indebtedness to the past. Even though Bausch tends to be regarded primarily as a choreographer, it makes sense to include her in a volume on stage directors: not only did her specific approach to 'tanztheater' combine theatre and dance to arrive at a particular form of theatricalized choreography but, as the Artistic Director of the Tanztheater Wuppertal, she also played a steering role in both the daily functioning of the company and the aesthetics of the dance pieces she developed with the dancers. As Mariama Diagne discusses in her contribution to this volume, Bausch had an 'astounding talent to direct moving bodies on stage', which Diagne understands in a fairly literal sense as she zooms in on 'Bausch's innovative ways of giving directions to get bodies moving'.

Much like Pina Bausch, the other two artists this volume focuses on expand any purist understanding of the stage director as someone who works exclusively for the theatre. Both Castellucci and Fabre had their primary education in the visual arts, which obviously left a formative mark on their theatrical work. In the case of Fabre, along with his practice as a theatre director, he continues to produce visual artworks turning him into a genuinely interdisciplinary artist who shows an astonishing mastery in various art forms, while often also combining them. Castellucci's work, too, still testifies to his affinity with the fine arts, since he is known for his highly visual theatre that often abounds in references to art history. In contrast to Bausch, Castellucci and Fabre's body of work is still a steadily expanding organism that continues to grow, breathe, transform or even sweat in the immediate presence of contemporary audiences. While both artists took their first steps in the theatre in the early 1980s, almost thirty years later they keep on creating theatrical works that – as this volume hopes to show – testify to the persistence of particular artistic and aesthetic interests, but not without continually revising and reinventing them. One can rightfully imagine that their persistent search for the expressive potentialities of the theatrical medium will lead to yet undiscovered areas, perhaps even inciting them to produce new work that, from a historical point of view, will prove to be most incisive.

Whether or not the oeuvres of these directors are still subject to the whims of time, it is beyond any doubt that Bausch, Castellucci and Fabre's work had an exceptional resonance in late twentieth-century theatre. To make such an assessment, historical distance is not the sole and sufficient prerequisite. On the contrary, as historian Mark Salber Phillips rightly argues, 'temporal distance alone does not determine our engagement with the past'.[2] Any retrospective look is necessarily informed by our own affective involvement in the subject we choose to historicize as well as by the formal conditions imposed on us by historiography. These tenets are particularly relevant in the context of the current volume, in which all of its authors engage with work they have not only discovered through scholarly research after the event, but also through personal encounters and as embodied spectators. Their interest and expertise bears the mark of the individual relationship they have developed with the director's performances on which they write, giving first-hand accounts of productions they have seen but which may no longer be staged, or providing vivid descriptions of archived works they have turned to after becoming intrigued by the artist's poetics. From this perspective, the absence of distance might turn out to be a promising avenue for a volume that critically probes the legacy of three most remarkable directors.

Even though subjective choices necessarily underlie not only the composition of the volume but also the individual chapters, the book deliberately foregrounds Pina Bausch, Romeo Castellucci and Jan Fabre as three artists whose oeuvre incorporates some of the most conspicuous tendencies that can be identified in director's theatre as it developed from the 1970s onwards. Rather than offering a kaleidoscopic overview of this period, the contributions collected in this volume develop in-depth discussions of the genealogies, aesthetics and influences that have shaped the work of three leading directors. Implicit in this approach is the assumption that the specificity of these artist's creative practices is indicative of broader shifts in the recent history of theatre. Consequently, while the book obviously cannot claim to be exhaustive, it does hope to work in two directions: by immersing readers into the particularities of a director's oeuvre, it wants give flesh to the skeletal structures of larger categorizations that often implode under the weight of labels that are too general.

Specifically with regard to this volume, the first such label that immediately springs to mind is, of course, Hans-Thies Lehmann's seminal notion of 'postdramatic theatre'. With this newly coined term, Lehmann heralded nothing less than the emergence of a new paradigm in theatre, which began to announce itself around the 1960s when the dramatic text as the privileged epicentre of theatrical creation was increasingly displaced in favour of other theatrical parameters – such as the body, sound, light and space – which conquered their own autonomous role as viable means of expression to be exploited on stage.[3] Ever since Lehmann first introduced his ideas on 'postdramatic theatre' in Germany in 1999, the term has gone through several rebirths. Every time his book was translated into a different language, it reached a new audience, which could familiarize itself with the aesthetic innovations his encyclopaedic approach aimed to chart. Unsurprisingly, the English translation played a major role in the currently widespread use of Lehmann's categorical token. The somewhat unfortunate side-effect of the general acceptance of 'postdramatic theatre' as an overarching term, however, is that it risks becoming an empty signifier that might justly point to a new direction in twentieth-century theatre, but which fails to account for the individual poetics that gave rise to the term in the first place.[4]

Fleshing out the precepts of this new doctrine called 'postdramatic theatre', while at the same time also challenging the wide application of this label, is one of the undercurrents running through this volume. Even if not all authors engage directly with the idea of post-drama as such, the insights they offer into the theatrical poetics of Bausch, Castellucci and Fabre do give substance to the generic term introduced by Lehmann. By singling out specific themes characteristic for their respective oeuvres, each chapter works towards a more thorough understanding of the incisive transformations theatre has undergone ever since the dramatic text was overthrown and a new realm of theatrical expression began to manifest itself. Formal principles and aesthetic innovations – such as the juxtaposition of images in Bausch's work, the transgressive iconoclasm in Castellucci's theatre or the negotiation between theatricality and reality in Fabre's performances – all give new contours and content to the prodigious influence these directors have exerted on twentieth-century theatre.

Considering context

It is a common truism that no artist operates outside time, insofar as any artistic work is always an expression of and a response to the cultural context in which it was created.[5] Because this book's primary focus lies on the trajectories, oeuvres and poetics of the individual directors, it is less concerned with excavating the influence of social, economic, political or institutional circumstances on the practice of these artists. Methodologically, the intentions behind this volume are obviously historiographical, but rather than construing a cultural history of the period running from the early 1970s until today, it adopts a case-study-based approach by offering predominantly aesthetic analyses of individual works as well as larger thematic concerns.[6] It is nevertheless useful to frame the more topical discussions provided in the various chapters against the larger background of historical events and decisive developments within the theatre scene, which – whether directly or implicitly – informed the work of Bausch, Castellucci and Fabre. Such contextual considerations might also reveal a common ground between the otherwise disparate practices of these three directors, who are each steeped in the cultural climate that followed the tumultuous 1960s.

Bausch, Castellucci and Fabre belong to a generation of artists who were confronted with a world in which collective dreams were shattered and calls for social and cultural reformations seemed to have shrunk down to pointless resistance. The ardent desire for alternative modes of communality, a new gender balance or valuation of age, a revised distribution of capital and prosperity or different models of economic and global exchange was gradually pulverized under the supremacy of conservative forces that upheld the societal status quo.[7] In the ruins of the euphoria that, during the 1960s, had promised revolutionary movements in various countries all over Europe, a fairly cynical individualism re-emerged, which found its economic pendant in the ultraliberal ideology of Margaret Thatcher in the United Kingdom (1979–90). The utopian impetus that fuelled the 1960s and peaked with a flood of protests in 1968, shrivelled in the face of the socio-economic climate that followed shortly afterwards. The two major oil crises of 1973 and 1979 lead to a dramatic collapse of the international monetary system and economic growth, whose effects became most palpable in the startling unemployment numbers, especially for younger people. What followed was a policy of draconian cutbacks in expenditure in various areas of the public domain, including healthcare, education and culture. While trimming down was everyone's task, salaries and allowances were drastically reduced.[8]

This admittedly dystopian image of the post-1968 economic reality and cultural climate bears uncanny resonances with the global financial crisis of 2008, which resulted in the so-called Great Recession as well as the European debt crisis that similarly had a real impact on people's everyday lives. While it has already become clear that these severely altered economic conditions also changed the institutional infrastructure of the arts and theatre with several belt-tightening measures, especially with regard to governmental subsidies, the manifold ways in which this new socio-economic reality also impacted theatrical aesthetics is a history that still needs to be written, not the least since tendencies such as these only manifest themselves after some time of incubation. For the 1970s – the period when Bausch, Castellucci and Fabre made their first steps into the art world – it is easier to ascertain how theatrical practices were reshaped by the austere socio-economic reality during that time, and which found its probably clearest expression in the demise of what is known as political theatre.

At least in Europe, the 1970s marked the end of the heydays of various theatre troupes or directors that aimed to repoliticize theatre in an attempt to keep the revolutionary spirit of the 1960s alive. The encroaching grasp of the individualist liberalism promoted by the governments in various countries, however, increasingly rendered such efforts unavailing, if not obsolete. Artistic collectives such as 7:84 in Great Britain (founded by John McGrath in 1973 and named after the 7 per cent of the British population that owned 84 per cent of the country's wealth), the Internationale Nieuwe Scène (International New Scene) that was also founded in 1973, and the Werktheater (Working Theatre) in the Netherlands (established in 1970) are just a few of many examples of a vehement political tendency running through European theatre that found itself challenged by the gloomy atmosphere of crisis that saturated people's minds and lives. By the end of the 1970s, a politically straightforward intervention such as Peter Stein's production *Viet Nam Diskurs* (Vietnam-Discourse, 1968) for the Müncher Kammerspiele – which caused a major scandal at its premiere when Stein and his actors asked the audience to donate money for the Vietcong – no longer seemed possible.[9] The macro-political concerns that inspired much of the work produced during the late 1960s and the early 1970s made way for a heightened interest in micro-stories that focused on personal experiences and subjective situations in which affective and emphatic identification regained validity.[10]

The social and political turmoil that arose during the 1960s obviously had a significant impact on the structures of theatre-making, both institutional and aesthetic, that went well beyond the intensified emergence and subsequent demise of political theatre *pur sang*. Also those directors, performers or groups that were less interested in drawing the reality of everyday life into the allegedly safe spheres of the theatre contributed to what might be considered a range of seismic changes in the theatrical landscape that radically redefined the division of labour while also expanding the possible approaches to creative work as such. This is the time of the so-called 'neo-avant-garde' – also known as the 'second avant-garde' – which was greatly inspired by the revolutionary innovations of their historical precursors, most notably the various '-isms' that emerged in the early twentieth century, such as Expressionism, Futurism, Dadaism and others. In theatre, the resurgence of the avant-garde spirit incited both playful and critical experiments with form and theatrical conventions; directors, collectives and individual artists began to overhaul theatre's standard ingredients, including location, duration, acting, text and the spectator's position.

Just as the historical avant-garde in the early twentieth century used art as a means to process and challenge the rapid modernization of society that followed closely after the Industrial Revolution, so too is the neo-avant-garde often regarded as a response to the changing face of the world after the Second World War. The field of art and culture has only increased in complexity ever since. The encroaching expansion of new technological media, the globalization of politics and economy, the burgeoning grasp of capitalism on the art market, the floods of immigration mobilized by continual violent conflicts, the protectionist restrains of nationalism and, of course, the advancing professionalization of the cultural sector have soaked deeply into the DNA of theatre, also affecting – as we will discuss in the following section – the role of the director therein.

Redefining directors

Because the position and the function of directors can obviously not be isolated from the local institutional infrastructures in which they work, any attempt to articulate broad changes in directorial practices unavoidably overlooks the ways in which specific conditions influence this kind of creative labour. It is nevertheless instructive to chart at least a few of the most conspicuous tendencies that occurred during the second half of the twentieth century, especially since this relatively recent legacy also informs the profile of directors such as Pina Bausch, Romeo Castellucci and Jan Fabre. In the decennia following the Second World War, the artistic innovations pursued by key pre-war figures – such as Erwin Piscator [see **Volume 2**], Antonin Artaud and Bertolt Brecht – were continued and amplified by theatre artists seeking new ways to develop their own distinctive directorial signature. While the emancipation of the director had already set in by the mid-nineteenth century, with the growing acceptance that someone else besides the playwright could be responsible for the staging of the piece, the actual recognition of the director's individual artistry has been a considerably lengthy process – it took almost fifty years before the director was acknowledged as an artist in his or her own right. As David Bradby and David Williams point out in *Director's Theatre*, it was only from the 1910s onwards that the theatrical apparatus began to open its doors for the director, with Edward Gordon Craig, Jacques Copeau and Max Reinhardt playing an instrumental role in this gradual legitimization [see **Volumes 3 and 4**].[11]

One of the most remarkable trends in the post-war theatre scene is the further expansion of the director's autonomy to the point of a complete extrication from the dramatist's traditional authority. Rather than putting a text on stage, an increasing number of directors started to create their own scripts, taking responsibility for various dimensions of the theatrical event (including lighting, scenography, costume, sound etc.), leading to the emergence of the 'director as *auteur*'.[12] In *Authoring Performance*, theatre scholar Avra Sidiropolou traces this development, claiming that:

> Avant-garde directors in the West have been developing their own singular methods and stage idioms, contributing to the resolute establishment of auteur theatre, which is more than ever present in the wake of the twenty-first century.[13]

The term 'auteur theatre' is, however, somewhat misleading, since the director's attainment of artistic independence progressively spread out to the position of the actor, who likewise conquered an unprecedented sovereignty in creating theatre. In the wake of the 1960s rise of political theatre, which fiercely questioned the pyramidal hierarchical system of both the arts and society, new and allegedly more democratic forms of collaboration increasingly emerged as an alternative to the established structures of traditional theatre companies. Characteristic of these so-called theatre collectives was that their members took over nearly all aspects of the creative process – the selection of (text) material, translation and adaptation, dramaturgy and scenography – as well as performing the piece itself. Especially in the Netherlands and Flanders, such models of collective theatre-making found a particularly fruitful ground, as evidenced by the emergence of various troupes such as Maatschappij Discordia, Compagnie De Koe and tg STAN.[14] Even in the United Kingdom, often regarded as the area where sweeping commercialization has impregnated the cultural sector more intensely than in Continental Europe, collective models of theatre have been gaining an increasingly firm foothold. However, the terminology used in the Anglo-Saxon world is slightly different, as these collaborative forms are generally captured under the term 'devising theatre' which stresses, perhaps more emphatically, that a given piece was newly *devised* by its makers.[15]

Even though it is tempting to align the democratization of theatre-making with groups that overtly present themselves as collectives or devising performance groups, it would be wrong to assume that this interest in unmaking conventional hierarchies is their exclusive attribute. There is indeed a certain tendency to conceive of the director as a domineering figure who, ever since he or she cast off the yoke of the playwright, simply took possession of the same authoritative position. While this assumption might hold up in some cases, there are various directors whose practice contradicts the view that directing equals commanding. In this respect, Peter Boenisch makes a pointed remark in *Directing Scenes and Senses* that is important to bear in mind, particularly in the context of this volume: 'Writing a history of *the* director', he states, 'as a celebration of original inventions of "great men" (and mostly they still are [men] ...), immediately pushes issues of authorship and authority to the fore', which makes it all the more pressing to develop an 'understanding of direction, and *Regie*, as the recognition (and, indeed, celebration) of an *essentially collective, social and political practice*'.[16] The discussions of the direction of Bausch, Castellucci and Fabre offered in this book show how, at least in their work, they are not concerned with asserting their singular superior power, but with channelling the inspiration and input coming from different sources, including the performers. Indeed, as we will explain in more detail below, the performers' quite recently acquired autonomy not only pertains to explicitly collective practices, but also spills over into what came to be known – perhaps for lack of a better term – as 'director's theatre'.

In much the same way as directors have shown themselves open to the creative contributions of performers, the role of the dramaturg has become increasingly substantial. Ever since the publication of Gotthold Ephraim Lessing's seminal *Hamburgische Dramaturgie* (1769), a collection of texts he wrote during his appointment as the first official dramaturg at the Hamburg Theater, drama has been open to allowing an extra onlooker who can reflect, fuel and assist in the creative process.[17] During the second half of the twentieth century, the collaborations between directors and dramaturgs have only expanded. More and more, the dramaturg's working terrain has moved from the desk towards the rehearsal studio, as he or she came to fulfil a co-artistic function next to and especially with the director. As Katalin Trencsény and Bernadette Cochrane point out in their introduction to *New Dramaturgy*, 'the dramaturg is no longer a critic or a "third eye" … brought in during the later stages of the work', as it is currently common practice that 'the dramaturg brings to the company's attention the ways they've chose to work by articulating, challenging, or, at times, disrupting the creative process(es)'.[18] The more active involvement of the dramaturg in the creation of the work is obviously not an infringement of the director's artistic autonomy, but rather indicates how the latter's authorial voice is anything but absolute, just as dialogical working methods have become more common practice than unilateral hierarchies.

Another conspicuous feature of director's theatre, both historically and contemporary, concerns the professional background of the director. While the group of practitioners who profiled themselves as directors has always been very diverse, this heterogeneity has expanded considerably during the past few decennia. Many of them – such as André Antoine, Vsevolod Meyerhold and Leopold Jessner – started off as actors who could rely on their own experience, charisma and recognition for taking up a leading role in creating new work [see **Volumes 1, 2 and 4**]. Others – such as Konstantin Stanislavski or Jerzy Grotowski – are primarily known for their pedagogical interest, coaching actors to help them to amplify their theatrical expression [see **Volumes 1 and 5**]. But there were also writers, journalists or critics – such as Bertolt Brecht, Luis Valdez and David Hare – who sometimes found their vocation in the theatre, as it gave them the means to put their dramaturgical proficiency into practice. The circle of directors spreads even further when architects, visual artists and graphic designers – such as Edward Gordon Craig, Tadeusz Kantor or Robert Wilson – also start to create theatre. Their proclivity for the visuality of theatre will open up new horizons through a heightened attention for the function of space and imagery. The apparent interest of directors in interdisciplinary crossovers also comes to the fore in the present volume: whereas Pina Bausch's so-called *Tanztheater* (dance theatre) seeks a rapprochement between two distinct traditions within the performing arts, Romeo Castellucci's education in the fine arts – as well as his early experiments with visual media – clearly shapes the image-orientated aesthetics of his theatre. Jan Fabre likewise began as a visual artist, but he has always continued his visual art practice next to his theatre work, with both areas mutually informing one another, evidenced by the fact that the overt theatricality of Fabre's visual art is ostensibly mirrored in the visuality of his theatre. Undoubtedly, it is the unique mixture of individual histories and artistic appeals that accounts for the distinctiveness of these directors' poetics.

The last and most recent trend we want to point out began to appear from the early 2000s onwards, when various directors who had been building their oeuvre for several years began to feel the need to look back on some of their earlier pieces as well as securing the afterlife of their work. This primarily led to substantial efforts in archiving the manifold kinds of documentary materials related to particular performances, including videos, sketches, notebooks, scripts and technical riders. It must be emphasized that this concern for archivization might seem more obvious than it actually is, since in most cases there is hardly any systematized preservation of the documents of both the creative processes and the stagings of pieces.[19] The directors in this volume are exceptions to this predominant negligence, as important initiatives have been set up to preserve their work for future generations. Shortly after Pina Bausch's death, for example, her son Salomon not only established the Pina Bausch Foundation, which holds the copyright to her pieces, but he also initiated the Pina Bausch Archive, which preserves and – if possible – digitizes the vast collection of archival materials she left behind.[20] Romeo Castellucci has been working with the team of the ARCH Research Project to collect and digitize both his personal archive and all documents of the Socìetas Raffaello Sanzio, the company he founded together with his sister Claudia Castellucci.[21] Jan Fabre founded two institutional structures, Troubleyn and Angelos, that provide production support for his visual art and theatre work respectively, and which also take care of the archivization of his oeuvre. Several contributions to this volume demonstrate how these archival resources are crucial for scholarly research on theatre, as they often provide the only traces of an art form that, precisely because it is performed live on stage, tends to disappear into the folds of time.

It is, however, this lived quality and embodied instantiation of the work that gets lost whenever it is preserved in traditional archival media, such as video, photographs or writing. Two-dimensional images or verbal impressions do not live up to the actual experience of 'being there', to sit in the theatre together with other spectators who are all witnessing the creation of the work as it happens on the stage. In recent years, the awareness of the archive's limitations resulted, most interestingly, in the rise of what is sometimes called 're-enactment' or 'revival', which signals an intensified interest in building a *living* repertoire by restaging earlier performance pieces. In this respect, the concern with conventional forms of archivization is only one aspect of the ongoing efforts to keep artistic legacies alive, as a concomitant search for alternative formats aspires to complement those dimensions of theatre the archive cannot capture. Admittedly, the idea of maintaining repertoire is anything but new, both in theatre and in dance, and most often associated with large companies or established institutions that build considerable parts of their programme around restaging canonical theatre texts or classical dance pieces. Yet, in recent years, the meaning of the 'repertoire' has been shifting to include other modes of keeping the practice of theatre alive. As Jeanne Bovet and Yves Jubinville rightly claim, repertoire is no longer 'confined to the idea of a collection of masterpieces' that, by tapping into cultural memory and shared referential frameworks, could appeal to 'prestige and stability', while also legitimizing and eternalizing artistic choices. Instead, contemporary theatre impels us to consider repertoire 'in its minor, singular and heterogeneous variations, which attest that the historical or memorial thickness of the theatre is a constantly re-evaluated and never definitively acquired fact'.[22]

The mnemonic function of repertoire to which Bovet and Jubinville allude is an important reason for its diversification. One of the most far-reaching implications of Hans-Thies Lehmann's thesis that theatre entered the era of postdrama by dethroning the dramatic text is that, along the way, theatre has removed itself from the most tangible substratum that facilitated its transmission. From the moment that text is no longer the epicentre of theatrical creation, there is hardly any base to secure a solid tradition that goes beyond individual artists and can be passed on to new generations of both performers and spectators. Paradoxically, then, post-dramatic theatre appears to constitute an emerging tradition that, in the very act of taking shape, undoes itself by relying heavily on non-traditional modes of creation and expression. Within this context, it is hardly surprising that theatre directors, as well as smaller collectives, are undertaking various efforts to prolong the life of their work. The scope of repertoire consequently expands from reinterpreting canonical classics to keeping performances on tour for several years to reviving older pieces that have not been shown for a considerable amount of time. The directors in this volume cover this broadened range of the repertoire. Pina Bausch's Tanztheater Wuppertal, for instance, continues to travel around the world, acquainting contemporary audiences with her work. Romeo Castellucci and Jan Fabre have restaged a few of their earliest pieces, as a first step towards exploring how their work might survive, but also changes over time.[23]

The retrospective undercurrent that is slowly beginning to articulate itself in contemporary theatre is not only geared towards preservation, but it also crucially allows for reinvention. Whereas some of the restagings do attempt to stay as close as possible to the original piece, there are also significant endeavours to adapt the works to the contingencies of our own time or to broaden their poetical force. It is at this point where the validity of 're-enactment' as a term comes into play, since it helps to distinguish deliberate re-interpretations from mere restagings or reconstructions.[24] Already during her lifetime, Pina Bausch showed herself aware of the potentially enriching effects of transforming the conceptual format of a piece, as exemplified by the re-enactments of her iconic *Kontakthof*, first created in 1978, and which she reinvented in 2000 by restaging the piece with elderly people as well as in 2008, when she created yet another version with teenagers. In addition, Bausch's work continues to inspire other artists of younger generations who are gradually beginning to approach her legacy from new and invigorating angles. In 2016, for example, the Dutch theatre collective De Warme Winkel created a compelling piece in which they framed an integral reconstruction of Bausch's *Café Müller* (1978) in a larger story revolving around issues as plagiarism, the weight of historical traditions, epigones and artistic innovation.

Above all, both the directors' own attempts to keep their legacy alive as well as other artists' interest in reviving this heritage demonstrates how the current expansion of the repertoire primarily serves to continually create new memories of performance works or to reactivate older ones, by using the stage as the primary arena for such mnemonic labour. Even though the live performing arts have often been glorified for their allegedly transient nature, this passing away is increasingly being turned into a passing along. It is precisely this tendency to which the present volume hopes to contribute.

The directorial poetics of Bausch, Castellucci and Fabre

Bringing together three distinctly different directors into one volume offers a unique opportunity to look for common interests and shared aesthetic principles, while such a juxtaposition also immediately points to substantial differences as to how these key figures realize their individual artistic projects on stage. Of the manifold cross-connections that can be drawn between the six chapters in this book, we want to spell out the most perspicuous threads that weave together the otherwise singular practices of Pina Bausch, Romeo Castellucci and Jan Fabre. As searching for similarities allows for articulating differences, the reflections we offer below provide readers with a first entrance to the more detailed discussions offered in each of the chapters, just as it serves as an invitation to discover other undercurrents that tacitly run throughout the volume as a whole.

Our broad sketch of the cultural climate in Europe during the post-1968 era already indicated that a certain defeatist stance towards the possibility of forcing structural changes in society superseded the initially buoyant belief in a new geopolitical order. Bausch, Castellucci and Fabre belong to a historically decisive period, as the 1960s idealism gradually eroded and gave way to the rise of so-called post-modernity that, as Jean-François Lyotard infamously proclaimed, marked the end of grand narratives. Lyotard's *La condition postmoderne: Rapport sur le savoir* (The Postmodern Condition: A Report on Knowledge), first published in 1979, had a profound influence and its impact on not only twentieth-century intellectual life but also on artistic practices as well as popular culture cannot be underestimated. The rise of punk music can be considered as one of the first responses to the post-modernist condition, as the 'no future' slogan similarly aimed to make a drastic end to any stubborn faith in progress that might have survived from the 1960s.

In theatre, the impact of post-modernism made itself felt primarily in the emergence of *fragmentation* as a central aesthetic feature. Rather than using the stage for creating a self-enclosed, fictional world through a causal chain of situations, it was the theatrical event as such that came to the fore, insofar as seemingly isolated actions and images supplanted the previous predominance of one overarching narrative. Even though the encroaching grasp of consequential storylines has never been as powerful in dance as in theatre, the outwardly fragmentary nature of Pina Bausch's work did cause a stir in the reception of her work, which testifies to a certain discomfort with, if not an animosity towards, her approach to making dance theatre. As Raimund Hoghe wrote in 1986, 'for years, Pina Bausch has been exposed to violent aggression and attacks with her work'.[25] A case in point is Bausch's radical reinterpretation of Shakespeare's *Macbeth*, which she redubbed *Er nimmt sie an der Hand und führt sie in das Schloß, die anderen folgen...* (He takes her by the hand and leads her into the castle, the others follow..., 1978). The premiere of the piece became a notorious scandal, as it divided the audience into ardent supporters and heavy opponents, with the latter causing a riot of shouting and loud door bangs as they left the theatre before the end. Despite the initial resistance Pina Bausch's aesthetics might have provoked, she would persist in turning fragmentation into a constitutive principle of her choreographic oeuvre. As Mariama Diagne demonstrates in her contribution to this volume, key notions such as 'montage', 'collage', 'repetition' and the 'deconstruction of narrative structures' can already be detected in some of Bausch's earliest pieces. These aesthetic strategies eventually coagulated into her poetics of fragmentation. One of Bausch's greatest merits, but also challenges, is indeed that her choreographic montages only become sensible when one leaves behind the successional logic of narrative, opening up instead to a 'dramaturgy of numbers'.[26]

Jan Fabre's performances can equally be regarded as assemblages of seemingly disparate scenes that are loosely tied together by one thematic concern or under a piece's title. In this regard, it is interesting to see how various working methods pursued by Bausch recur in Fabre's directorial practice, even if they lead to an entirely different theatre aesthetic. Just as Pina Bausch relied heavily on her performers, who provided the primary material for composing the eventual piece, Fabre devotes large parts of the rehearsal period to improvisation sessions in which he and his team explore all aspects of a given theme. As we will elucidate in more detail below, the creative responsibility granted to performers is indeed one of the primary hallmarks that distinguishes the directorial practice of both Bausch and Fabre, raising questions as to what kind of 'characters' are featured in their pieces, insofar as the staged personalities are always to some extent the result of the performers' individual subjectivity. While the intensive collaborations with performers are crucial for creating the piece, the eventual decision of which material is used and how it is arranged does fall to the director, who – after all – guides his or her team in giving the best possible expression of the theme at hand. Fabre, for instance, will work to condense the material, often giving it an unexpected twist that challenges the public not only to find their own way into the piece, but also to recognize the cyclical patterns, superimposed layers and paradoxical entanglements that are typical for Fabre's oeuvre as a whole.

In the absence of one singular narrative line, both Jan Fabre and Pina Bausch find a counterpoint to fragmentation in the use of repetition as a poetical principle. Probably the most famous example in Bausch's work is the scene in *Café Müller* in which one dancer moulds the arms of two performers into an embrace, then helps the female dancer into the arms of her male partner and puts her mouth onto his. As soon as he has finished his living sculpture, he wants to leave the stage but, on his way out, the female dancer falls to the ground as her partner does not seem to have the strength to hold her up. Unwilling to yield to the inability of holding themselves together, she springs back up and strongly embraces him. Having heard the fall, the third dancer returns and redoes his sculpture, but as he wants to leave, the woman ends up lying on the ground again. This sequence is repeated several times with an ever-accelerating pace, with the couple carrying out the same set of movements as slavish automatons, since the rapid succession no longer requires the intervention of the third dancer.[27] In many of Fabre's performance, repetition is a structural element as well. For example, in one scene in *It is theatre like it was to be expected and foreseen* (1982), performers undress and redress themselves, repeating the same gestures at an increasing rhythm until they stand exhausted front stage. At another point during the piece, they start running on the spot, and again Fabre unrelentingly extends the duration of this scene in order to let the real physicality of the performers' bodies overtake the theatrical framing of the action.[28]

In the case of Fabre, the inspiration for using repetition as a compositional principle clearly comes from the visual arts, not least from Marcel Duchamp, one of the artists Fabre greatly admires. In this regard, Emil Hrvatin refers to the doubling of the female figure in Duchamp's *Nu descendant un escalier n°2* (Nude Descending a Staircase, No. 2, 1912), which resonates with how Fabre exposes the living bodies of his performers to a similar kind of virtually endless repetition.[29] Luk Van den Dries takes this a step further in his chapter in this volume, arguing that Fabre's conjunction of visual and performing arts leads to a tension that is at the core of his work and which results from the confrontation of two distinct structures of time: the immobile 'stillness' of the painting and the unfolding 'movement' of performance. Hans-Thies Lehmann also identifies in his contribution the central importance of repetition in Fabre's oeuvre, not only in his directorial practice but also in the various texts he wrote for the theatre.

Repetition appears to be the flipside of fragmentation, but both strategies serve the same end: to disrupt the consequential logic that typifies traditional drama and to replace it with a more associational mode of composition that makes a strong appeal to the audience's own imagination. This interest in creating a theatrical universe that follows its own rules and laws is what connects Pina Bausch and Jan Fabre to Romeo Castellucci. His theatre, as Thomas Crombez amply demonstrates in his chapter, is built out of an amalgam of often disparate material: images, text, sound and bodies are assembled in the most capricious ways, even if this outright accumulation makes the work 'illegible', at least for the rational mind. The performances of the Socìetas Raffaello Sanzio, the company Castellucci founded together with his sister Claudia Castellucci, often leave spectators perplexed, if not shocked, because they are confronted with a disconcerting labyrinth of enigmatic imagery that seems to offer neither a single entrance nor a clear-cut clue that could guide them through this eccentric world. Theatre scholar Freddy Decreus describes Castellucci's performances as 'narrative, visual and acoustic chaos', but at the same time he recognizes how they attempt to penetrate the primal mythologies of Western civilization.[30] There certainly is a radical deconstructive gesture behind Castellucci's theatre, which Eleni Papalexiou discusses in her chapter as the iconoclasm that permeates his poetics. This iconoclastic thrust in Castellucci's work is, in the first place, a vehement attack on the traditional function of the theatrical image as a symbolic signifier, which Castellucci opposes by composing scenes whose meaning cannot be easily deciphered. It also applies, as Papalexiou shows, to the manner in which he assails the Western canon of literary and dramatic texts. While various of Castellucci's productions are inspired by the writings of classical authors, such as William Shakespeare, Dante Alighieri or Aeschylus, these texts are never kept intact and subjected to an irreverent deformation. 'I hammer at the text', Castellucci claims; 'I hammer, I hammer it, until I make it disperse'.[31] What remains are traces, remnants and ruins, which is why it is sometimes overlooked that there is a distinctly constructive side to Castellucci's iconoclasm. As Timmy De Laet and Edith Cassiers have argued, the process of ruination that typifies his theatre is, in fact, deeply dialectical in nature, 'as it hovers between the hostilities of destruction and the potentialities of resurrection'.[32] From this perspective, the insurgent undoing of drama's conventions and canon is only a first step towards creating a new, alternative reality on stage in which spectators can indulge and which might impel them to question their own habitual modes of looking at both the theatre and the world.

The absence of one signifying centre that drives the theatrical event and which abridges the possible meanings one might ascribe to it, is one of the primary characteristics that connects the oeuvres of Pina Bausch, Romeo Castellucci and Jan Fabre. These directors not only honour but also radicalize Umberto Eco's famous notion of the 'opera aperta', the open work, which signals how art works may deliberately reject one singular meaning and allow instead for a multiplicity of interpretations.[33] Art that is 'open', in Eco's sense of the term, requires an ongoing dialogue between the work and its onlookers, who can bring to it their own imagination, ideas or recollections, which – in turn – can only temporarily complete 'the' work. In *Postdramatic Theatre*, Hans-Thies Lehmann points to a similar dynamic, when he writes about 'parataxis' or 'the de-hierarchization of theatrical means' as a fundamental feature of post-drama. Whereas scenery or music often served an illustrative function aimed at embellishing the staging of the play, post-dramatic theatre grants autonomy to the different parameters of the theatrical apparatus, insofar as different media, language, objects and bodily expression are allowed to tell their own 'story', without subsuming the expressive force of each of these elements under one totalizing narrative. This paratactic reorganization of the theatrical event also implies that spectators are faced with the responsibility of finding their own way into the piece. The meaning of a performance, therefore, is never given or fixed, but – as Lehmann explains – is always the result of a perceptual process that appeals to the audience's discursive understanding and sensory involvement:

> Everything depends on not understanding immediately. Rather one's perception has to remain open for connections, correspondences and clues at completely unexpected moments, perhaps casting what was said earlier in a completely new light. Thus, meaning remains in principle postponed.[34]

But even if there is not a single semiotic centre structuring the performance and even if a recalibration of the senses is typical of so-called post-dramatic theatre, this does not mean that *language* has become obsolete.[35] On the contrary, one of the most remarkable reformations Pina Bausch has introduced in dance is precisely that she wanted her performers to use their voice as they had never done before in the entire history of dance. As Mariama Diagne argues in her chapter, Bausch's profile as a director should not be misunderstood as authoritatively imposing a preconceived choreographic structure on the dancer's bodies, but rather – quite literally – as 'giving them direction by making them move, interact and sense'. The very fact that, in order to accomplish this, she attaches great importance to the dancer's speaking voice indicates how language does remain a crucial means of expression, even in so-called post-dramatic practices. It is the function of text that changes, insofar as it no longer serves the creation of a fictional world, the development of the dramatic action or the explicit expression of opinions or thoughts.

Discussing 'the new variants of text' that emerge in post-dramatic theatre, Lehmann refers in passing to Jacques Derrida's concept of 'espacement' (spacing), which helps to explain how the purely symbolic signification of language is replaced with some of its other qualities, such as 'the phonetic materiality, the temporal course, the dispersion in space'.[36] According to Derrida, spacing points to a fundamental condition of linguistic meaning, since language can only make sense through the double-sided dynamics of difference and deferral, or what he calls 'the general law of *différance*'.[37] This implies that language can never be fully self-coincidental and requires an exteriority breaching into the linguistic system, which consequently fulfils an intermediary role between the external means of expression and the content that is expressed. It is the Derridean externalization of language that theatre brings to the fore by substituting narrative with text as a formal principle. Rather than meaning, it is the sonic, visual and referential dimensions of language that become a primary interest, leading Lehmann to speak of a 'textscape' to emphasize how text becomes part of the general scenic landscape that grants equal importance to other theatrical elements, such as light, sound, space and bodies.

Romeo Castellucci's theatre provides an exemplary demonstration of how text can function as an autonomous 'actor' on stage. While his work is sometimes erroneously characterized as a theatre of images that does away with words, verbal expressions are omnipresent in his pieces. Text appears on screens, placards or in neon, or it is carved in stone or wood. But even when words might briefly light up, giving a glimpse of what appears to be some form of signification, any sense of comprehension is quickly – and often also repeatedly – destabilized. Letters are erased or burned, words appear backwards, or the projected text does not correspond at all to the actions on stage. An emblematic scene in *Democracy in America* (2017) aptly illustrates Castellucci's stance towards language, which for him is anything but a medium of fixed signification. At a certain point during the piece, the performers appear on stage, carrying a flag with one letter, which they use to form at first the title of the performance, but soon they start to move through space, construing a range of other words, such as 'decay crime macaroni', and completely nonsensical phrases, such as 'caiman marry ecocide'. Whereas some of these combinations evoke the stereotypical image of the United States, others primarily highlight how Castellucci treats language as a material to play with, since its virtually endless self-regenerative potential offers an effective means to disturb the conventionalized and confined use of words, letters and text.

Language in the work of Jan Fabre is likewise far from being a descriptive or denotative means of communication. Instead, he is interested in the plasticity of language. Using words for their poetical expressive force, lyrical leitmotifs, puns, alliterations, onomatopoeia and rhyme abound in Fabre's texts. He juggles with different rhythms and registers, and he also often integrates repetition into his writing, just as in his theatre oeuvre. Fabre's texts are hardly dramatic in the traditional sense of the term; nor are they calling for any form of straightforward *re*presentation. They seem to touch upon something else, which Sigrid Bousset has described suggestively as 'the voice of the absent'. In her opinion, 'Jan Fabre is a poet who gave words to the inner silence, to the lack, to the unknown in himself'.[38] On stage, this endeavour to give voice to silence is channelled through revolting bodies that scream, sweat, struggle and transform, as if reaching into the depths of our interior existence requires breaking through the physical boundaries and surfaces on which cultural conventions have inscribed themselves.

As Pina Bausch wanted her dancers to appear as individual subjects on stage, letting them speak and use their own voice was one of the strategies to fulfil this aim. However, as Gabrielle Cody observes, in her work, 'speech is never at the service of exposition or communication. Rather, words act as spontaneous emissions, states of mind and being, utterances that simply make audible the traces of a moment'.[39] Bausch could arguably only achieve this refunctionalization of speech by granting her performers a greater responsibility in the creative process. This brings us to the third and final point: besides fragmentation and language, there is another important strand structuring the directorial practice of Bausch, Castellucci and Fabre. This concerns the function of the performer, which – in contrast to the previous two – constitutes a ground of both con- *and* divergence.

A common feature that each of these three directors share is that in their work there are no preconceived characters the performers must relate to, in terms of either impersonation or a rather Brechtian distance [see **Volume 2**]. As such, they partake in the tendency that began to announce itself in the theatre from the late 1970s onwards and which encouraged Elinor Fuchs to proclaim 'the death of character'.[40] After the rise of so-called post-modernity had brought about an already startling range of 'deaths' or other kinds of endings – of metanarratives, of history, of metaphysics, of the author, and so forth – it seems as if the sweeping grasp of the post-modernist current had finally reached the core of theatre by destabilizing the largely tacit assumption that bringing a character to life is one of the constitutive traits that defines theatre as theatre. According to Fuchs, the ways in which post-modernist theorists were questioning the fixity of the subject, replacing it for constructivist angles that emphasized the ongoing and culturally conditioned constitution of an individual's identity (which several years later became a topic of debate itself), found its theatrical correlate in the decline of the character. While Fuchs offers a valuable historicization of this tendency, pointing out that pioneers such as Strindberg, Brecht and Pirandello had already precipitated the gradual demise of the traditional dramatic character, she nevertheless emphasizes that the late twentieth century amplified and deepened these early reconsiderations of the character's function in theatre. Interestingly, Fuchs herself anticipates Lehmann's later emphasis on the landscape as a founding metaphor for post-dramatic theatre:

> The human figure, instead of providing perspectival unity to a stage whose setting acts as backdrop and visual support, is treated as an element in what might be described as a theatrical landscape. Correspondingly the spectator's focus on this stage is no longer convergent: it is darting or diffuse, noting some configurations, missing others, or absorbing all in a heterogeneous gaze.[41]

It might well be argued that since the turn of the millennium the character has been replaced with the 'figure', which may be the most felicitous term to describe the human actors still populating the theatrical stage (and perhaps even also the non-human objects that take up an increasingly central place in what is currently known as posthumanist performances). From this perspective, Pina Bausch seems to stand on the threshold between the dramatic and post-dramatic or post-modernist aesthetic paradigms, as many of her pieces focus on the human individual or the singular subject with its own history and background, though she shows great mastery in abstracting these personal circumstances into larger and perhaps even universal conditions. Raimund Hoghe, who worked as a dramaturg with Pina Bausch from 1980 to 1990, describes how the staging of the particular might also touch upon deeper layers of human existence: 'The seemingly personal and yet general movements: as they are not wrapped up in a (theatre) history, they are history itself, referring to clear traces of lived and unlived lives.'[42] In her directorial practice, Bausch starts from the personality, input and inspirations each of her performers bring to the creative process. However, as Mariama Diagne rightly remarks in her chapter, Bausch is not interested in exposing the private intimacy of the performers, but rather in balancing the specificity of the individual with the potential generality of his or her condition.

Bausch is arguably the first choreographer to show the individual *behind* the dancer, which is probably most clearly signalled by the fact that in most of her pieces the performers were called by their own names. Jan Fabre's landmark 1982 production, *This is theatre like it was to be expected and foreseen*, contains a scene that playfully engages with this individualization of the performer. Near the end of the piece, all actors are summoned one by one by calling out their name and profession. Sitting naked on a chair, they respond by standing up, bending over until they fall onto the ground and then going back to their initial seated position. As with many other sequences in *This is theatre ...*, this series of actions is repeated in a seemingly endless loop until the actors are left exhausted. For all its bold simplicity, this scene is quite remarkable, since it seems to offer the audience something that resembles a bow, which in the end turns out to be a fall, while the naming of each performer emphasizes that the bodies we have seen running, jumping or undressing throughout almost eight hours are actual human beings whose life extends beyond the confines of the theatrical cocoon the piece had been creating for us. 'Their outside body fully coincides with what is being demonstrated in this fictional space', Luk Van den Dries observes, 'these ordinary bodies repeat the statement that they are ordinary bodies. They sweat out themselves'.[43]

This particular 'naming-scene' primarily indicates how, in Fabre's oeuvre, the performers are less coupled to individual histories or personal remembrance than in Bausch's pieces, while it still upholds the importance of the performer's identity as a crucial input for the eventual embodiment of the work. If a spectrum could be drawn that runs from character to figure, Fabre is moving more closely to the latter, as the bodies appearing in his pieces are often ecstatically visceral and abundantly physical *creatures* whose identity is hard to recognize, let alone to pinpoint. As Luk Van den

Dries shows in his contribution to this volume, while 'transformation' is a key principle in Jan Fabre's acting methodology, it is the transformation into *something* else, rather than someone else, that interests him the most. However, the seemingly simple act of ending *This is theatre* ... with calling the performers by the name can be regarded as Fabre's theatrical credo that his work could not exist without the individual personalities giving shape and reshaping his own artistic imagination. It is hardly surprising, then, that – as in the case of Pina Bausch – improvisation is a vital part of Fabre's creative practice as a theatre director.

Romeo Castellucci can be positioned at the ultimate end of the spectrum. He radicalizes the notion of the figure by creating a kind of theatre that starts completely from his own imagination and only allows the performers to enter into the process just before a piece is about to premiere, when Castellucci is ready to test out his ideas on stage. The performer's input does not function as a potential source of inspiration for Castellucci; it is rather their particular physicality that convinces him to work with certain actors. This is tellingly illustrated by the call for auditions issued by the Socìetas Raffaello Sanzio for the restaging of Castellucci's *Oresteia* in 2015. For the role of Electra, for example, Castellucci is looking for an actress who is 'rather short. Corpulent. Aged between 25 and 35. Only a few lines to recite', while Aegisthus must be 'a young actor, very muscular and with a perfect stature' and Pylades 'a very tall actor, at least 190 cm. Extremely thin. No recitation. Aged between 30 and 40'.[44]

The emphasis on weight, height and age demonstrates that bodily facts and physical appearance are more important to Castellucci than personal background or experience in acting. It is the dramaturgy of corporeality he is interested in, instead of the performers' aptness for transformation (as with Jan Fabre) or their individual personality (as with Pina Bausch). As Eleni Papalexiou discusses in her chapter, Castellucci's bodies are often 'deviant' or marked by illness; they are, as Thomas Crombez points out, 'anomalous bodies'. These body types infuse Castellucci's theatre with a realness that punctuates the autonomous universe he aims to create, as highlighted by the immense gauze curtains he often inserts between the events on stage and the audience, challenging spectators to pierce through this porous border in order to enter the enigmatic world of Castellucci's imagination. Next to (ab)normal bodies, Castellucci also includes animals and even small children in his productions, since they too complicate the representational machinery of the theatre by referring only to themselves instead of coinciding with a role or character. Nonetheless, even though the corpo*reality* of these bodies, animals and children is what motivates Castellucci's choice to work with them, once they are absorbed in the poetical microcosm he puts on stage, they unavoidably also turn into figures with a distinct sculptural quality. Not only their physical contours and bodily traits, but also their movements, actions or poses become part of the scenic imagery. As a director who first started in the visual arts, Castellucci can rightly be described as a sculptor of the stage, who uses all theatrical means at hand to craft a world that simultaneously parallels and exceeds our own.

Staging directors

There is no straight line to be drawn in the history of theatre as innovations, ruptures, changes or tendencies are all part of a whirling vortex that runs in circles, sometimes expanding its reach to affect large parts of the landscape while at other times condensing into a local incision whose impact will resonate only with a delay. Swirling between the macro-developments in post-war theatre and the micro-level of the artistic practice of three leading theatre directors, this book documents the trajectories, poetics and oeuvres of Pina Bausch, Romeo Castellucci and Jan Fabre to flesh out the most cardinal directions in director's theatre during the late twentieth and early twenty-first centuries. The contributions in this volume connect personal histories with iconic theatre pieces, key poetical principles with concrete stagings, archival documentation with critical analysis. Even though each chapter looks to chart which characteristics make the directorial practices of Bausch, Castellucci and Fabre unique in their kind, their attention to the underlying lines of influence leading up to their work and eventually emanating from it testifies to this volume's premise that the recent past, necessarily and intriguingly, reverberates with older histories whose imprint continues to sprawl among different times. Similarly, the discussions and insights collected in this book will undoubtedly resonate with various other volumes in the *Great Stage Directors* series, which offers ample opportunities to seek cross-temporal connections and unexpected correspondences. Ultimately, then, the chapters in this volume and the books in this series might throw multiple and different lights upon each other, perhaps even enlightening the epoch we are living in today.

Pina Bausch

1

Directing Bodies in Dance: A Visit to Pina Bausch, Now and Then

Mariama Diagne

Pina Bausch is known for an unconventional repertoire of theatrical dance works she created together with and nearly exclusively for the Tanztheater Wuppertal, an ensemble of dancing artists she brought together and directed from 1973 until her sudden passing in 2009. With legendary signature pieces such as *Le Sacre du Printemps* (The Rite of Spring, 1975) and *Café Müller* (1978), Bausch is recognized as the pioneer of 'Tanztheater', as it developed in WestGermany during the Cold War.[1] The aesthetics of her work as well as her specific approach to creating and directing dance have greatly influenced various generations not only of dancers and choreographers but also theatre and movie directors. Both her work and her life have been discussed by numerous scholars and critics,[2] leading to worldwide recognition of Pina Bausch as the founding mother of 'Tanztheater' in the twentieth century. This high praise made Bausch into one of the most successful female German choreographers in the recent history of the performing arts, who, quite exceptionally at the time, managed to be appointed as a director of her own dance company.

Bausch's work can still be seen on contemporary theatre stages, as the Tanztheater Wuppertal continues to perform pieces from the repertoire. While her unexpected death left a deep void within her company, both the ensemble and the Pina Bausch Foundation maintain the work to commemorate her achievements, even if this continued tribute is tinged with a shade of grief.[3] Keeping Bausch's legacy alive also means that it necessarily changes, since the transmission of dance between different bodies and through audio-visual media or subjective memories never leaves the work entirely intact. The efforts of the Tanztheater Wuppertal to prolong the life of Bausch's oeuvre by continuing to engage new dancers to work with longstanding members, who pass their knowledge of the choreographies on to newer generations, are a vital complement to the Pina Bausch Archive, which was founded in 2010. Whereas the archive preserves and also attempts to digitize most of the documentary material Bausch had left after passing away, it is the Tanztheater's ongoing engagement to perform her work that constitutes a *living* archive of its own, granting access to Bausch's legacy through live performance, the medium in which it was meant to exist.

The idea of *infinity* as ongoing movement that seems to steer the Tanztheater's current activities has always been at the core of Bausch's choreographic practice. As a closing remark of the speech she gave when she was awarded the Kyoto Prize in 2007, she said: 'the search never stops. It contains something that is endless, and that is the beauty of it. Whenever I look at our work I have the feeling that I only just started.'[4] In her Kyoto speech, which has often been quoted ever since she delivered it,[5] Bausch recounts personal memories of her life and work, beginning with her childhood in Solingen, a city close to Wuppertal where she was born in 1940. She goes on by looking back at her education as a dancer, first at the Folkwang School in Essen where she studied from 1955 until 1959, after which she moved to New York City, to study at the Juilliard School for the Arts with a scholarship. Bausch thereafter describes her encounters with artists, her first steps as a choreographer creating smaller works and her eventual function as an artistic director of a large ensemble. She also offers insight into her creative process and how she, in the 1970s, started to develop her by now famous method of asking her dancers personal questions to generate the basic material for the work. The speech ends with a reflection on her continued aim to initiate and explore encounters with people and their passions, not only within her company, but also in the various countries to which the Tanztheater Wuppertal has travelled to show her work.

Following a similar trajectory, this chapter starts with the early stages of Bausch's education and career, moving on to her first years at the Tanztheater Wuppertal. By looking closely at this period in which the foundations for Bausch's particular approach to making dance were laid, it becomes possible not only to articulate how her longstanding interest in theatricalizing everyday life radically redefined what choreography is or can be, but also to flesh out the specificity of her directorial practice, which I will describe as her astounding talent to direct moving bodies on stage. Bausch's innovative ways of giving directions to get bodies moving is currently continued in various acts of passing on her legacy outside the Tanztheater Wuppertal. These transmissions are the topic of this chapter's last section, which considers how Bausch's past can be secured for the future.

Formative encounters:
Pina Bausch's early period

When Pina Bausch went to study at the Folkwang School in 1955, it was Kurt Jooss (1901–79) who would become Bausch's first mentor. Jooss, who also founded the school in 1927, had trained in both expressionist dance and ballet.[6] His methods for generating movement shaped Bausch's education as a dancer and later her own choreographic work, while also his efforts to establish dance as an autonomous discipline within the performing arts had a formative influence on her. What connects the typically German traditions of 'Moderner Tanz' (modern dance) and Tanztheater is that they were each built on a naturalistic approach towards body movement, which means that instead of subjecting the body to the shape of a pose, choreographers and dancers would follow the movements generated by the body itself.[7] So too the relationship between effort and shape – as it was formulated by Rudolf von Laban – played an important role.[8]

Together with his colleague Sigurd Leeder (1902–81), Jooss created the 'Jooss-Leeder-method', a hybrid of principles that were adopted from both classical ballet and expressionist dance, leading to new approaches to German modern dance.[9] Jooss valued the 'merits of the classical movement systematics' of ballet, but rather more for its disciplinary technique than its aesthetics.[10] At the Folkwang School, dance techniques were thought to enhance the development of a singular but also repeatable movement vocabulary, in order to arrive at a contemporary form of the so-called 'Handlungsballett' (narrative ballet).[11] The most significant piece of this kind is Jooss' *Der Grüne Tisch* (The Green Table, 1933), a choreography that is often considered timeless in its poignant evocation of the excruciating losses that people suffer in times of war while others try to gain profit from warfare.[12]

As a student at the dance department of the Juilliard School in New York – which at that time was led by Alfredo Corvino (1916–2005), who was a former member of the Ballets Russes de Monte Carlo[13] – Bausch took classes with Antony Tudor (1908–87). His approach to dance was influenced by Wigman, Jooss and mostly Michel Fokine, choreographer of the Ballets Russes.[14] His interest in Sigmund Freud and Carl Jung's theories of the human psyche led to the creation of his so-called 'psychological ballets' for which he chose 'imaginative dancers' who were 'extremely musical and malleable people, with emotional breadth and warmth'.[15] Other instructors were choreographers such as José Limón (1908–72) and Paul Taylor (1930–), which enabled Bausch to gain deeper insight into the distinct characteristics of American modern dance and ballet. Bausch must have made a strong impression on her teachers, as she was invited to dance with Antony Tudor at the Metropolitan Opera Ballet while she also worked with Paul Taylor at the New American Ballet in 1962.

During her time in the United States, Bausch performed on numerous occasions. She danced, for instance, the third leading role in *In View of God* (1959), a piece choreographed by Paul Sanasardo (1928–) and Donya Feuer (1934–2011), who each danced the other two leading parts. Bausch also presented her solo *Girl in the Big City*, choreographed to musical arrangements by George Gershwin at the festival *The World of Dance and Fashion* (1960). Another notable example is Bausch's role in *Four Seasons* (c. 1960), which was created by American dancer and choreographer La Meri (1899–1988) and was based on Antonio Vivaldi's music of the same title (1725). Bausch also appeared in dance sequences in operas at the Metropolitan Opera, including *Tannhäuser* and *Alkestis* by Tudor and *Carmen* and *Turandot* by Alexandra Danilova.

By performing in a variety of works, Bausch was exposed not only to different types of choreography, but also to several kinds of music, including baroque chamber music, compositions for bigger orchestras, opera music and compositions specifically made for dance. But it was especially her time at the Metropolitan Opera that had an important influence, since it was there that she would 'learn to distinguish between voices' and 'to listen very exactly'.[16] Later in her own work, music was a vital instrument to help generate the emotional atmosphere she aimed to provoke in her audiences and she used any style of music to achieve this, including folklore, jazz, pop music and *Schlagermusik* (German lyrical pop songs).

Bausch returned to Essen in 1960, as she was asked by Kurt Jooss to become a leading dancer in his newly founded Folkwang Ballet. When Jooss retired in 1969, Bausch succeeded him as director of the company and held the position for four years.[17] During this period, she also began to choreograph her own works, such as *Im Wind der Zeit* (In the Wind of Time, 1968) and *Nachnull* (Afterzero, 1970), while she was also commissioned by the Wuppertal Theatre to create two pieces, which became *Aktionen für Tänzer* (Actions for Dancers, 1971) and *Wiegenlied* (Lullaby, 1972). This eventually led to her appointment as director of the Wuppertal Ballet, a position she took up in 1973 after renaming the company Tanztheater Wuppertal.

Towards a new vocabulary:
Early dance works in Wuppertal

With her first evening-length dance programme as the newly appointed director of the Tanztheater, Bausch paid tribute to the formative encounters with dance and the arts she had experienced both in Germany and the United States. The programme, which premiered on 5 January 1974, consisted of Kurt Jooss' *The Green Table*, American choreographer Agnes de Mille's *Rodeo* (1942) and ended with Bausch's own new creation *Fritz* (1974).

With *Fritz*, Bausch confronted the audience with an unfamiliar aesthetic that only a few years later would dominate her entire way of directing movement on stage.

Fritz presents an assemblage of disturbing figures: a man named 'Mantelmann' (coat man) seems to have no neck as he is wearing a black hat covering his head; a woman called 'Mannfrau' (man-woman) has a huge mouth stitched onto her stomach; an old child named 'Mädchengreis' (elderly girl); a woman without hair called 'Kahle Frau' (bold woman); a 'Großmutter' (grandmother) who sits in a chair and, when rising up, transforms into a giant.[18] These figures seem eccentric and lonely, as they rarely interact. Moving sporadically in unison and performing popular songs from the 1920s or just experimental noise, the dancers create an oppressive atmosphere, while fragments of Gustav Mahler's third movement of Symphony No. 1 add a sense of melancholy to it as well. The movement material originated from daily events at rehearsals. One dancer, Dominique Mercy, suffered from a nervous cough during rehearsal, so Bausch asked him to repeat the sound and exaggerate the stagnant movement that followed each noisy and scratchy cough. The situation evolved into a movement phrase of repetitive, abrupt jumps, which were passed on to the 'coat man'. Situations such as these were embedded in the uncanny, fragmented narrative of the lonely child 'Fritz', performed by the female dancer Marlies Alt and later by Hiltrud Blanck. 'Fritz' stumbles through a loony environment of adults, including his or her parents.

The early 1970s post-war German audiences reacted to *Fritz* with anger and lack of comprehension. Bausch's Brechtian estrangement [see **Volume 2**] of everyday family life by means of repetition, exaggeration and an unconventional use of the dancer's voices cumulated in a non-comprehensible, psycho-social texture that seemed to overstrain the audience. Bausch's intention was to follow her interest in the dark German folktale of a *Märchen von einem, der auszog das Fürchten zu lernen* (The Story of a Boy Who Went Forth to Learn What Fear Was), written by the Grimm Brothers in 1812–18. It is a story about a boy who does not know fear and embarks on several adventures seeking for eerie encounters with the dead and the undead to experience the feeling of being scared, which did not happen until his later wife, a princess, one morning empties a bucket of cold water and fish over his head. Dominique Mercy, a classically trained dancer, remarked that 'for the first time I had the feeling that I, Dominique, was on stage and that I was giving and saying something of myself'.[19] Bausch's *Fritz* is one of the first pieces to demonstrate to what extent montage, collage and repetition were key strategies to deconstruct narrative structures and to theatricalize everyday situations. They shape the modes of composition that underlie Bausch's entire oeuvre.

Immediately after *Fritz*, Bausch choreographed the two dance operas *Iphigenia on Tauris* (1974) and *Orpheus and Eurydice* (1975), which – in contrast to most of her work – tell a comprehensible story based on a given music composition. Although they remain choreographic exceptions within Bausch's oeuvre, these dance operas nevertheless testify to her exceptional ways of directing music, props and moving bodies on stage. For *Iphigenia*, Bausch denied the singers the prominent position usually assigned to them, relocating them instead backstage into the wings. In *Orpheus and Eurydice*, the soloists joined the dancers during some of their movement sequences. The choir was intended to be seated on extremely high chairs during the opera's second act, titled 'Gewalt' (Violence), the singers ultimately refused Bausch's scenographic idea, preferring to be placed in the orchestra pit. The act eventually showed the soprano interpreting the role of Orpheus walking through a setting of fabric strings, woven across the stage by the dancing ensemble. At the end of the fourth act, 'Sterben' (Dying), the two dancers and two singers, who each represented Orpheus and Eurydice, sink one after the other as if they are drifting off to death on the concluding tones of the last aria.

The third piece in Bausch's oeuvre that translates an existing music score into dance is her widely praised *Le Sacre du Printemps* (The Rite of Spring, 1975). It was first presented as the last part of an evening-length programme, called *Das Frühlingsopfer* (which is the German translation of 'The Rite of Spring'), together with *Wind von West* (Wind from the West) – also called *Cantate* – and *Zweiter Frühling* (Second Spring). The Tanztheater Wuppertal eventually stopped performing these last two pieces, whereas *Le Sacre* continues to be staged, often together with *Café Müller* (1978).[20]

Wind from West and *Second Spring* contain fragments of a story, but do not provide a coherent narrative. In the first part of the programme, the stage is equipped with several layers of black, gossamer curtains, hanging from floor to ceiling and with their irregular width creating a maze-like room. Because of the scenography, no movement across the stage can be observed sharply, which creates the effect of dancers slowly disappearing while walking upstage. Practically the only prop is a table, which is placed off centre and used as a bed for one of the main characters, a young woman who seems either to be remembering scenes of her past or visiting figures and situations of her dreams. *Wind from West* offers a poetic, often sensual and figurative, but at times also abstract, choreography, resembling closely the aesthetics of contemporary ballet in those years and especially the work of choreographers such as Antony Tudor. At the same time, the setting of the stage and the use of the props bespeak Bausch's own directorial signature, whereas the influence of ballet is primarily visible in the lyrically choreographed steps.

Even though the three parts of the programme were presented together, there is a remarkably stark contrast between them. The stage setting, figures, time period and narrative structure of *Second Spring*, for example, refer to a completely different world. As opposed to the rather poetic universe of *Wind from West*, this piece unfolds in a space that might be as real as the living room of most audience members in West Germany in 1975. The everyday

FIGURE 1.1 Wind von West. *Photograph by Rolf Borzik, 1975, courtesy of the Pina Bausch Foundation.*

look of the setting arises primarily from the furniture and the objects that are placed on stage, including an old red couch with velvety fabrics, a small set of two wooden chairs, a table with porcelain and silverware that is set for two and real food such as soup, bread and wine. The apparent realism is enhanced through the costumes and actions of the performers: a woman and a man impersonate an elderly married couple, called 'Älteres Ehepaar' (elderly couple), that enjoys a dinner for two at home. Announced as 'Die Erinnerungen' (the memories), a group of dancers gathers next to them, with each dancer presenting a different figure, such as a young woman in a red dress, dancing flamenco steps. The title of the piece feeds into the assumption that it presents the couple's second spring being interrupted by recollections of past moments and companions. The dreamlike structure of this piece also dominates the movement aesthetics and stands out against the scenography, which is primarily composed of items of everyday life, including furniture, objects and activities.[21]

The third piece of the *Frühlingsopfer*-programme is *Le Sacre du Printemps*, a choreography that would grow into one of Bausch's signature pieces.[22] The dancers struggle to move across dry turf that covers the entire stage. The use of turf is exemplary of Bausch's interest in using real elements from nature, which also recurs in other pieces such as the water in *Arien* (Arias, 1979), leaves in *Blaubart* (Bluebard, 1977), or sequoia trees in *Nur Du* (Only You, 1996). The choreography presents a pagan rite which culminates in the final sacrificial dance in which a woman, the 'Chosen

One', dances to death in order to satisfy the gods of spring. Despite being highly individual, Bausch's interpretation ostentatiously echoes the ground-breaking choreography that Vaslav Nijinsky (1989–50) had created in 1913 for the Ballets Russes, together with composer Igor Stravinsky (1882–1971). *Le Sacre du Printemps* was nothing less than a revolutionary piece that subverted several of the reigning conventions in both music and dance. In Nijinsky's choreography, a group of dancers and a soloist, who interprets the victim, appear with inward rotated feet, stumbling and pitching to the ground. Their style of dance stood diametrically opposed to classical ballet's orientation towards upward movements and jumps to create the impression that dancers briefly float through the air. Nijinsky also substituted the traditional tutus and leotards of ballet for costumes that conveyed imaginative impressions of a primitive tribe in pagan Russia. To reinforce this tribal look, the dancers appear with heavily painted faces instead of wearing make-up that underscores one's beauty, as had been common in Europe.[23] These innovations, together with Stravinsky's unsettling music score, came as a shock to the audience attending the premiere at the recently renovated Théâtre des Champs-Élysées in Paris. This ended in a riot because the piece caused loud protest among spectators. Despite – or perhaps, rather, partly because of – the scandal it provoked, *Le Sacre du Printemps* and its notorious 'crime against grace' went down in history as one of the greatest masterpieces of twentieth-century dance.[24]

It is the tension between theatrical abstraction and real physicality that becomes evident in Bausch's interpretation of *Le Sacre du Printemps* and which will continue to inform nearly her entire oeuvre. While, dramaturgically, she held on to Nijinsky's abstraction of movement and stage design, she added a physical aspect that was not present in the original: as the dancers give expression to the human condition of shock and fear, their dismay is not mimicked or narrated but follows immediately from the 'rite' and the movements they are executing. This close connection between the actual choreography and the affective states of being the dance eventually expresses is again reminiscent of the psychological aspects in Tudor's work. The costumes are also different in Bausch's reinterpretation of *Le Sacre*: as if to intensify the dancer's physicality, she chooses to dress the women in transparent flesh-coloured chemises while the men are wearing black suit-like trousers with their torsos kept naked. Another important alteration is that Bausch left out the first part of Nijinsky's choreography, called 'The Adoration of the Earth', which he had introduced to establish the naturalistic atmosphere that had to envelop the entire piece. Instead, Bausch worked with abstract action: both women and men are running and stumbling across the turf in a fearful search to select the chosen one, who later during the piece will appear in a red chemise, being the only dancer dressed in a colour.

In interviews, dancers recall how, during the rehearsal process for *Le Sacre*, Bausch compelled them to search for a quality of realness. Jo Ann

Endicott, for example, remembered how she exceeded her own physical limits in order to appear as 'really dead'.[25] Bausch asked her 'to die' but 'not like a dying swan',[26] by which she obviously meant that Endicott should not pretend to be dying, as in a classical ballet, but rather evoke the feeling of dying as a real human being.[27] Bausch's advice for Ruth Amarante was to feel the 'mortal fear of death'.[28] The same emotional involvement was demanded from the group: observing the sacrifice, they ought to become filled with the fear of seeing a colleague dancing herself to death. Endicott remembered that 'the choreography unfolded and there we were, sweaty and breathless, the whole room trembling as we watched Marlies fighting against death ... Then, at the end, she fell down, dead ... I couldn't bear it and I ran off stage sobbing'.[29]

Going along with Stravinsky's disharmonious composition, Bausch's choreography picks up the intensity provided by the musical score. Groups of dancers gather together, directed as one forceful body that moves within a choreography of multiple, contrary tensions. While heads are thrown sideways, the torsos are twisted the opposite way. The arms and legs also move in opposed directions. Bausch choreographed a fight between the limbs of the dancers' bodies:

> The lower stomach, the solar plexus and the sternum are essential. It gets visible when the victim dances herself to death. Many movements are initiated in the sacral bones, and quite often the movements direct the span of the sternum in combination with the sacral bones. Most concise are movements of the hands and arms directed between the legs.[30]

Bausch's choreography shifts between dances for the group and smaller movements for single dancers to break away from the tribal ceremony. As described above, the roots of Bausch's dance training and choreographies from her earlier period are easily retraceable in works such as *Wind von West*, but also in *Le Sacre*, where patterns from Tudor's melancholic piece *Dark Elegies* (1937) are visible.[31] Several publications put great emphasis on Bausch's *Le Sacre*, while previous pieces are more often regarded as choreographic pre-work.[32] Even at the Tanztheater Wuppertal itself, *Le Sacre* continues to be treated as a standard, since, up until today, sequences from the work are still used for auditions to probe the aptitude of the candidates.

Defining the work of Pina Bausch is considered to be a challenge precisely because the aesthetics of her dance theatre refrain from offering spectators a set of signs and hints that could support a clear-cut interpretation or straightforward understanding. And, as Norbert Servos points out, despite her own strong technical background, 'Pina Bausch has always insisted, quite reasonably, that her work cannot be judged as choreography. Her dance theatre is not a technique'.[33] The difficulties that Bausch's work raised for interpretation led to a certain depreciative tendency in the critical discourse on her work. Already in 1977, dance critic Edmund Gleede stated that he 'is tired of having to consider suicide after every Bausch performance' and that he 'will reject her' as long as she does not offer 'more spirit, more tenderness and more charity' in her work.[34] Swiss dance scholar and critic Christina Thurner reads Gleede's statements, among other sources, as symptomatic of the ambivalent attitude that audience members and critics had towards Bausch's work. On the one hand, they acknowledged her talent as a choreographer in staging dance theatre pieces, whereas, on the other hand, they mistrusted the way Bausch directed movement without displaying technical virtuosity.[35]

Looking at the aesthetics and structural composition of Bausch's work, it is readily clear that she turned away from the narrative structures of classical ballet while also dismissing the illusion of weightlessness through tulle skirts and pointe shoes.[36] There is one piece in which Bausch directly references the tradition of ballet but only to comment upon it. In *Viktor* (1986), a woman covers her naked toes with raw meat before entering the stiff pointe shoes and then aggressively binding the satin ribbons around her ankles. The role is danced by a female company member who is trained in dancing en pointe and can float across the stage with fairylike arms for about seven minutes.

This sequence is obviously meant as a critical demystification of the ballerina's apparent ease in dancing en pointe, while it actually requires enormous strength and effort. But the reference to ballet in *Viktor* also opens up for consideration of the idea that Bausch did not entirely skip the core of technique. In general, dancers must have the ability to balance while being connected to the ground only with a small surface, whether that surface is one foot or just the tip of the toe. This technique, which is also called equilibrium, is also necessary for walking in high heels which the dancers, both male and female, do in almost every piece by Bausch. By trading pointe shoes for high heels, Bausch again inserted an element from everyday life into her pieces, while costumes and movements often recall popular theatrical genres as well, such as the revue or the musical which typically combine singing and dancing.[37]

At first sight, the movement language that Bausch started to develop during her first years as director of the Tanztheater Wuppertal seemed to be rootless, since it consisted of jumps, walks or falling, with virtually no traces of poses and figures that were known from modern dance or ballet. In this respect, Bausch somehow morphed what she had learned during her education and work as a dancer into a whole new language of her own. 'It would have never crossed my mind', she once said, 'to use any movement phrase of Martha Graham or Kurt Jooss or from anyone else. And that is why I started to search for something else, mainly because I just did not want to use a specific vocabulary'.[38] Bausch did not create a fixed vocabulary that led to a specific technique or a 'Bausch-school', even though her specific approach to directing dance did leave an indelible mark on the history of twentieth-century dance and theatre.

Working methods:
Asking questions and staging *Macbeth*

The work of Pina Bausch is often praised for the overwhelming emotionality it generates through seemingly banal and mundane situations. Her search for a different theatrical language and movement idiom may perhaps not have led to a clearly circumscribed technique but it has resulted in a specific poetics, which arises from everyday life but works to theatricalize this material and turn it into a skilfully crafted work that is familiar in its concreteness and at the same time thought-provoking in its abstraction.

One pivotal and well-known strategy to arrive at this peculiar mix of concreteness and abstraction is Bausch's reliance on asking questions as a method to generate ideas for single movements, a series of actions or particular situations. In a 1998 interview with the German talk show host Roger Willemsen, Bausch concisely describes her working procedure. After asking a question such as, for example, 'What do you do when you are tender?', the process would go as follows:

> Everybody thinks of a gesture, like: what does one do to him- or herself, in terms of tenderness? And then I just say, okay, six different gestures that deal with tenderness, for example. And these questions aren't just some random questions, but rather I try to narrow something down that I intrinsically know, but which has neither a form nor a word.[39]

Questions are used to initiate a process of finding movement and of defining situations that could surround these movements. The ensemble often spent weeks exploring possible answers to Bausch's questions, while the eventual selection and moulding of the material into a performance piece fell under Bausch's directorial responsibility. Creating transcripts and developing a notebook were an important part of this process. As Bausch explains: 'Everybody writes down everything they had done themselves. And I write down everything. And we film all the things that are connected with movement. All this is just like a notebook.'[40] One of the reasons why everything had to be documented so meticulously stemmed from the fact that, when the phase of experimentation was about to end and Bausch felt ready to start with the actual composition of the piece, she asked her dancers to redo some of the material in order to assess its potential value. 'And then the time comes', Bausch says, 'when I want to see all the things that have been left again. The dancers need to be capable to demonstrate it again, and then we see how it feels now.'[41]

The questions and tasks that Bausch confronted her dancers with during rehearsal were always personal but they were emphatically not intended to expose the privacy of the individual: 'I never ask for something private; I always ask for the specific. When a dancer answers, there is something in his answer we all have inside of us. We are aware of it, but it does not emanate from an intellectual perspective at first.'[42] Questions were not always understood the way Bausch hoped. During the rehearsal process for *Viktor*, for example, she prompted her dancers to come up with a possible response to the following cue: 'something, that one does, doesn't work'.[43] Bausch did not give more specific information about the question, or what she wanted to achieve with it. The dancers apparently understood Bausch's request in a literal way, as they offered gestures such as trying to light matches on teeth. In order to redirect them, Bausch rephrased her question and gave some additional explanation: 'It's something that you can do – don't look for anything very absurd. Actually, I thought that something very sad would come out it. I thought that something stops because one doesn't have the strength anymore.'[44] In her analysis of this rehearsal moment, dance scholar Heidi Gilpin reads Bausch's own clarification as indicative of her aim to search for 'movement [that] would stop because the originary force is no longer present', which in Gilpin's opinion 'calls into crisis the identity of movement performance, if not life itself', insofar as it puts 'absence – and failure – of movement' at the very heart of choreographic practice.[45]

The misunderstanding between Bausch and her dancers points to the subtle nuances of the language that Bausch used in order to develop her thoughts and her work. The paradox is that she needed language – and, related to this, her method of formulating questions and tasks – to create a radically new form of dance theatre that had no coherent narrative and instead took the dancers' and her own input as its primary material:

> It is something very different, when one creates a piece that does not yet have a plot or a theme. There is no piece, we start working, and there is nothing except ourselves and the situation that is present – simply our situation. Who we just are, today on this earth, so to speak (smiles). And there is no music as well, no stage prospect. So literally just us by ourselves.[46]

The first time that Bausch started to work with questions was in 1978, when she was invited by Peter Zadek, director of the Municipal Theatre in Bochum, to create her version of Shakespeare's tragedy *Macbeth* for the acting ensemble in the context of the festivities of the German Shakespeare Society in Bochum. Instead of adopting the original title of the play, she used, quite significantly, one of the stage directions appearing in the Shakespearean text: *Er nimmt sie an der Hand und führt sie in das Schloß, die anderen folgen* (He takes her by the hand and leads her into the castle, the others follow). As the title already indicates, Bausch's choreographic adaptation of the play did not stick to the letter of Shakespeare's *Macbeth*. Instead, she fragmented and deconstructed the original text into an associational system of loose references, combining movement and speech to create a piece that can be considered a form of dance theatre in the most literal sense of the term.

FIGURE 1.2 Er nimmt sie an der Hand und führt sie in das Schloß, die anderen folgen. *Photograph by Ulli Weiss, 1978, courtesy of the Pina Bausch Foundation.*

Bausch was very conscious of the particular circumstances in which she would be creating her *Macbeth*. While she took a few dancers from the Tanztheater Wuppertal with her to perform in the piece, the other members of the cast were actors without any professional experience or education in dance whatsoever. She started to audition the actors by asking questions such as 'What did you have for breakfast?' She then gave the task to 'walk while remembering what you had for breakfast'.[47] Bausch's intention was to make the actors think about something else in order to distract them from being too conscious of the way they were moving while walking. Assignments such as these are nowadays no longer considered new or innovative in theatrical practices. In 1978, however, theatre actors were usually not confronted with the request to respond to a question that had seemingly nothing to do with a given drama text or to carry out a task that did not involve the use of their voice, especially not the kind of actors who worked at institutions such as the Municipal Theatre Bochum.[48]

Bausch's version of *Macbeth* demonstrates how her method of asking questions melts into a series of repeated movements, actions, motifs or figures, as she seemed to convert the narrative development of Shakespeare's play into a distilled time and space. For about two-and-a-half hours, spectators followed the inner state of ambivalence and undecidability that haunts the piece's protagonists. Should Macbeth obey the whispers of the ghosts telling him to kill in order to obtain power or should he follow his own moral compass and spare many lives? Men and women scream and speak fragments from Shakespeare's tragedy, but not enough for the audience to follow a narrative thread. A man slaps a woman in the face, but with tenderness; a woman stands and commands herself to 'sit down, relax, walk towards the wall, smile, put your hands through your hair'. These phrases invoke an almost desperate execution of power and the actions cause discomfort for the audience as well as for the actors and dancers.

The complexity of Macbeth's tragic condition is mirrored in the lavish and technically elaborate scenography of the work, which was developed by Rolf Borzik who had been creating the sets and costumes for Bausch's work from the very first performance she made at the Tanztheater Wuppertal until his death in 1980. Oversized windows, a jukebox and seats from a movie theatre refer to public spaces. The shower cabin that is placed on stage seems to be an extraneous element within this setting, even if it is used as a functional prop. The shower is connected with a pipeline behind the stage to make it actually work. Whenever it is used during the piece, the water runs down the stage forming a small lake in an area that had been lowered. Another pipe brings the water underneath the stage and back to the shower cabin and, from there, down the drain.

Bausch's use of water on stage, which became a recurring element throughout her oeuvre, was part of the reason why the premiere of her *Macbeth* generated unease and even outrage among audience members. Glenn Loney, for instance, recounts that because the water was splashing from the stage, 'members of the West German Shakespeare Society who had bought out the front, high-priced rows of seats had to retreat to a safer distance'.[49] The fact that spectators did not get the *Macbeth* they were perhaps expecting to see caused such an outrage that they tossed objects on stage, screamed and roared at the performers.[50] The potential expectations of audience members were even further disrupted by the radically challenging structure of Bausch's piece, which Norbert Servos has described as an 'endless work in progress'.[51]

There is one particular scene in which this alleged endlessness becomes poignantly palpable. Starting from down stage left, the performers walk in a diagonal across the stage[52] and disappear behind the scenery. One performer after another continues to walk while making gestures (washing their hands or lifting their arms as if they had to explain something complicated), making noises with their feet or screaming words that might belong to Shakespeare's text. At some point, music by Verdi is played. It is not the action by itself that troubles the viewer, it is the ongoing repetition of the sequence, without any hint of its ending. By repeating the same movements over and over again and continuing to walk across the stage for about ten minutes, the ensemble puts the audience's patience to the test.

Within this repetitive structure, links between the figures of Macbeth and Lady Macbeth are suggested through the tension created between men and women. At a certain point, the women are carried around like dolls. They do not move until they are relocated at a different spot on stage. One might interpret this action, which also returns in several other pieces by Bausch, as men inflicting their power on passive, repressed women. However, even though a feminist agenda has often been assigned to Bausch's work, she never wanted to privilege the position of women:

> I am interested in the man and his relation towards the woman, and vice versa, both of them are interesting to me. I cannot think of a woman alone without at the same time thinking about the man, and the other way around. But that does not mean, I am not interested in things that are given. I would like to be allowed being interested in both.[53]

Of great importance is her last remark, 'being interested in both', which could also mean being interested in both sexes *at the same time*. Cross-dressing is a recurring motif throughout Bausch's oeuvre, as can be seen in pieces such as *Die Sieben Todsünden* (The Seven Deadly Sins, 1978), *Bandoneon* (1980) or *Nelken* (Carnations, 1982). Male dancers wearing female costumes or vice versa is obviously meant to reveal how clothes play an important part in the culturally constructed codification of gender identities. As dance historian Hedwig Müller states, in Bausch's pieces 'the clothes are protection for the body and at the same time a constrictive ascription of gender roles'.[54]

In her choreographic adaptation of *Macbeth*, Bausch addresses the dynamics of gender power not through costumes but through movement. The image of the female dancers being carried around like dolls actually contains in it the profound shift the character of Lady Macbeth undergoes in Shakespeare's play. Whereas Lady Macbeth is first presented as a decided advocate of committing murders in order to obtain power, she ultimately turns into a tormented figure who, burdened by the blood that is shed, eventually dies, allegedly by suicide. The question whether Shakespeare's tragedy seeks to assert female power or, conversely, ends up reasserting male dominance through Lady Macbeth's fatal ending has been much debated among scholars.[55] Bausch seems to take no position, insofar as she is interested in – again – both sides of Lady Macbeth. This is reflected in the choreographic technique required to create the image of women being carried around like dolls. In order to achieve the stiffness of a non-living object, the female dancer who is being lifted needs to maintain a great amount of inner tension. While it might look as if she is carried around as a passive, repressed figure she is, in fact, using real physical power to appear as a non-moving object. In other words, it takes strength to create the image of being weak. These lifts can thus be seen as a method of creating something significant and concrete out of something that might be less noticeable and abstract. In this manner, Bausch presents both qualities of Lady Macbeth at the same time: her forceful insistence on committing murders vis-à-vis her being oppressed by the situation, which ultimately leads to her death.

Body concepts: Autography and memory

To clarify the specific manner in which Pina Bausch directed moving bodies on stage, it is useful to look at those instances in which she herself appears in her own work. In *Danzón* (1995), for example, there is a melancholic solo slowly performed by Bausch. She enters the stage from left to right, dressed in black, with loose pants and a wide shirt.[56] The backdrop is an oversized video recording of swimming goldfish that move their fins through sea grass and yellow-green algae. Bausch walks gradually across the stage, with a spotlight on her body so that her own shadow accompanies her. She pauses and begins serpentine arm movements, gracefully meandering along her body. As if waking up from a dream, she opens her eyes, raises her hand, smiles and waves. A few minutes later, after repeating the serpentine arm movements and extending the curves through her torso, she slowly continues to walk across the scene, from left to right, leaving the stage with closed eyes, waving farewell. The spotlight ceases and her body disappears, followed by her shadow.

The shadow that accompanies Bausch's body throughout the entire *Danzón* solo has a doubling effect as it echoes her own physical appearance. This brings to mind another and probably more famous piece in which Bausch performed herself. In *Café Müller* (1978), Bausch danced one of the main roles: a woman who stumbles across the stage as if she were sleepwalking, hitting chairs and tables in a setting that is reminiscent of an

FIGURE 1.3 *Pina Bausch in* Danzón. *Photograph by Ulli Weiss, courtesy of the Pina Bausch Foundation.*

abandoned restaurant at night. Her movements give the impression that she is powerless and controlled by an external force, only there is no suggestive sign of something or someone being in charge of her. It is striking that some of the photographs that show Bausch dancing in *Café Müller* also capture her shadow as if in this performance too she is haunted by her own body. But the motif of the double is also present in a more direct manner. Next to the sleepwalking woman, there is another figure on stage, a woman who is dressed like Bausch and echoes her in certain movement sequences, such as the scene in which both of them are standing against a wall and sinking down. Even though most photographs of *Café Müller* show only a single woman (Bausch) and her shadow, the piece actually presents two people, a second body that occasionally melts into a single figure when doing the same movement.

These pieces in which Bausch can be seen dancing herself illuminate the role that her own body played in creating her work, while the motif of the double hints at her intention to pass the movements on to others.[57] While it is obvious that, as a choreographer, Bausch's profession was to produce movement or danced steps, it actually would be more accurate to state that Bausch directed other bodies, in the literal sense of giving them direction by making them move, interact and sense. In this process, Bausch's own body operated as a vessel that channels the ideas, themes or affects that underlie the work. Regardless of whether it was the role of Iphigenia, Eurydice, Orpheus or the Chosen One in *Le Sacre du Printemps*, for each Bausch accentuated her bodily autograph: 'These roles had all been written with my own body.'[58] Bausch's body seems to function as the primary avenue that allows her to direct other bodies, while at the same time crystallizing into a non-scripted but retraceable signature that permeates her entire oeuvre.

Based on these considerations, one could say that Bausch ultimately pursues a deeply embodied kind of theatrical directing. This particular approach to directing has, in turn, further-reaching implications that stretch beyond the ways in which Bausch developed a highly singular aesthetic and which challenge our habitual views on the body and dance. The underpinnings of Bausch's embodied directorial practice can be clarified by looking at recent theorizations of the body that stress its inherently relational nature. What philosopher and anthropologist José Gil calls 'the paradoxical body', for instance, is 'a body that opens and shuts, that endlessly connects with other bodies and elements'.[59] For Gil, it is because the body and its skin not only inhabit space, but also constitute space themselves that the body demarcates its limits while at the same time reaching beyond them, which underpins the deep connection between the body and its environment. Relying on Laban's use of the icosahedron to visualize how a kinesphere surrounds bodies and objects such as a spatial cover, Gil proposes that the body's movements are always 'a fluid circulation of intensities over a given matter, a skidding of energy fluxes one over the other'.[60]

In *Always More than One: Individuation's Dance* (2013), philosopher and dancer Erin Manning takes up Gil's concepts of movement and the body's relation to space. The title of her book reflects her view that 'A body is always more than one: it is a processual field of relation and the limit at which that field expresses itself as such'.[61] According to Manning, however, the human body is not only related to the environment that surrounds it, but it also plays an active role in the construction of social identities that mark a body as 'black, gendered, sexed'. Acknowledging that these markers seem to function as 'irrefutable givens that situate the body within the realm of fixed form', the crucial issue for her is to ask which processes bring about these kinds of fixation.[62] To tackle this question, Manning posits that the body is 'an ecology of processes ... always in co-constellation with the environmentality of which it is part. A body is a node of relational process, not a form per se.'[63] A body that is open to change and multiple appearances bears the potential to move across its anatomical borders and to enter other, or even new, social categories.

Bausch's approach to directing bodies in dance demonstrates a similar relationality and flexibility as foregrounded by Gil and Manning. Her interest in theatricalizing everyday life proposes a larger environment for dance to operate in, while she also uses motifs, such as repetition or doubling, to lay bare how the body and its movements actively co-construct the subjective identity that gradually becomes attached to it. In this way, the bodies that populate her work reveal the process of their own becoming, even if they sometimes seem to get stuck in it, unable to escape from the constraints that the world in which they move appears to impose on them. Yet there is also another important sense in which these expanded conceptualizations of the body are pertinent to Bausch's choreographic practice. This sense concerns the ways in which relationality applies to the transmission of Bausch's works and the function of corporeal memory therein.

A rehearsal of the solo for the Chosen One in *Le Sacre du Printemps*, which was recorded in 1987 but only released in 2013, reveals the manner in which a relational bodily memory is key to Bausch's practice. The video shows how Bausch directs dancer Kyomi Ichida who is about to replace Beatrice Libonati in the leading role of the Chosen One. Bausch is dressed in wide pants and a casual shirt with a pilot cap and black rubber boots. The choreographer directs movements that she once had choreographed for herself. When Bausch is demonstrating or correcting specific positions of the arms or movements of the legs, she is clearly inserting her own memory of the choreographic sequences, even though she experiences difficulty in translating into words the expressive qualities she is looking for. 'It's about this movement, and that one', Bausch says at a given movement, 'and doing them at the same time. ... it's like ... what Beatrice does all the time isn't right either. It's more like ... I've told Beatrice not to do it anymore.'[64] The manner in which Bausch's own moving body and comments are intended to correct the dancer's execution of the choreography by demonstrating the appropriate amount of intensity or the right shape of the movements gives an insight as to what extent body-to-body transmission or the relational interaction between two bodies being present at the same time in the same space, is a necessary prerequisite for passing on the work.[65]

While Bausch is using her own body to remember the movements as when she first created them, her reference to Beatrice when giving instructions to Kyomi indicates that she is simultaneously remembering other bodies learning and performing the sequence. Transmitting the dance during rehearsal thus seems to cause certain shifts in time and space, gesturing towards a dynamic that might be effective whenever one of Bausch's pieces is performed. That is, given the close connection between Bausch's own dancing body and the choreographies she created, any performance of Bausch's work can be considered a reincorporation of the choreographic knowledge that she once embodied and which, now that she has passed away, continues to be passed on through different generations of dancers. It is telling that Mechthild Grossmann, actress and long-time member of the Tanztheater Wuppertal, once stated in an interview that the subtitle of most of Bausch's works, *Ein Stück von Pina Bausch* (a Piece of Pina Bausch), needs to be understood more literally, since 'every piece was always a piece of her, a piece of Pina Bausch'.[66] The interview mentions how Grossmann, when making this claim, 'grasps her right upper arm with her left hand, as if she would tear out of her body a piece of meat', as if she wanted to underline the importance of her statement through a theatrical and corporeal gesture.[67]

Bausch's reliance on a relational employment of physical memories is not restricted to the process of transmission that took place between her and the dancers, but it also extends to the spectators, who equally become part of the mnemonic dimensions on which her choreographies rest. It is especially Bausch's renowned talent for theatricalizing everyday life that allows the audience to connect with the aesthetic universe she puts on stage. Bausch choreographs gestures an audience can relate to because they are recognizable and, in their very recognizability, these gestures point at movements that reside both in the past and the future, as they are part of the physical vocabulary we rely on through everyday life. In this respect, the last movement that Bausch performs in the *Danzón* solo is exemplary of her attempt to reach out to her audience. When she lifts her arm and starts to wave her hand, accompanied by a warm smile, she is clearly making a sign of communication, trying to relate to the spectators who are sitting in the darkened auditorium. In the words of José Gil, what Bausch is trying to achieve here is that she 'reconnects (her) body with another', like the observer's body, in order to create a 'passageway for energy and for movement that … increases their flow and intensity'.[68]

Reviving movement: The legacy of Bausch

Ever since Pina Bausch passed away in 2009, the dancers of the Tanztheater Wuppertal can of course no longer be rehearsed through her own corporeal memory. But it seems that, already during her lifetime, Bausch was aware that one day she would no longer be able to guide the ongoing process of passing on the dances because she took various initiatives to ensure that the work could continue to be transmitted. An important step was her decision to select dancers to supervise either an entire work or certain sequences of a piece when it was taught to other dancers within the Tanztheater Wuppertal (in case of a change in the cast, for instance) and also when the work was passed on to other companies.[69]

The Paris Opera, for example, was the first company allowed to perform *Le Sacre du Printemps* in 1997. About ten years later, they would also include the dance opera *Orpheus and Eurydice* in their repertoire. The rehearsals for the dance opera were guided by former Wuppertal company members (Malou Airaudo, Dominique Mercy and Mariko Aoyama) who supervised the solo and group dances, whereas Bénédicte Billiet coordinated the movements of the opera singers and the dancers. When Pina Bausch wanted to create two new versions of her famous *Kontakthof*, she asked Jo Ann Endicott and Bénédicte Billiet to teach the movements to the two new casts. They first worked for an entire year with elderly people to create *Kontakthof mit Damen und Herren ab 65* (Kontakthof with Seniors, 2000) and later with teenagers for *Kontakthof mit Teenagern ab 14* (Kontakthof with Teenagers, 2008).[70]

After Bausch's death, the Tanztheater Wuppertal continued their efforts to disseminate her oeuvre among wider audiences by sending out company members to guide the rehearsals. In 2015, for example, the Bavarian State Ballet in Munich asked for permission to stage *Für die Kinder von gestern, heute und morgen* (For the children of yesterday, today and tomorrow, 2001).[71] All the dancers from the original cast went to Munich to pass on their roles to the ballet dancers. The complex procedure of transmission took nearly two years. Current company member Barbara Kaufmann also assisted in the rehearsal process of *Le Sacre du Printemps* by the English National Ballet in London, which premiered at Sadler's Wells Theatre in March 2017.

It is remarkable that most of the companies that gain permission to restage major pieces by Bausch are classical ballet ensembles.[72] Through her dance education in Germany and the United States, Bausch was well trained in the principles and structures of classical ballet, especially in its modern variant. In this respect, it can be surmised that the apparent preference for ballet companies to revive Bausch's oeuvre stems from the fact that they are used to executing existing works, which also ensures that Bausch's pieces maintain her artistic voice and visible signature. Whether the highly trained bodies of classical ballet dancers are the most appropriate choice for performing Bausch's dances, however, is a debatable question, insofar as the predominance of dance technique risks undercutting the theatrical quality that typifies Bausch's oeuvre.

Along with the strenuous efforts of both Bausch and the Tanztheater Wuppertal to ensure the active transmission of her work to other companies and newer generations of both dancers and spectators, the other key pillar that supports the continued afterlife of her oeuvre is the archivization of her legacy. Earlier in this chapter, I mentioned how Bausch, as well as her dancers, documented the development of the rehearsal processes by taking notes so that they could revisit the material at a later stage during the creation of a piece. Bausch required this from her dancers in the same manner as she imposed the task upon herself. Even early in her career, Bausch notated in an almost dainty manner the creative process of entire pieces or of specific movements she did either by herself or together with other dancers.

While Labanotation was taught at the Folkwang School and also informed Bausch's later notation of movement and action-based sequences, she did not use the principles of Labanotation as such in devising movements or in capturing the choreographic phrases her dancers came up with.[73] Instead, she developed her own way of notating dance, using columns that looked like spreadsheets and which combined the names of the dancers with time indications and spatial instructions. These notations testify to the manner in which Bausch was looking for an expanded form of choreography, one that exceeds the arguably more common practice of creating merely technical steps for trained dancers, searching instead for a highly theatricalized form of dance that would also incorporate the individual personalities of the dancers performing in the piece.

Once she started working in Wuppertal, Bausch continued what can be described as her systematic mode of 'auto-archivization'.[74] Next to handwritten notes, she began using videotapes when creating new pieces and, later on, for restaging existing productions. Just as she assigned individual dancers to supervise the transmission of certain pieces, so too did she select dancers to annotate the video material and to add labels or information that would make the gradually growing archive of her work not only accessible but also more workable. These tapes are stored in Wuppertal and are still used by the company for the restaging and circulation of the repertoire. The archive that Bausch had started to build, which continues to be rebuilt and adapted to the current needs as well as the possibilities of a digitized culture, is astonishing. It not only provides dancers with the necessary means to continue to pass on Bausch's legacy, but it is also, for dance scholars, a tremendous source of information that enables research on Bausch's oeuvre and invites ongoing revisitations of the archival material to assess the impact of her directorial legacy.

In 2016, the oeuvre of Pina Bausch was opened up and distributed through yet another format, as the Pina Bausch Foundation collaborated with the Bundeskunsthalle Bonn to organize the major exhibition *Pina*

Bausch und das Tanztheater (Pina Bausch and the Dance Theatre).[75] The exhibition aimed to make visible to what extent Bausch was influenced by her encounters with different styles of movement, types of music and experiences at various schools and art venues as a student, dancer and young choreographer who had lived and worked in Germany and the United States. The curatorial concept basically consisted of presenting two distinct but complementary categories of material: on the one hand, it drew from the Pina Bausch Archive to display documents (including personal photographs, playbills, private notes and video footage of Bausch's early period), many of which had never been exhibited before; on the other hand, by incorporating into the programme movement workshops and warm-ups led by current as well as former company members, the exhibition wanted to offer a genuinely *living* archive, acknowledging how Bausch's work lives on to a large and important extent in the dancers' bodies that once enacted it or still do so.[76] The exhibition thus reflected the same interaction between the archive in its traditional sense and the intangible embodied memories that also fuelled Bausch's own choreographic practice.

In an attempt to deepen the visitor's experiential immersion into Bausch's aesthetic universe, all events included in the exhibition took place in an exact reconstruction of the 'Lichtburg', which is a German term for movie theatre but also the name of the rehearsal space where Bausch developed most of her work and which, up until today, is still used by the Tanztheater Wuppertal. Upon entering the reconstructed Lichtburg, visitors find themselves in a 1950s-style space with art nouveau-like lamps and green carpets covering part of the walls, while also clothes and costumes are hanging on the sides of the space, as if the room was just left after a day of rehearsal.[77] However, despite these efforts to 'enliven' the exhibition, there is no doubt that Bausch's choreographic oeuvre and her connection to it as a dancer, resists being displayed in a museum. In his inaugural address at the opening of the exhibition in its second venue in Berlin, Salomon Bausch stated indeed that a prominent paradox adheres to any attempt to exhibit movement, insofar as the representation of what is in essence an embodied 'object' (whether it concerns dance itself or the life and work of a dancer) will always remain in tension with the museal setting in which it is placed, which in the end is designed for non-performative arts.

Yet the inclusion of the reconstructed Lichtburg as the centre space of the exhibition does hint at a fundamental aspect of Bausch's directorial practice as a choreographer. As a former movie theatre, the Lichtburg served as a showroom for filmic sensations of a depicted reality or projective imaginations. Bausch turned it into a workspace for real-time explorations of everyday life that infuse her choreographies of the sensual. Isolated from the world outside, the Lichtburg provided the noiselessness that was necessary for Bausch to create a world full of noise and life, developing imaginary spaces for seemingly daily scenes that the audience in return can relate to. Similarly, the exhibition in its entirety mirrors the duality that impregnates the afterlife of Pina Bausch's oeuvre, as it hovers between the relatively stable support of archival resources and the dynamic restlessness of embodied movement. As José Gil says: 'In the beginning was movement. There was no rest because there was no cessation of movement. Rest was only an image that was too vast of what moved, an infinitely tired image that slowed movement down.'[78] The archived material presented at the exhibition can be seen as the image of rest itself, transformed and reified in installations, photographs, videos and texts. It only remains vivid to the extent that it connects with what Pina Bausch had in mind when thinking about movement: 'I had to dance, simply had to dance.'[79] It all began with Bausch wanting to dance; it will continue with others, wanting to observe and incorporate that dance.

Acknowledgement

I would like to thank Dr Elizabeth Kattner for her generous and incredibly helpful comments on earlier drafts of this chapter.

2

Imagistic Structure in the Work of Pina Bausch

Royd Climenhaga Word

At one point in Pina Bausch's film, *Die Klage der Kaiserin* (The Plaint of the Empress, 1989), we see a man walking across a lush green field with a huge bureau on his back. The camera stays with him for quite a while as he struggles with the sheer enormity of the task of transporting this bureau across the open field. It is not clear where he has come from or where he is going. All we are given is the event itself: a man struggling to carry a bureau. That struggle becomes palpable as the image lingers. The man's legs begin to wobble under the strain until finally he must put the bureau down. The only sound is a plaintive drone buzzing throughout. After a brief rest, the man once again tries to lift the bureau and balance it on his back. He tries to get himself positioned under it and carefully, rises, but the bureau slips to one side and falls. He tries again, but again the bureau slips to the side and falls. He tries a few different strategies for getting the bureau up; once he seems to have succeeded, but it falls again. Eventually, he gives up and stands, resting against the bureau, with a look of frustration and resignation.

This image clearly lays the ground for many of Bausch's images. It forces us to attend to the event itself rather than referring to some other context. That event takes place primarily in bodily terms in that our experience of it comes largely through our connection to the physicality of the expression. And yet the image calls up a host of similar experiences any one of us may have had, from having to carry something, to struggling with an idea in writing, to trying to make a relationship work. The image is not placed within a direct context in the piece, as part of a linear story structure, or as an expression of character. We don't know who this man is or what his reasons are for moving this bureau. The event is not specifically referred to later in the piece, nor is this character seen again. The image stands on its own. It is a pure distillation of a feeling – struggle and frustration coupled with nobility in effort and the persistence to keep trying – presented in corporeal terms. The image alone may capture our attention, but placed with other similar images that surround it, a mood begins to develop. The images coalesce, joining together precise moments built around a common feeling now displayed as various facets of a larger experience. The image is startlingly clear in its simplicity, yet its function within Bausch's film is complex, demonstrating the way images in Bausch's work are put together to develop a contextual narrative of association. It exists as if in a dream.

Images and dreams

Bausch's pieces have often been compared to dreams.[1] To provide only one example, the American dance critic Joan Acocella once said that Pina Bausch 'is an image-maker with an imagination half-visual, half-narrative. And she can turn a stage into something like a corner of a dream'.[2] The analogy is valuable on more than simply a surface level. It is not just that the images feel dreamlike, but in many cases their production and reception follow the cognitive pathways we walk in dreams. Ever since Freud highlighted dreams as windows into our cognitive world,[3] writing on dreams in both scholarly and popular literature has steadily increased, with many following Freud's seminal view that dreams are carriers of encoded messages bespeaking psychological processes. In art theory and theatre studies, the distinction between manifest and latent content has been employed to analyse artistic processes and uncover the allegedly hidden meaning of the work. In the case of Pina Bausch, however, the images she chooses are not repressive of some hidden content, not keys to a hidden meaning, but are fully expressive of a situation as experienced. The image as represented on Bausch's stage is feeling embodied in action.

Theatre theorist Bert O. States has described an alternative view of the function and structure of dreams[4] based on active experience rather than repressed content (that is, we experience the structure of the moment in a dream as an active enactment of feeling rather than as a marker for hidden meaning). States' perspective is particularly helpful to gain insight into the development, use and impact of Bausch's performed images, as I go on to explore here. He provides a structural approach, with formal principles drawn from aesthetic and cognitive roots and with a particular emphasis on the performative nature of dream imagery that creates an analytical template to help us understand our experience of life events. I apply that approach to Bausch's dreamlike performed images to help uncover our lived connection to the performed event. In dreams, States writes, 'we process the patterns and qualities of life, never its precise content – memory being less like a computer than it is like a metaphor, that is a kind of orderly mistake'.[5]

To understand States' essential shift to metaphor, it is important to underscore the process of perception and memory to which he refers. Perception is never simply a recording of data transmitted to the brain through discrete sensory impulses, but is always a reaching out and contextualizing of experience through prior associative pathways. We do not experience the colour blue, for instance, as a particular saturation and reflected wavelength of light, but as a relationship to past experiences of blue. That does not mean we carry with us precise records of all past experience. Instead, we create feeling structures[6] or interconnected frameworks for varying experiences of, in our example, blue and every experience of blue with all of its contextual heft either confirms or confronts the underlying form, subtly altering our established conception of blue. The process becomes more intricate when we encounter complex associational patterns of emotional or ideological expression. The experience of love, for instance, is always conditional on past experience and always revelatory at the same time, in that the new experience alters our previous ideological pathway even as it uses that path to arrive at a new point of meaning. Essentially, our cognitive processes do not consist solely of the input and analysis of data, but rather work accretively and metaphorically to absorb new experience and transform it, to continually redefine our particular connection to the world.

For States, the dream makes present the creative images our mind produces through everyday perception and memory. He postulates that the specific purpose of dreaming is to induce a creative process that helps to make sense of the events of our daily lives by placing them within the metaphorical context of past experience. Dreams act as a way to catalogue experience within a referential system of likeness, a metaphorical system based on deeper-feeling structures that connect analogous events. States imagines that dreams create images of action that serve to transform discrete experience into structures of feeling. Dreams utilize sensory and contextual data to imbue a new image with performative potential. These images are not repressions of latent content, as in a Freudian model, but are substantively themselves, as they do not stand in for something else. The dreamer is enveloped in a perpetual present, where the past intertwines with the now and individual history is subsumed into the developing moment.

Dreams bring us to a particular feeling structure and let us inhabit it anew as the current dream image is placed within the context of its emotional precedents. Dreams have a special relation to waking reality and, as States says, 'we use them much as we use maps to find our way through the terrain of waking reality. Maps do not resemble the reality they refer to; but we are not surprised by this fact when we arrive at the place to which they have directed us.'[7] Dreams act as an emotional map that places the present experience within the realm of past like experiences to encompass an amalgam of similar events into an overall feeling structure. This crystallization endows the dream with the ability to forge connections between our being in the world (experience) and our response to it (emotion). States continues:

> Dreams gravitate toward base-level emotions: fear, anger, desire, embarrassment, sadness, guilt, or, simply, frustration – trying to do something that, for some unspecified reason, has to be done against a resistant world. One might say that dreams worry or ramify the emotion by giving it a representational structure made of things that are personally associated with the emotion.[8]

Of course, the same could be said about Bausch's pieces. They too tend to deal with base-level emotions and work with the ramifications of those emotions within experience. In approaching the broad range of human emotions through the lens of experience, Bausch is able to call upon particular, personal moments to explore deep structures that affect our own behaviour and way of being in the world. We are connected to the moments Bausch stages not because we have had similar experiences, but because we can identify with the underlying feeling evoked in response to those experiences; we recognize the form of the emotional response in the image itself. Rather than simply feeling the impact of the moment as staged, the act of performance asks us to become active in gathering the associations we find. Bausch transforms her and her dancers' experience to create more open, metaphoric vessels for the emotion that the experience elicited, much as States claims for the dream; we respond to that deeper structure rather than what often appears as the absurdity of the event, such as a man carrying a bureau across a field.

The building blocks of Bausch's pieces are the images she creates. For Bausch, however, these images are more than skilfully crafted visual moments: they act as patterns of experience, as ways of being in the world. The image of the man carrying the bureau, for instance, has contained within it a feeling of effort, persistence and struggle against the odds. There is beauty in the effort because of the tie those emotions have to larger feeling structures we all can recognize in our own lives. The moment is particular, but uses that particularity as a referent to larger themes. It is Sisyphean in the archetypal sense and brings with it the full force of that metaphoric expression. We enter the moment empathetically, feeling the struggle with the man and relating it to our own experience. The idea that images function as active links to a referential world of ideas and emotions within a complex event of representation is precisely the role that art theorist W.J.T. Mitchell assigns to the image. In his view,

> Images are not just a particular kind of sign, but something like an actor on the historical stage, a presence or character endowed with legendary

status, a history that parallels and participates in the stories we tell ourselves about our own evolution from creatures 'made in the image' of a creator, to creatures who make themselves and their world in their own image.[9]

In Bausch's work, images exist for themselves. We are not intended to see beyond them, but merely to see them or to see because of them. Images are themselves, they don't necessarily directly refer to something else, but in being themselves they are paradoxically caught in a web of meaning and reference. They are not naive or pure, but stained with the vitality of reference to our own experience and bring with them the history of their context in past forms of expression. States also points out how each image in the dream is a condensation of context and history, asserting that the image

> carries to an extreme a basic condition of perception. We think we see a person or an object as if it were all there before us in plain sight. But we are really seeing it contextually, or perhaps cubistically, if we redefine cubism as being a superimposition of associations on a spatial object. … So perception, as Sartre says, is always contaminated by knowing. But in the dream state, where all objects and people are 'chosen' because of associations, contamination is an especially strong factor.[10]

States goes on to say the function of the image is not to 'point cryptically to, or move away from, the primal source of a particular emotion but to enact the emotion in its entirety as a psychic state that can only be represented cubistically – that is, as a fusion of past and present experience. Cubism is the all-at-onceness of an object; the dream is the all-at-onceness of an emotional history'.[11] Bausch captures that emotional history as it is expressed in bodily behaviour, specifically in behavioural patterns in which we find ourselves enmeshed. She sets up image pathways that relive experiential frameworks; all the moments are centred around an interconnected structure that reveals the underlying pattern of experience.

The structural dynamics of the image

To better understand the relationship between Bausch's work and dreams, I want to start with a description of the opening sequence of images from a specific performance. On entering the theatre for Bausch's 1980 piece *Bandoneon*, the curtain is raised to show a squared-off stage with a high ceiling and panelled walls on which hang large old-looking black and white photographs of boxers. The space is littered with small brown tables with brown chairs placed around them to more or less evenly cover the stage. There is a piano against the back wall and two stage doors, one on each side, as well as one high door in the stage left wall. Variously coloured coats and dresses hang from hooks on the walls.

Before the house lights come down and as the audience continues its pre-show settling in and chatting, a man dressed in a suit from the 1940s or 1950s enters sheepishly, stands centre and cautiously looks out into the audience. He picks his nose, smiles and appears nervous. He says, 'I have to do something', to someone seated in the first few rows of the audience. He wanders to the back of the stage and looks at the pictures. He appears nervous at being watched, shrugs his shoulders and starts to leave, but is prevented from doing so by two men, also wearing suits from the same period, who enter through the door. They do not acknowledge him, but take off their jackets and move silently to various chairs. The first man eyes them warily, as if they are a group to which he does not belong. The entering men go about their actions as if the audience were not present and the original man turns to us and shrugs his shoulders when the two men appear not to recognize his presence.

The original man speaks to one of the men who has entered, but he does not respond. The first man continues trying to speak to the second man, who finally responds, 'I am Maria, the immaculate conception.' The original man nervously says, 'Oh, good, good. I can't think of anything on the subject of Mary.' The other two men are going through a repeated series of actions: selecting a seat, draping their jacket over the chair and settling in at the table. Then they each get up, move to another table and repeat the process. The first man nervously tries to come up with a response to the statement about Mary. 'Tia Maria, Maria Callas, Mary had a little lamb. Hail Mary.' He tries to leave again, but is stopped by a line of women dressed in evening wear, also from the 1940s or 1950s, who enter and form a group in the downstage left corner. He asks them about Maria and they each hold their nose as they respond with a variety of associations concerning Maria or Mary. Quiet tango music begins to play as the women become more and more confrontational with their replies, attacking the man with each successive answer. One of the pair of men, who had left the stage, re-enters wearing a white tutu while the women begin reciting the lyrics to 'Maria' from *The Sound of Music*.

The man in the tutu sings quietly and pulls up a chair as the other performers exit. He says 'Hi' to the audience in a manly voice and, as another song starts, his eyes glaze over and close and he starts to do a slow ballet warm-up, using the chair as a barre. The stage has begun to fill with people; two of them begin slapping each other with increasing force and rapidity. The performers all run to sit against the walls as the man in the tutu exits. A woman moves centre, falls down and screams in horror while another woman reads a card matter-of-factly that says 'pain, the sound of pain'. Each person comes centre and says a few amusing words about childhood. They all begin to jump around and scream, leaving two people, zombie-like, frozen in a kiss. The stage clears and the man who was wearing the tutu re-enters in a suit, sits down and tells stories of simple bodily pleasures. Just to pee after a long drive and not being able to. To undo your belt after a large meal.

A woman comes forward, appearing desperate. She calls out, 'Jacob! Jacob!' and a man comes forward and furiously scratches her back, but it fails to satisfy her. She asks another man to help. He looks apologetic that he cannot complete the task. The women all sit facing the front, patting their faces. The back scratching moment is repeated. People move furtively from chair to chair; eventually everyone leaves and the stage is empty. A couple enters as if entering a restaurant. They try to decide on a table and reject each one as they consider it. They move to a space down stage left and the woman rolls up her sleeve, the man undoes his tie, unbuttons his shirt and pulls it aside to reveal his collarbone. They touch the exposed patches of skin.

This series of seemingly independent images begins to coalesce into a more unified scene brought together by the emotional tenor that connects the images, rather than from any storytelling function that may be more typical in the theatre. Nor does the series of images described above attempt to create an illusory world. The physical representation of experience in action, as well as the trappings of the staged world – costumes, sets, etc. – are stripped of all pretence in this instance and on Bausch's stage in general. Hedwig Müller and Norbert Servos identify this mode of telling as an abandonment of traditional plot structures: 'the aim no longer is a logical, accurate development of plot and character, but an unfolding of groups and motifs, along the lines of free association with images and actions. Instead of representing human characters, the problematical aspects of a subject become the focus of interest.'[12] The mode of telling exposes inner experience rather than describing a series of overt actions. The reality depicted is personal, but it is also open to individual understanding because the presentation concentrates on common structures of experience.

The idea that the images find their source in a deeper feeling structure comes close to what Bert O. States writes about the dream. 'The dream image does not arouse feeling', he claims, 'it is instead the feeling that arouses the image, which is so deeply saturated in the feeling that it is impossible to distinguish one from the other.'[13] The event is saturated with the feeling that stands as its base. The images appear strange as isolated moments, disconnected from any context that might heighten their affective potential. They rely on that associational context to create a connected whole. In Bausch's pieces, we place each image in the context of those surrounding it, while also relating it to similar events we have experienced. In seeing the collected images in *Bandoneon*, we attempt to come to terms with an overall feeling for the piece, even as that feeling is contained within each image. The images live in context and draw that context within their own walls.

Der Fensterputzer (The Window Washer, 1997) further illustrates the idea of contextual structure described above. The piece ends with the image of an endless series of people walking on stage to ascend the 20-

foot mountain of bauhinia blossoms piled upstage right. A range of pictures projected on the backdrop changes the visual environment as we see the line of people climb the mountain and descend off stage, only to return to the other side of the stage so the process can continue. The action remains the same whether against a backdrop of a desert landscape or a cityscape, or finally the glistening lights of Hong Kong. This final visual image remains as the line of people keep moving up the mountain and the window washer of the title returns to be hoisted up in his chair, continuing the process of washing the myriad windows.

The end scene of *Der Fensterputzer* works independently as a distillation of the feeling structure of persistent struggle that is developed throughout the piece. No matter what the setting in time or place, people keep ascending the mountain of blossoms only to confront it again and make the ascent anew. However, even while the image exists on its own, it unavoidably resonates with the similar expressions that preceded it during the performance. Moreover, spectators will likely add to the perception of the event their own memories of effort and persistence, whether experienced personally or recalled through other images, such as the man with the bureau. This final image thus expresses its own purpose while it also remains open to similar feelings any audience member may have encountered in his or her own life.

There is a rhetorical richness to the theatrical images Bausch presents on stage, derived from the fact that they transcend the particularity of the actions performed by her dancers to create a full instant that is replete with its own underlying feeling and able to provoke cross-connections within the overall structure of the work. In this sense, Bausch's images act as a choreographic variant of the immediate expression that characterizes the lyric mode of poetry and narrative. Antonin Artaud (1896–1948) most clearly and completely inaugurated a lyrical theatrical expression in this way.[14] Reacting against the dramatic mode of Stanislavsky's psychological realism or the distance implied in Brecht's epic structures, Artaud emphasized the immediacy of presence in order to recover the transformative potential of the theatre.[15] Specifically, he states succinctly that: 'The theater must give us everything that is in crime, love, war, or madness, if it wants to recover its necessity.'[16] Bausch continues and refines the Artaudian lyric tradition by creating a world where moments exist as condensations of feeling structures with no need for the causality of linear narrative to develop their intensity. She transforms directorial intent away from the interpretation of a text and towards the careful construction and linking of staged images. However, while each image speaks for itself in purely theatrical terms, it also speaks metaphorically for all events that might be associated with it. It does not need outside influence to make sense, but in its path towards meaning it does – inevitably perhaps – carry outside influence with it.

Meaning is problematic here as well, for the image is ultimately not concerned with revealing a concrete meaning that stands outside it.[17] The question becomes not what do images mean, but *how* do they mean? Is meaning the best way to consider the effects of the moment? To pin down an image to a specific meaning is to limit its possible realm of influence and the associations it may call up in any given onlooker. Ideally, the image is an embodiment of a feeling that, if successful, captures feeling structures so completely that it achieves what Samuel Beckett said about James Joyce's writing, 'it is not about something, it is that something itself'.[18] It is precisely this potential of images to act with their own expressive force that enables them to offer a way to channel and categorize experience. Whether encountered in a dream or in one of Bausch's pieces, images do not offer meaning or an imitation or description of experience, but instead the progression of images provides a structure whereby we can recall the emotional contours of experience without representing the experience itself.

Capturing an event's emotional contours speaks to the way we see the world and organize our perceptions into meaningful experience. We piece things together within an associative framework that is personal, creating our sense of self out of an interaction between our own experience and elements of the outside world.[19] We create reality from the objective elements of our experience and our own subjective organization and placement of those details within an expressive context. Reality bends towards a more subjective concern, begging the question of whose reality is under consideration and how images function within that frame from the standpoint of an involved observer?

This process of attempting to make sense of the world by placing it within a personal system of reference finds its correlate in expressionist art. Expressionism describes a worldview represented through powerful emotional connectives and it is upon those condensations of emotional content that both dreams and Bausch's pieces are based. Many people have noted Bausch's connection to Expressionism, specifically her reclaiming of the roots of expressionist dance. Anna Kisselgoff has gone so far as to dub her the 'indisputable star of neo-expressionist dance theater'.[20] But Expressionism is more than a convenient label to affix to Bausch's art, insofar as Bausch is effectively expressing the world in subjectively affective terms. Kisselgoff recognizes how Bausch's expressionist aesthetics leads her away from any kind of realism: 'I don't find tanztheater realistic. Bausch's work is expressionistic in that there is a very strong distillation of a prime emotion in every episode and every character. It's personal experience as expressed in a form of distortion, which is very common to expressionist art, especially expressionism in Germany.'[21]

Bausch's compositional process is built on individual expressive moments developed out of the dancers' experiences in rehearsal.[22] But it is the connection of those moments into an affective whole – one that does not tell a story, but rather continually re-presents various connections to larger emotional structures – that carries the burden of content in Bausch's pieces. Content becomes what you are willing to make of it, given the connections provided by the specific pathway Bausch treads. Because each image relies on context and belongs to a larger flow of information, it becomes difficult to talk about images without talking about the way they are pieced together. Conversely, it is just as difficult to talk about the organizing structure, or the form that propels the piece, without talking about individual images, for they are both born of the same stuff. They both draw their life not just from a feeling, but also from a feeling structure, a deeper imprint of how a feeling works. The image opens the potential for different ways of relating to it because it does not evoke one specific feeling but is derived from the feeling itself.

Recognizing those larger emotive patterns that Bausch imbues in the performative moment is nothing short of revelatory. The image compels us to probe deeply into the structural grid of our own awareness. In both dreams and Bausch's pieces, what the connected series of images duplicates is the structure of experience. Just as experience is based not on single moments, but on the overall connection of those moments in the piecing together of an event, it is Bausch's particular way of establishing connections between images that calls up our own associative feelings and our feelings move along with the development of the piece.

The succession of images in Bausch's performances entails a transformation of ideas and emotions into corporeal, dramatic events. Consequently, Bausch's images are never static, but continually transforming into each other, affecting the way latter images are perceived and former images are remembered when we try to consider the piece as a whole. We stitch together the interplay of images on the stage in the same way that we take a succession of images in life and, through their context and presentation, develop an impression of the overall event. This process of integrating ideas and images into a larger structure mirrors the very way we process information from a subjective perspective in our creative construction of our world. In both cases, the attempt is to capture a broader form by placing things within a field of likeness and compatibility. In adapting the constitutive principles of cognition, however, Bausch creates a new deep structure: instead of utilizing the constituent elements of what might be defined as a language (of movement, for instance), she is invested in what comes *before* language and develops much of the physicality in her works out of those generative sources. In other words, the pieces do not speak through the recognized patterns of dramatic intent, or the language of the theatre, nor do they operate through an established movement vocabulary as might be the case in more conventional dance structures. Instead, they think themselves into being and involve us in the process of constructing a new sense of meaning. The examples from *Bandoneon* described above create a participatory pathway that does not impose any preconceived and fixed direction on spectators, but rather functions as an open invitation to engage in the construction of a form of meaning that – much like the piece itself – comes only gradually into being.

Dream images develop structures out of the memory of experience to test and evaluate our own patterns in reality. Images are not simply representations, but ways of entering into the very process of imagination and Bausch presents precisely that kind of principle in her work. The images in both dreams and on Bausch's stage are not blocks of representative material that carry meaning, but are a way to work towards understanding.

A tropological approach:
Metonymy and synecdoche

Dreams are full containers of experience, replete with the feelings they evoke. The feeling of what happens in a dream, or in Bausch's choreographies, is often enveloping, making it difficult to grasp the elements that come together to create the overall effect. In order to help understand the structural principles at play in the dream, States embarks on an analysis borrowing what he calls the four 'master tropes' from literary theory: metonymy, synecdoche, metaphor and irony.[23] The template he suggests is remarkably fruitful in unpacking the same kind of complexity in Bausch's oeuvre. In *Metaphors We Live By* (1980), George Lakoff and Mark Johnson argue that literary tropes relate to the structure of consciousness itself as '"primitive" and "undecomposable" strategies of thought'.[24] States agrees and in his analysis of dream structures, tropes are considered precisely for their active potential as mental events, rather than simply as static figures of speech.[25] They act as ways to describe our own processes of categorizing experience and developing meaningful patterns of connection. The four key tropes that interest States have distinct characteristics as well as considerable areas of overlap and just as they help to structure experience, they can function as analytical tools to gain deeper insight into the images that appear on Bausch's stage.

Metonymy is generally defined as an instance where 'the literal term for one thing is applied to another with which it has become closely associated. Thus the "crown" or the "sceptre" can stand for a king'.[26] States, however, quotes Kenneth Burke's more specialized description of metonymy as a strategy used '"to convey some incorporeal or intangible state in terms of the corporeal or tangible" (as when we speak of "the heart" instead of the emotions)'.[27] In both cases, it is clear that metonymy functions to concretize that which is ephemeral, or to reify something for affective purpose. But, unlike metaphors that draw connections between seemingly unrelated constituents, metonymies stay within a tight referential framework, insofar as they reduce a broader experience to its component parts and keep the affect within the same conceptual domain. However, because metonymies emphasize the physical or active substance of as well as the relation to the idea in question, they may cause us to revaluate what we before may have taken for granted.

Metonymic operations are key to the imagery that Bausch develops in her work. The image of the man carrying a bureau, for example, could be considered as a metonymy in that the idea of endurance is presented within corporeal terms, giving substance to that which was before conceptual and, in so doing, both particularizing it and opening its affective potential. In *Keuschheitslegende* (Legend of Chastity, 1977), Norbert Servos encounters a similar metonymic moment, which he ranges under the feeling of 'vulnerability' and describes as 'A man in a black evening suit stands at the front of the stage with his back to the audience. A second man outlines the vulnerable parts of his body with white chalk and explains the best way to injure them.'[28]

Many of Bausch's metonymies are seen as violent because the performer's body is either put at risk or put through some process of subjugation or degradation. *Kontakthof* (1978) famously contains several images of abasement enacted on the bodies of the performers. The piece ends with several men surrounding a lone passive woman and subjecting her to a series of small pokes and tweaks that become an emotional onslaught. Rather than depicting a specific event, the violence acts as a metonymically condensed physicalization of a larger intangible idea of subjugation. Images such as this are often difficult to watch because the violence implicit within the image is tied to a more universal feeling, rather than located in a specific context that we can easily hold outside ourselves. As Ann Daly says, 'In Bausch's pieces, violence comes in bursts of dense repetition. These acts of violence are neither conventional nor naturalistic, rather, they exist on the plane of metaphor [or more precisely metonymy]. They deal with the violation of woman's bodies but, more so, with women's autonomy'.[29]

Bausch's metonymic images never occur as a static field, but as a verb, an action within a temporal framework that not only relies on a latent past, but which also hints at a possible reconfiguration in the future. The metonymic image stays grounded in a common referential framework, but also immediately broadens its field of reference by drawing on and reflecting wider arcs of experience. In *Palermo, Palermo* (1989), a man stands down stage right. A woman is carried on by a group of men and placed before him. They all look at the man accusingly. The woman has a plastic seltzer bottle between her knees, which she points at the man. She unscrews the cap to let the water inside cascade out to pee on him. She gives her knees a little shake as the bottle empties to get the last drop out and is carried off. Metonymically, the action gives tangible form to the ideas of accusation and condemnation, but its effects reach further. Even though the scene is funny in its absurdity, the attitude of the performers belies something dire going on beneath the surface, something that we do not know. Implied in the scene is a history to which we are not alerted, but which informs the peculiar relationship between the performers. While the image is a concretization of abstract feeling, it is also open enough to allow us to have this image stand in for any similar experience we may have had. By means of this metonymical scene, Bausch gives us a way to relate our own feelings to something that is both concrete and unspecified at the same time.

In contrast to metonymy, which condenses a general idea to a substantive corporeal image, synecdoche enacts a condensation into representative units, usually those that are most functional in the whole (ships into sails, workmen into hands). As with the other tropes, however, it is important to think of synecdoche as an active potential, especially when it is applied to the making of images. More than a simple replacement of a whole for a part, synecdoche explicates a close relationship between the element it represents and the object, idea or feeling to which it refers. From this perspective, synecdoche provides a cohesive element that demonstrates how the whole is always already contained in the parts as the part is contained in the whole.

According to States, synecdochic structures are also present in dreams, insofar as 'the business of the dream-work is to preserve the quality of certain experience by seeing that it is quantitatively represented by the appropriate parts. The dream must add up to the feeling of which it is the carrier.'[30] In Bausch's pieces, distinct parts similarly adhere to a founding experience and eventually coalesce into an overall feeling structure that is consistent with and revelatory of experience, whatever that experience may be for any given audience member.

The series of images from *Bandoneon* described above were developed from the company's exploration of the underlying structure and motivating principles behind tango culture (a Bandoneon is a small accordion often used in tango music). The images that result and the way they are assembled serve to uncover the root of the feeling associated with the tango; this is then enacted on the bodies of the performers. The image of the women having an itch that the men fail to scratch despite their best efforts is a synecdochic condensation of the feeling of unmet desire contained within the tango. This feeling can have different meanings for individual spectators. When I saw the piece for the first time, for example, I was at a point in my life where I was moving frequently without having the opportunity to establish connections that I found meaningful, and I felt that the piece captured my experience of physical dislocation of self in my desire for connection. During the intermission, I overheard a woman say to her friend in response to the piece, 'I just started chemotherapy last week. That's what it feels like.' The women spoke of how the piece captured what I can only imagine was her experience of being physically removed from her own sense of self that processes such as chemotherapy enact. It was the piece that gave us each the language to articulate that feeling structure through embodied action.

States goes on to further qualify synecdoche as 'always a seed, or germ cell, that carries a set of instructions, or even better a structuration in which a wholeness inheres'.[31] The idea that the synecdoche adds structure to an otherwise undifferentiated whole can perhaps be seen most clearly in the editing process Bausch goes through during rehearsals. The choice whether individual fragments are maintained and developed, while others are discarded is ultimately based on their relation to the developing whole. At the same time, the whole of the piece only emerges along with the sequences that make it up, as Bausch and her performers discover the full parameters of its subject as it evolves. The synecdochic quality of Bausch's work thus consists in the structuration of seemingly isolated parts under the rubric of a cohesive idea.

While synecdoche acts as a compositional principle in Bausch's creative processes, it also recurs in the aesthetics of the eventual pieces. In *1980* (1980), for example, there is a scene in which a woman stands alone, apart from a slowly coalescing group. After a moment of silence, each member of the group comes forward to offer rather flat recitations of clichéd goodbye lines ('It's a pity that you have to go so soon, best regards.' 'Please don't forget us here, we'll be thinking of you.') After everyone has offered their line to the lone woman, there is a moment of silence before the group disperses and the piece simply continues. The image works as a condensation of the idea of departure, where the structure of the event is revealed as a simple enactment of the feeling in question. The moment possesses a quality of 'goodbye-ness' that we can recognize and compare to our own experience, but that sense is attendant on an even larger structure in the piece (which was developed just after the death of Bausch's long-time companion and collaborator, Rolf Borzik and one of the dominant elements is incorporating a sense of loss). This moment is prefaced with that overarching theme and carries the weight of that and our own personal connections with it throughout the rest of the piece.

This departure scene works archetypically, if we think of archetype as the whole that lies behind and inheres in all the parts. Archetype here describes a standard form of a particular event, such as departure, whose structure and conventions can be appropriated to prompt associational links drawn from our own experience. Archetype works as a master-synecdoche, in a way, by concretizing and formalizing classes of experience. Besides the formal reuse of archetypal situations, Bausch's imagery also comes close to James Hillman's description of the archetype as 'a rich image that gets deeper as we go deeper into it'.[32] In this case, Bausch condenses any particular goodbye party to its simplest and most evocative functional units, while retaining the feeling of awkwardness that often comes with having to say goodbye. The image draws on the archetypal foundation of that experience and goes deeper into it by means of the synecdochic relationship to the whole of the piece and its exploration of loss. Both the archetypal and synecdochic aspects of the goodbye scene point to the deep structure of the moment.

States argues that these archetypal moments might more usefully be described under the idea of gestalt structure. He more specifically refers to Mark Johnson's definition of gestalt structure as 'an organized, unified whole within our experience and understanding that manifests a repeatable pattern or structure'.[33] Johnson develops this idea and gives it active potential, transforming it into what he calls 'image schemata' or 'schema':

A schema consists of a small number of parts and relations, by virtue of which it can structure indefinitely many perceptions, images and events. In sum, image schemata operate at a level of mental organization that falls between abstract propositional structures, on the one side, and particular concrete images, on the other ... it is important to recognize the dynamic character of the schemata. I conceive of them as structures for organizing our experience and comprehension.[34]

Following Johnson, we tend to look past the particulars of a situation in our attempt to categorize events and perception into preconceived scripts of behaviour, despite how the new experience may revise the script under which we are operating. Bausch similarly renegotiates image schemata by forcing us to attend to the details that challenge the behavioural pattern. While the schemata underlying the image provide the audience with a base to recognize the event, Bausch's particular way of staging the event also forces you to address its structure and reconsider what you may have taken for granted in order to account for the presence of new terms and conditions. Gender is an image scheme that Bausch addresses in this way. In *Palermo, Palermo*, Jan Minarik often returns to a small area downstage set up with a locker and where he cooks a steak on an iron while watching a documentary about sharks. Minarik steps into his masculine terrain, but removes his suit and tie, applies lipstick, dons a feather boa, heels and a crown of cigarettes to become a grotesque version of the statue of liberty, holding aloft an apple with one lit birthday candle as the torch. The unquestioned expression of gender roles is challenged through specificity and incongruity, while still drawing on the way we enter into our performance of gender. The subjective presence of the individual is maintained and used to help us revaluate the underlying image schemata of human experience. It is this structural dynamic that is in play in many of Bausch's performances, as she simultaneously produces images that are open to a broad level of interpretation while remaining specific expressions of a particular person.

Metaphor and irony

In common understanding, a metaphor occurs when 'a word or expression which in literal usage denotes one kind of thing or action is applied to a distinctly different kind of thing or action without asserting a comparison'.[35] Like the other tropes, however, metaphor is not simply a functional unit of speech and most definitions do recognize its potential to open imaginative possibilities. But metaphor has also been considered even more broadly as a central principle of cognition and creation. It can be seen as a metamorphosis of daily life into elements of appreciation, part of the process by which we think and tell the story of ourselves. In short, it is a way of processing images into dynamic, meaningful sequences based on association. As States argues,

> metaphor is the spirit of movement, or progression from one image to another. Here I am emphasizing not likeness or resemblance but the drive

of the figuring mind to find likeness. The urge to make metaphors is really a refinement of a basic fact of perception, that things are perceived both as themselves and as members of a class, that every movement of mind is a relevant movement rather than a random one, a leap based on attraction.[36]

Metaphor is essentially a creative process, an assemblage of likenesses that envelop the idea or feeling at hand within an organizational structure of underlying connections despite apparent differences. It brings with it the fullness of the moment and the history of past associations. In this case, not only do we adopt the structures that we see in our experience, we transform them through associative power. Metaphor is not simply a way to describe a specific product of thought; it is a process that changes our perception. In this sense, metaphor not only brings about likeness, but also functions as an active force in the way things are linked together. 'As a movement from one object, event, or thing to another via the path of a resemblance, we may say that metaphor is a seeking action, a restlessness born of the inability of the image to remain self-contained. Thus metaphor, this escape from the stasis of identity, is the very momentum of thought.'[37] Whereas metonymy and synecdoche work to assign things to their likeness, metaphor works to push feeling into new contexts. The idea is advanced along pathways of association to create a rhythmic flow of images. This is the sense in which metaphor is not a thing but an action.

Describing Bausch's images as metaphors is almost a tautology, not only because they establish connections between seemingly disparate events, things or feelings, but also because all theatrical images are creative interpretations given concrete form. But the metaphorical operations in Bausch's work run deeper, since together with their ability to connect images, they also reveal the way in which sense is derived not out of a telling, but out of the enactment of essential feeling structures placed within a variety of contexts and linked through associative means. *Palermo, Palermo* begins with an image of a woman in desperate need of something that the men who are with her cannot provide. She screams 'Thomás! Hug me!, Hug me!!' but, despite his best efforts, Thomás cannot satisfy her demands. The piece continues with other images, including the one described earlier that consists of a woman damning a man by letting a seltzer bottle which she holds between her knees empty on to him. Each of these images has its own specific affective sphere and could call up a variety of associations for any given audience member. But the larger, metaphoric questions would be: how do these two images connect? How do they both create and draw from the context of the whole piece? In this case, both images bring up a certain sense of feeling disconnected, of the inability of a given situation to provide what is really needed and the attendant frustration, anger and condemnation that may go along with that feeling. This connective tissue is the beginning of a larger structure derived out of the company's experiences of decrepit beauty and permeated history in Palermo on which the whole piece rests and out of which it draws its strength, as the images build up and begin to reflect and expand the growing sense of the metaphoric condition of Palermo that the piece contains.

For dance critic Joan Acocella, Bausch's earlier pieces are primarily strings of images, whereas the connective tissue of metaphoric process is what holds the later pieces together, as for example in *Palermo, Palermo*, where the images 'range more freely; they obey internal laws, they flower'.[38] Even though the coalescing element of *Palermo, Palermo* is clearer than in … some of the earlier works and while that clarity … can be used to cite Bausch's growth and maturity, a similar connectedness of internal laws and flowering can also be discerned in the earlier performances. In *Kontakthof* or *1980*, for example, the themes of tenderness and loss are clear; the range of images surrounding those ideas do indeed flower. In an interview with Nadine Meisner, Bausch clarifies this process when she says that the connection to larger themes by the audience 'can only work if we avoid anything explicit – anything where we see something and we all know what it means. We think oh, this is a sign for that: you know it in your head. But if we avoid this and if the audience are [members] open to experience or feel things, I think there is a possibility of another kind of language.'[39] Rather than providing a direct representation of a larger idea, the images work as a combination of that idea with the thing that is found to express one aspect of it, connecting the synecdochic work of individual images with the metaphoric structuring principles that govern the full piece.

Since I.A. Richards's seminal analysis of metaphor in *The Philosophy of Rhetoric*,[40] metaphors have usually been broken down for analysis into a tenor (the underlying idea) and a vehicle (the metaphorical figure that carries the tenor).[41] While we can look at images in Bausch's productions as maintaining this structure, it is not how we experience them. We see the images not as standing in for something else, but because the tenor is collapsed into the vehicle, they shimmer with potentiality in their connection to an overall theme. This is the sense in which Servos says that Bausch's work is not like something, it is the thing itself: 'It does not pretend. It is.'[42] Again we come to understand that the question of what a particular image or connection of images means becomes irrelevant in sight of the more encompassing question of what it does.

Metaphor does not simply replace one thing with another, but initiates a dialogic relationship between things; they begin to infect each other and move on to something new. We uncover the hidden potentialities of an idea or feeling by exposing its deeper structure and by realigning that structure along associative pathways. Feeling is metonymically condensed into image, while the schema that engendered the image also pushes the feeling metaphorically to a new mode of being. In other words, metaphor is what drives the piece, as it enables the transition from one image to another.

Irony could be considered simply as the process whereby the expected associational link between images is subverted. But even this description points to the complexity inherent in irony, because rather than talking about the thing as it is, it speaks specifically to the thing as it is perceived, while that perception relies heavily on context and viewer. It demands interpretation. Irony involves a subversion of expectation, often a sudden reversal. One technique Bausch frequently uses in rehearsals is to ask her performers to take an image or gesture and quickly and efficiently get it to mean its opposite. Caresses become attacks through an increase in intensity or attention becomes torture through an increase in duration. We are arrested by the revelation of the unexpected connection between these seemingly opposite actions. We see how different and yet structurally similar they are.

Irony gives us a way to realign contexts because it moves the image beyond the context which seeks to contain it. Within an exploration of a given idea or feeling, irony pushes the limit of possible connotations by forcing likeness into the realm of opposing structures. Irony serves to give us access to emotions that may be too powerful to be dealt with head-on without tipping into cliché. As a self-conscious device, we knowingly put ourselves in a position to confront feelings we thought had been safely placed at a remove. When the feeling does infect us, it comes as a shock, a sudden awareness of the power of expression and our placement within it.

The ironic process also works to alter the affective potential of any given image. When two performers were asked to remember situations in which they laughed (I discuss this rehearsal moment at length in the section on memory below), Bausch does not allow them to indulge in the feelings of lightness and mirth that laughing usually connotes. She asks them not to

FIGURE 2.1 Nelken. © *Bettina Stoess, 1982.*

engage in the moment that makes them laugh, but the act of laughing itself. Stripped of its context, the eventual image works to evoke a sensation of loss. As spectators, we feel the tension of being denied access to the moment as it is experienced and the subsequent sadness that comes with the loss of that moment. We read the scene as ironic because we recognize how it refers to a past event or experience while emphasizing that it is beyond our reach. We are brought up short by the sudden reversal from laughing to loss and are forced to reconsider our attempt to understand the image.

The beginnings of connectedness

Analysing Bausch's synecdochic version of choreography sheds light on her particular approach to the structuration of her pieces and demonstrates her version of direction. With the whole being contained in each part, the images within each performance begin to connect, showing how Bausch's characteristic juxtaposition of scenes is in fact held together by means of a vital structure (such as loss in *1980* or connection in *Kontakthof*), expressed through different enactments. The images acquire an accumulative quality, establishing relationships between those around them and providing the substance for what is to come next. The series of images produced along a given theme begin to delimit the possibility of subsequent images while also providing a fertile ground for deeper explorations along the associative pathway. In Bausch's pieces, we see images striving after some general significance and framework. Seemingly disparate things are shown to have a value in connection for their evocative power of a deeper structure, as in the series of images from *Bandoneon* described above.

The final outcome may appear to lack a coherent line of development, because the structure did not precede the images as the skeleton upon which the meat of the piece is attached. Instead, the images come first, although they are based in a common ground; the structure of the piece arrives with the process of connection that is called for by these images. Eventually, then, the further development of the structure starts to merge with the selection and creation of images, as both dimensions mutually inform and form one another. The piece begins to come to life as it starts to provide its own rationale. Also in this regard, Bausch's approach to directing comes close to the manner in which States describes the process for the production of dreams. 'The dream usually supplies the next incident as a response to what is already there', he states, and goes on to explain this as follows:

It is … like the structure that children build out of blocks of various shapes and sizes. The child establishes a foundation and builds upward, instinctively observing elementary laws of balance, tension, centralization, and support. Each new block advances, changes, and limits the dynamics of the structure, inevitably to a point of collapse. Hence there is a kind

of self-determination in the process: it is a 'What now?' situation, a way
of getting from here to the next point by established means, which in the
case of the dream would be metonymic evolution.[43]

States continues describing how the process of accretion in the dream follows
Darwin's notion of natural selection, where 'the fittest variations (even those
occurring by chance) are retained and the poorest discontinued'.[44] Bausch
follows exactly this pathway in structuring the images in her pieces, but
– unlike dreams, which operate beyond our conscious control – she has
the advantage of seeing what comes out of the suggestive process and then
making decisions as to what has the greatest value. She responds to the events
the performers suggest in rehearsal and then is able to shape and refine those
events into a cohesive whole. But much of the cohesion is actually already
in place, if Bausch listens carefully to what is being offered. The images have
contained within them the possibility for connective action, in that they are
built from the same base. However, even though each image that is created in
rehearsal is equally valid as a response to the underlying theme, they are not
all equally effective. The work of rehearsal and Bausch's particular genius
lies in sifting through the enormous amount of material that is generated to
discover those images and their connective pathways that most powerfully
present the underlying themes and open up the potential for interaction.

Another aspect of this process is to find linkages to move from one
image to the next. In Bausch's work, one image calls up another through its
evocative connection to a larger structure, rather than establishing a causal
relationship between the images. In dreams, this production of images leads
to sudden changes in the event or unexpected locations. As States says,
'the sequence of dream events tends not so much toward the "And then"
structure as toward "And suddenly" or "I found myself"'.[45] This produces
a path of images that seemingly jumps from event to event without the
transitional structure that links events into a story: 'Unlike the reader of a
story, the dreamer does not require transitions, because each new event is
all-emersing [sic] – as it were, a new throwness into a complete world.'[46]
This is only partly true of Bausch's images: they too have the 'all-immersing'
completeness, but the connection or bridge is still needed to lead an audience
through the complex web of associations. It is this associative link that
many reviewers miss in criticizing Bausch's pieces as being disparate strings
of disassociated images.[47] When we look for a conventional narrative stream
of 'and thens', but fail to find that, we refrain from making the effort to ask
ourselves what might really be connecting the series of images. Conversely,
once we discern the associative links in Bausch's pieces, it is often easy to see
how images are connected as facets of complex experiential and emotional
structures.

Servos makes just such a claim in analysing the structure of Bausch's
pieces when he writes that 'the freely associated images and actions form
chains of analogies, spin a complex web of impressions that are connected,

as it were, "beneath the surface". If a logic exists, it is not a logic of the consciousness, but of the body, one that adheres not to the laws of causality but rather to the principle of analogy'.[48] Associative pathways have been an overriding structural principle in Bausch's work at least since her Brecht-Weill performance of 1976, *Die sieben Todsünden* (The Seven Deadly Sins).[49] Servos describes the key dynamic of that performance as follows:

> the functioning stylistic principle is the fusion of an apparently loose dramaturgy, contextually bound by alternating, associative mood values, here compressed by Bausch for the first time in her own special brand of dance theater, a theater of movement which makes variation of motif possible without the encumbrance of narrative strictures and allows the subsequent illumination of these motifs from a variety of angles.[50]

Bausch had begun experimenting with a structure built on associational connections earlier, but it reaches the fully fledged position of a 'functioning stylistic principle' with this piece. It is precisely this approach to the openness of narrative that becomes a defining characteristic of Bausch's performances and which sets Tanztheater or dance theatre apart as a distinct practice.

Even though Servos rightly intimates how Bausch deliberately refuses to conform to the limitations of linear and causally structured narratives, it is by looking through the lens of metonymy, synecdoche, metaphor and irony that we acquire a deeper understanding of the compositional principles that characterize her practice. What develops in rehearsal is the overall theme the piece is to inhabit. Whereas in the early works, these themes are often derived out of simple prompts that begin to uncover Bausch's and her company's experience, during the later period, they are rather based in the company's experience of a distinct locale in many of their co-productions. Those themes then come to stand as the deep structure to which all images turn, while they also furnish these images with the dramatic potential to move forward and establish connections with those around them. This process of developing the overriding idea or feeling structure in the rehearsal studio (instead of starting from a preconceived and clear-cut theme) and the subsequent step of using that structure to move the piece forward is not altogether new in either dance or theatre.[51] Yet never before was it developed and utilized so extensively as a method for both rehearsal and production. It is this process, more than any recognized stylistic technique, that is Bausch's creation and legacy.

The architecture of memory

In her discussion of Pina Bausch's dance theatre, Leonetta Bentivoglio relates the flow of associated images around a central theme to consciousness itself and, more precisely, to our own attempts to place present experience within a referential system of memory so that our experience can be made useful and give us the opportunity to move on. In her opinion, 'the associative criterion that guides the montage of images, by which each of these bodily histories is communicated, is determinably elliptical. In Bausch's theatrical collages, a freedom of connections is in force, recalling a flow of memories or of consciousness'.[52] Uncovering that connective force that Bentivoglio describes, however, is not always so straightforward, as repeated viewings are often needed before the dominant motif is recognizable. And even then, there may be some pieces of the puzzle that do not appear to fit. Bausch does not adhere to a strictly narrow thematic structure, but the range of images she presents does provide a way both to support the piece itself and to allow for one's own explorations within the associative world she creates. The field is not so firmly delimited as to deny spectators their own participation in the event, even as each successive image does tend to gravitate towards a common emotional root. That this root is not always clearly defined speaks to the subtlety and complexity of the worlds Bausch chooses to explore. According to Servos, there is great merit in this distinct openness of material structure. 'Instead of every detail being absolutely interpretable', he writes, 'the dominant features of the pieces are a multidimensionality and complex simultaneity of actions that offer a wide panorama of phenomena.'[53]

The thematic root is derived from experience, such as tenderness or love in *Kontakthof* or the persistence of desire and will to continue in the city of Hong Kong as evoked in *Der Fensterputzer* (The Window Washer, 1997). Servos uses the analogy of music in describing the way in which experience takes on a thematic structure in Bausch's works:

> The principle of the structure of dance theater resembles that of music, in that themes and counterthemes, variations and counterpoint are woven around a basic idea. The beginning and conclusion do not mark temporal limits in the psychological development of its characters. Its overriding principle is that of a dramaturgy of individual numbers, which deals with the motifs in a free but, at the same time, precisely calculated and choreographed order.[54]

Other critics have also found musical composition an apt analogy for describing Bausch's pieces. As Barbara Confino writes, 'like music, this theater does not tell a story; it conveys feelings via physical, vocal and visual images treated symphonically'.[55] States makes the same point about dreams, which 'seem to obey a theme – not in the conceptual sense, as we use the term in literature, but in the musical sense of key, or melodic continuity'.[56] The idea of a musical key is helpful, not just in terms of identifying an emotional base for the piece, but also in a compositional sense of controlling the possibilities of development and harmony within the structure of a given performance. Bausch is often obstinate in pursuing a certain theme from various angles and going along with her on that road is not always an easy path to travel. Once Bausch enters into a subject, she won't let go, as she is ardent to uncover, express or overturn all elements that could belong to a particular key. Bausch won't allow you to look away or ignore the aspects of love or relationships that trouble the surface in a piece such as *Kontakthof,* for instance, where intimate acts of both tenderness and cruelty are played out in exacting detail.

Bausch uses constructions of memory to pursue her musical themes, but memory serves not simply as a recollection of past events in this regard, but also as a ground that gives meaning to present experience. Rather than merely using memories for affective purpose, Bausch's pieces mirror the very process by which memories create a virtual imagination through recontextualizing them into common cores of experience and expanding upon the way they are linked across time. She pursues the way memory shapes the present, following Proust's construction of memory in the novel and placing it within the kind of stream of consciousness crafted by Virginia Woolf. The specific images she presents are combined in a similar way to the imaginative leaps we make when categorizing our own experience within a realm of remembered similar instances.

The mechanism by which Bausch links memory to imagination becomes palpably clear in the work on an image about remembered laughing, which I briefly touched on above in describing the function of irony. In the moment captured in a video of the rehearsals for *Waltzer* (Waltzes, 1977),[57] Bausch asks two ensemble members to dance together and describe how they laugh (in their real life), but to remain very serious in their description. She says, 'I want to hear not how you laugh, but how you laughed, how you used to laugh years ago. There's not much to laugh about nowadays'. When the couple begins, the man says, 'And when I was sitting there in the cinema, I got real cramps in my stomach'. Bausch interrupts and says:

No, stop, that's not what I mean. It's something different when you say I was in the cinema and there was this awful film, and that you laughed. Because then everyone thinks that what you're telling us is about seeing the film. You don't have to tell us the reason, only how you laughed, a long time ago. Otherwise it sounds like it was only that time, watching the film.

The couple starts again and the man begins to explain in the present tense what physically happens when he laughs. Bausch interrupts again and says that it is still not right. 'You have to tell everything in the past. What you're doing is telling how you laugh now.' The couple starts again and the woman says, 'I used to laugh without making any sound, like this' and she demonstrates. The man replies, 'I used to roll up in a ball in a chair' The woman says, 'Didn't you ever laugh like that, sometimes' and demonstrates again. And the man says, 'No, but I did sometimes hit my head because I was shaking so hard, and just used to roll right up in a ball' The woman responds, 'I only used to make small movements' From here they begin demonstrating a variety of laughs, from rasping to wheezing, high-pitched to low guttural, even spurting liquid. Bausch stops them and says, 'O.K., O.K., but when you do it you must stay completely serious. There were some good bits at the beginning, but later it sounded like really laughing'

Bausch is clearly impelling her performers to describe a state that they might have experienced once, while not allowing them to get carried away by it. The experience of laughter must remain in the past: a thing that is lost and which can never truly be recaptured. Even though the past contains all the feelings attendant in the original scenario, any direct access to them is denied as the performers are summoned to evoke them from a distance, as if they are looking at themselves laughing through glass, without direct access to the original experience. By stripping the moment of its context and focusing on the corporeal event, Bausch uncovers a new feeling of loss: loss of the very remembered moment that fuels our present and makes us real. The living possibilities of the moment are taken away and a feeling of disconnectedness becomes palpable. The transition into performance is even more complicated. This particular moment does not appear in the final performance, but the energy discovered in the moment in rehearsal is suffused throughout the piece.

Narrative possibility

Whether exposed through absence or made more singularly present, this development of patterned associative images within memory creates a grammar of suggestibility. This ultimately leads to a piecing together of images into narrative possibility. Because images are linked through constructions of likeness, we tend to notice pathways which we naturally build into a narrative. We tell ourselves stories or, more accurately, we make stories out of our experiences as a way to give them context and structure within the sea of our emotional lives. The forms of narrative we produce are largely based on the world of social conventions we see around us. We follow scripts or what Mark Johnson would call image schemata, that we encounter and enact everyday. The connection of images into meaningful patterns is essentially a plagiarizing of the world, insofar as we tend to construct our present based on social scripts borrowed to fit given circumstances.

It is this existential condition that Bausch has mastered by turning it into a choreographic reality, reorienting the process of directing away from an interpretive function and towards the constructive elements of the piece, making her a natural progenitor for devised theatrical practice. As she takes a social script under which we operate (about love, gender, or simply saying goodbye as described above) and uses it for affective purpose, she causes us to re-evaluate the conditions of the script itself, because her use has made it, perhaps for the first time, evident as just that: a script that modifies our behaviour and has the potential for change. The most obvious arena Bausch addresses in this regard is gender and the role of women in a male-dominated society. Those themes run throughout Bausch's pieces as both elements of content and as structural entities in that they show how the possibility of

FIGURE 2.2 Arien. © *Bettina Stoess, 1979.*

drawing meaningful connections between images also incites us to combine them into something that, though non-linear, could be considered as a story: the stories we create that ultimately are ourselves.

Marianne Van Kerkhoven claims that Bausch's dance theatre relies on a reconsideration of stories. She draws on the work of Oliver Sacks, who says:

> Each one of us is a story constructed by us in a permanent fashion within ourselves – by way of our experiences, our feelings, our thoughts, our actions and, certainly not least, by what we say, by our own spoken narratives. From a biological point of view, or a psychological one, we hardly differ from one another; from a historical point of view, as stories, as narratives, each of us is unique.[58]

This is another way of describing *Empfindnisse*[59] or the idea that we bring a sense of our place in time and space with us in the continual creation of our selves. If these stories of ourselves are shared with an audience, as they are in Bausch's pieces, they run the risk of spiralling down into an unintelligible solipsism, meaningful only to the person doing the telling.

However, even though the stories and images may have personal relevance to the performers or Bausch herself, they are never allowed to remain within the realm of individual expression. They derive from the personal, but Bausch's insistence on the link between the event and deeper-feeling structures is what pulls the pieces out of a narcissistic exploration of self and into a broader concern for what makes us human. Each individual's path through the framework Bausch provides is particular, but the connection of those pathways provides an opening for the common struggle towards understanding of our experience in the world. Van Kerkhoven comments on this use of story:

> The notion of identity covers a reality much larger than the notion of psychology. Psychology is only one minimal part of our being. Moving away from psychology in the direction of the essential, in the direction of that interior narrative spoken of by Oliver Sacks, can lead to a new manner of telling stories on stage.[60]

The practice of recombining experiences and memory into a series of connected elements that has the beginnings of a story structure is the work of imagination. It is the process that underpins our formation of self and that we engage in to attempt to come to know our sense of self in the world. It is the process by which new material is contextualized with previous experience, resulting in a constantly shifting imaginal whole. To simply replicate experience would serve no purpose for us, either within ourselves in the process of cognition or in the crafted mirroring of that process which Bausch attempts. We need a sense of transformation of experience, through either metonymic or synecdochic reduction or the expansion that metaphor and irony provide. As States explains:

A direct copy of experience without a tropological conversion would be virtually useless, except to the memory function, because it would always be only itself. It would possess no motility. The brain would then be a storehouse of rigid, isolated memories, or things that had no usefulness in making adjustments to the continually shifting and continually repeating demands of life. Art, among other things, would be impossible. The brain would be like a library in which the books were stacked indiscriminately on the basis of date of acquisition. In order to be fully useful, experience must be filed not only as memory but also as metaphor. This is the card-catalogue system of the self's history in time.[61]

The importance of this notion in relation to Bausch's work is its emphasis on process, specifically metaphoric process, rather than product. The process envelops material within its growing thematic folds so that individual elements or images of the production start to function as concretizations or corporealizations of abstract ideas or feelings. They are produced metonymically as a distillation of possibilities to one distinct image that has an affective base in the idea or feeling. The connection of those images is metaphoric, that is, it is not simply a string of metaphors, but the process itself is metaphoric – expansive, suggestive and open to a realm of possibility within a given feeling structure.

Bausch's pieces move through the connection of vital moments, rather than following a clear line of action. Whereas traditional theatrical representation might give us a linear sequence of events, Bausch's work is more combinatory than representational: it asks what are the essential connections between successive actions rather than what leads you from one to another in a consequential narrative. As Sally Banes explains, 'the pieces proceed not by causality but by accretion. An image is gradually, laboriously built, then abandoned. It is partly this structural disconnectedness among intensely lived events that creates the pervasive sense of alienation and angst.'[62] The alienation we feel comes from not being given a through line for the experience, which places us outside events. The images feel immediate, but we are distanced from them because they lack a conventional empathetic structure through which we normally identify with the people on stage going through an event. Within a conventional narrative frame, any feelings generated are connected to the context as it is developed on stage; we maintain that connection by considering those feelings. Even if feelings might relate to our own lives, we are essentially provided a way to leave them with their attendant context. But in Bausch's work, feelings become disconnected from the generating image; we are forced to take them with us to sort through within our own sense of self.

As we move through the images in Bausch's work, we are carried along on currents of association and personal connection. As States says of dream images, they are 'simply thought in transit, nothing formed but something forming, never an identity but always a passage'.[63] This continual dynamics of formation also applies to Bausch's creative process as well as to the actual productions: on the one hand, there is no theme first and then examples, but both emerge simultaneously; on the other hand, the structure of the piece is open, ideas and emotions are set apart and put in connection to things like them to offer a multiplicity of perspectives.

Bausch's pieces employ a looser structure of exploration and held tension rather than resolution so that the pieces are literally texted, that is, elements are woven into a whole as in a textile. Sometimes the weave is fairly loose, but if you look long enough the overall pattern of the fabric comes through, with its subtle interlacing and juxtaposition of likenesses. Following those associative pathways does not lead us on a journey of *what* is expressed, but places us within the effort of *how* the piece attempts to construct coherence. It is that effort to discern that we relate to. Bausch's work shows how the very persistence to go on trying is what makes us human; to continually attempt to reweave the bits and fragments of memory and experience into a fabric that makes some sense.

Bausch builds a system of awarenesses. It is not just what each successive image says about the underlying structure, but how they infect and affect each other, creating a web of sense or a weaving of ideas and images. This takes place both through the progression of the piece and in the density of simultaneous action on stage. Images occur in reaction to other images, sometimes overlapping and sometimes separated by other images or intermissions. The total work is so richly layered that we cannot contain it in our head as an instance of projected meaning. The pieces are felt more than they are understood. The series of images is connected in such a way as to add up to an overall feeling which is the piece. Bausch asks a question on the first day of rehearsal and the piece is the answer, with all of the weight of the exploration contained in the discovery.

Bausch reconfigures experience for specific affective purposes. She attempts to uncover the deep structure of the experience through association. But it is only through distortion effectuated by abstraction that the structure and connections become visible. As Van Kerkhoven explains,

> abstraction as method leaves its traces, its fingerprints on the material; the quality of the method employed determines the final result. Thanks to the use of abstraction, the nature of things changes – they are attributed a new value. By means of this added distance we are able to see them differently and become aware – with time – of their complexity.[64]

This sense of distortion through abstraction also recurs in the progression of images, where, again, the point is to determine what emotional or conceptual ties bind the various images together rather than concentrating on their apparent randomness, or their lack of linear development.

The most commonly commented upon structural strategy of distortion in Bausch's work is her use of repetition. In many cases, this sense of repetition partakes in the ongoing revision and reincarnation of related ideas and feelings in new materials of presentation. Bausch finds patterns of human behaviour and places them in and out of context to show their impact on individuals and groups. As Barbara Confino notes, 'unlike Robert Wilson's use of repetition, Bausch's does not hypnotize, but awakens … Intellectual as well as emotional associations come tumbling to mind'.[65] One frequently cited scene demonstrating this dynamic can be found in *Cafe Müller* (1978) when Malou Airaudo approaches Dominique Mercy and the couple slowly raise their arms into an embrace. Jan Minarik enters, gently takes Airaudo's hands off of Mercy, takes Mercy's hands off of Airaudo and places their faces together in a static kiss. Minarik then raises Mercy's arms up to a position bent 90 degrees at the elbow. He places Airaudo's arm around Mercy, lifts her and places her in Mercy's arms so that she is lying limply on her back. Minarik leaves and Mercy slowly drops Airaudo to the floor. She bounces up to hug Mercy in the same position in which the scene started. Minarik, who had been walking out, hears the activity and slowly returns to reposition the couple in the pose in which he left them, methodically repeating his actions in the same sequence as before. He turns to leave again, Airaudo is dropped, return to embrace, Minarik returns, the couple is rearranged again, Minarik leaves, Airaudo is dropped … etc. The action goes through several repetitions, getting faster and faster as the scene progresses. Finally Minarik leaves for good and the couple continues to repeat the action, working up to a frantic pace until they stop in an embrace and we hear the sound of their breathing, heavy from the exertion. Airaudo slowly moves off to continue her path around the room and Mercy slowly exits. This couple meets on several other occasions throughout the piece and always repeat the same series of actions before moving off in their own direction.

In this example, we see a metonymic condensation of a behavioural process (the course of love, here) into a single image. This image was derived out of the idea of a doomed relationship (think Romeo and Juliet), but the metonymic form the image assumes places the entirety of that idea into a clear set of gestural actions. That image is repeated and the context changed, to show the way we all fall into patterns of behaviour and allow them to dictate our actions rather than striking out to find something new. The moment started as personal, but through repetition it points to the larger idea of doomed love that is central to the piece. While the individual image is metonymic, the connection of those images and the dramatic move forward is metaphoric, since it requires weaving together the seemingly distinct scenes into an overarching fabric. To accomplish this, the metaphoric process takes the image out of the realm of the personal and opens it to our own considerations and associations.

The process described above is repeated in different forms in several of Bausch's pieces, showing us how the underlying framework of experience presents itself in a variety of contexts. In *Blaubart* (Bluebeard, 1977), for instance, a woman sits on the floor behind a table at which the man playing Duke Bluebeard is seated, passively looking out at the audience. We see

FIGURE 2.3 Blaubart. © *Bettina Stoess, 1977*.

her hand rise up and describe a tender path up the man's body towards his face and just as she reaches the point of tenderly caressing him; he violently shoves her head back down to the floor and out of sight, without moving his eyes from his distant goal. After a moment, we see the hand again and the action is repeated, again ending with a violent push to the floor. Again we see the hand rise up and the whole sequence is repeated several times, getting faster and faster until the woman finally stops, leaving the man to continue looking callously at the audience. There is a moment of stillness before we see the hand rise up once more.

Here the repetition serves to shine a new light on the image. Its expression moves from a moment of tenderness and cruelty to the persistence of desire and relentless brutality to find connection even in that. In addition, the continuous repetition also opens up the moment of personal struggle towards all moments of tenacity and futility we may have been involved in ourselves. As Deborah Jowitt explains in response to a similar series of repetitive actions in *Bluebeard*, 'although the gestures become more brutal with every repetition, they also move farther away from their original status as expressions of devotion and rejection, and the performers don't seem to own them anymore'.[66] By incessantly repeating the same scene, the performers are removed from the image as a direct expression of their subjectivity. However, even though they do seem separate from the action, the event ruthlessly subsumes them as characters, as they are lost within it and seemingly unable to escape. At this point, the image begins to take on the contingency of whatever the underlying tenor of the piece might be. It is not a moment in a linear story, but one possibility in an imaginal whole. It exists as if in a dream.

Romeo Castellucci

3

Romeo Castellucci or the Visionary of the Non-Visual

Eleni Papalexiou

'Every image we see in art should penetrate us, cause in us a kind of fire', Romeo Castellucci (b. 4 August 1960) once said in a 2015 interview.[1] Living up to his own expectations of what art should achieve, the work Castellucci has been creating for more than thirty-five years never ceased to set the art world on fire, as it continued to surprise – and, very often, also to shock – spectators, critics, artists and scholars alike. Together with the company he founded, the Socìetas Raffaello Sanzio, Romeo Castellucci has invented a new stage language and created a theatre that is immediate, vibrant, beautiful and violent at the same time. His theatrical poetics, which explores the limits between the human and the inhuman, is heretic, but it is also deeply rooted in primitive codes, replete with meaning but using a minimum of speech. His work is characterized by its constant change of style and its experimental nature, its audacity and its sense of danger and fragile balance. It already constitutes a major chapter in the history of modern theatre. As theatre scholar Marco De Marinis notes, 'Socìetas Raffaello Sanzio and Romeo Castellucci have contributed to a radical change in our way of thinking about and making theatre in our era'[2]

In the early days of the twenty-first century, Romeo Castellucci seems to be the director who responds more than anyone else to the expectations and visions of Antonin Artaud (1896–1948), who, already at the start of the previous century, demanded 'a kind of unique Creator who will bear the double responsibility for the spectacle and the plot'.[3] Romeo Castellucci does indeed take up various roles in creating his work, as he is not only a director, but also a dramatist, set and costume designer, lighting and sound manager, while he was for many years a performer as well. Moreover, as a 'philosopher of the stage', as Piersandra Di Matteo describes him, he has written several theoretical texts on the art of theatre.[4] In these writings, Castellucci develops a complex theatrical vocabulary that, much like the performances he creates on stage, is often quite obscure, but which testifies to a solid view on what theatre ought to strive for in contemporary times.

Refusing to succumb to the predicaments of our increasingly networked society that seems to thrive on the continuous flow of communication and images, Castellucci's theatre offers an antidote to the deceitful connectivity that marks our globalized condition. Instead, his work opens up a world of revelation and insight, as it gives us the opportunity to see images that derive from the inner regions of both our culture and our own individual existence. Accordingly, Castellucci attaches great importance to the role of the spectator, as he wants to highlight the creative force of the gaze and to activate the double ability of viewing and being viewed. In this way, this archetypal relation between onlooker and looked-upon is awakened and becomes conscious,[5] while the spectator becomes the master of the act of viewing, an attribute that makes his theatre intensely political.

The dazzling aesthetic universe that Romeo Castellucci presents on stage resists clear-cut interpretations that attempt to pinpoint the meaning of the work, allowing instead for a multitude of both reflective associations and affective sensations. But even while Castellucci's productions are open to different understandings and experiences, his directorial signature is highly idiosyncratic while also the theatrical oeuvre he has been building from the early 1980s onwards up until today demonstrates a solid consistency in that each production partakes in his overarching quest for what can be described as a theatre of non-representation. In this chapter, I will present the most significant steps in Romeo Castellucci's career in order to provide insight into his singular way of devising theatre. Starting from the very early beginnings and Castellucci's first explorations in the world of art in the 1970s, I will proceed with a more thematic discussion of his theatre work, singling out the key motifs, ideas and aesthetic features that undergird his artistic poetics. This brief journey through Castellucci's theatrical universe will lead us from the iconoclasm that defines his and Socìetas Raffaello Sanzio's relationship to images, the role of language and silence in his dramaturgy, as well as his noted fascination with the expressive power of human bodies, animals and children.

This chapter not only enjoys the benefit of hindsight, but also draws heavily on the archival material that has been collected, catalogued and digitized, as part of two large-scale research projects.[6] As such, it testifies to the continued importance of acquiring primary documentary sources for chronicling the development of an artist's oeuvre and for discovering patterns, themes or inspirations that are not always immediately discernible as they only emerge over time. As Romeo Castellucci himself avows, 'The archive demonstrates, finally, that all things return, forms resurface after having taken long journeys, frequently without the artist's knowing or wishing it. It represents for me the realization of the sources of my works, as I discover, through it, that these sources are few and always the same'.[7] Even though Castellucci might be slightly too moderate here in reducing the breadth of his work to only a few sources, the recursive dynamics by which he revisits, reworks and reinvents similar interests over and over again is indeed one of the hallmarks of his oeuvre. As this chapter will show, it is in this paradoxical tandem of recurrence and novelty where we can find some of the keys to unlock his singular theatrical language that has proven to be both challenging and fascinating for twentieth-century spectators.

The beginnings

In Romeo Castellucci's archive, one may encounter hundreds of loose pages with class notes, exercises and drawings, from the period when he was studying at the Liceo Artistico (Artistic Lyceum, graduated in 1978) and the Accademia delle Belle Arti (Academy of Fine Arts, 1983) of the University of Bologna, where he majored in set design and painting. It was Romeo's sister Claudia who seems to have ignited his desire to study art, as she was already before him a student at Bologna's art school, bringing home with her books, pictures and records that eventually would draw Romeo to the realm of the arts. Romeo's interest in art, however, came quite unexpectedly. As he explains himself, 'I had the desire to live with animals, I wanted to become a veterinarian', and while he had decided to do his high school studies at the Istituto Technico Agrario (Technical Institute of Agriculture) of Cesena, he found that 'my school was disappointing, the opposite of what I expected'.[8] Abandoning his dream to work with animals, Castellucci went on to pursue another one, even though – as we shall see more below – his deep fascination with animal life will return in his theatre work.

Browsing through the archived documents of Romeo Castellucci's period as an art student, one can readily identify several key themes that inform his later creations, even if they are still unrefined and rather inchoately present. There are traces of major works he will engage with (such as Dante Alighieri's *The Divine Comedy* or the biblical story of Moses and Aaron); his admiration for the ancient Greek spirit; his interest in not only animals but also machines, theology and the symbols of faith; his confrontation with dramaturgy and literature; the notion of motherhood and the figure of the mother; the issues of language, speech, rhetoric and the voice; and the corporeality of art.

Along with his interest for the visual arts and his first exhibitions,[9] Romeo starts to develop an ardent need to immerse himself in the world of theatre. Already as teenagers, he and his sister Claudia testify to a theatrical sensibility.

At the ages of 13 and 15, for instance, they met Chiara and Paolo Guidi, 13 and 11 at the time, at the local boys and girls scouts in Cesena, where they were confronted not only with 'their first audience', but also with the first 'rejection of their unconventionality'.[10] And even though Romeo and Claudia were completely ignorant about theatre and had never watched a theatrical performance, they decided to found together the Gruppo Espressione (Expression Group). Improvising short sketches in which they played with fire, the experiments of the Gruppo Espressione anticipated the central role of fire in the iconoclasm for which the theatre of the Sociètas Raffaello Sanzio is now notoriously known and which I will discuss in more detail below. In this respect, the group proved foundational for many years to follow, as it was here where the seeds for their later work in theatre were planted.

By the end of the 1970s, Romeo and Claudia resume their early interest in theatrical performance, as he takes his first steps in acting, whereas she assumes the more guiding role of director. The first work to come out of this collaboration was *Prometeo Incatenato* (Prometheus Bound) with the group Il Cantiere (The Yard), which was staged in 1977 at Cesena's Jolly Theatre. One year later, Romeo and Claudia Castellucci together with Chiara and Paolo Guidi founded a new group, the Explò–Esplorazione Teatro (Theatre Exploration), which marks the period when they start trying their hand at the classical repertory, including theatre pieces by Samuel Beckett, Henrik Ibsen, Eugène Ionesco and Albert Camus.[11] During the rehearsals, they train themselves in experimental acting techniques, and, in particular, they systematically train their voices and other expressive means:

> In the first years of work we did tremendous exercises for the voice and for the body. The first texts of theatrical history that we familiarized ourselves with were Aristotle's *Poetics* and Grotowski's *The Poor Theatre*; these were followed by Stanislavski's and Diderot's texts.[12]

After these first explorations in theatrical practice, Romeo Castellucci moves to Rome and starts working as a professional actor. In 1978–9, he interprets the role of the twentieth-century Italian painter Antonio Ligabue in the eponymous play written by Angelo Dallagiacoma and directed by the esteemed Italian avant-garde director Memè Perlini.[13] Having seen the piece at the Venice Biennale festival, Dallagiacoma recalls the interpretation of Romeo as 'molto giovane, molto fresco, molto bravo' (very young, very fresh, very good).[14] Despite this apparent acclaim, it seems that, for Castellucci, the experience was excruciatingly disappointing, only feeding into his intolerance towards conventional theatre with the result that he came to reject it completely.

Unsatisfied with the demands of the directors he had been working with, Romeo Castellucci decides to abandon his individual career as an actor, returning instead to his earlier collaborations with his sister Claudia and Chiari Guidi. In 1980, they found the group Raffaello Sanzio, laying the base for what eventually would grow into one of the most daring companies in twentieth-century Western theatre. Paolo Guidi, Chiara's brother, was still a student of fine arts at that time and would join them the following year. The name of the group exemplifies the close affiliation of its members with the visual arts, since it is obviously chosen to commemorate and honour the legacy of the Renaissance painter Raphael. According to Claudia Castellucci, their choice for Raphael as the nomenclature for their company was inspired by the idea that he prefigures the transition from Renaissance to Baroque. As the harbinger of a new visual regime, in which expressive power arises through the interior of the artistic creation itself, Raphael adumbrates the Baroque, which – in hindsight constitutes one of the most iconoclastic eras in art history, as representation is connected to rupture.[15]

On 1 November 1980, the newly founded group Raffaello Sanzio staged their first performance. The setting was anything but usual: rather than a theatre, they decided to show the piece in Romeo Castellucci's apartment in Rome in front of one single spectator, the famous drama critic Giuseppe Bartolucci. *Cenno* (Nod) was based on John L. Austin's posthumously published collection of lectures, *How to Do Things with Words* (1962). The performance revolved around interviews of the girls by their mothers and of the boys by their fathers, a concept that corresponds to their first manifesto, in which they state, 'it is probably as a result of the Christian truth, according to which the Son is also his own Father, because God is three in one'.[16] The apartment was used as the setting for the show: the floor, the walls, the windows, the table, even the heaters were parts of the stage. Symbols, such as the miniature house, the features of the face (eye, nose, mouth, ear), the reflecting mirrors were the main props. The group performed on the floor and on the table and they were all wearing blouses with a long cut on the back. Despite its biographical wrapping, this was not a type of a devised theatre performance but a totally pre-fixed and well-rehearsed show.[17] The performance made a strong impression on Bartolucci, who was impressed by this 'theatre of tautological heroes [in which] to say means to do … to create by the simple movement of the imagination'.[18] Despite the raw appearance of the piece, Bartolucci realized that a potentially innovative aesthetics was germinating here, so he encouraged the members of the group to go on.

After *Cenno*, the group managed to acquire funding to rent, for seven performances, the theatre La Piramide, which was one of the more experimental venues in Rome at that time. There, in front of about twenty spectators, they presented *Diade incontro a monade* (Dyads versus Monads, 1981), the performance that, according to their own writings, 'open[ed] the way for the weird logic of the group, through a theatrical form fully dedicated to symbolic thought'.[19] In the first review ever published on a work by Raffaello Sanzio, Giuseppe Bartolucci wrote about the piece:

This group, 'Raffaello Sanzio' is completely primitivist, to all appearances to a scandalous degree. The primitive aesthetics are expressed through

Dyads versus Monads with such grace that it is impossible for one to remain indifferent to it. Words, images, thoughts, feelings are bandied about, seeking ways and paths for an interior exploration and an expressivity of the surface.[20]

The next experiment the four protagonists of Raffaello Sanzio presented on stage was called *Persia-Mondo 1a1* (Persia-World all one, 1981), which they described as 'an exclusive performance ... on how to be dogs'.[21] It was a daring performance that confronted the audience with an unexpected reading of ordinary dialogues and situations, such as 'whom would you kill first, your dad or your mum?'[22] The central staging elements were 'horns of bulls and goats horns, hooves, teeth, intestines and eyes preserved in formalin jars'.[23] *Persia-Mondo 1a1* was a breakthrough for Raffaello Sanzio, as it not only raised the interest of drama critics and the art scene, but also led to various articles in which the group was recognized for their innovative approach to theatre.[24] Eventually, the success of the piece would lead to the group's first tour of Italy,[25] while they also succeeded in securing the support of the distinguished nonconformist art critic, Francesca Alinovi,[26] who encouraged them to present *Persia-Mondo 1a1* at the Galleria d'arte moderna in Bologna. Thanks to her intervention, the group started to attract interest from various other leading figures in the Italian art scene, such as the renowned writer and art critic Pier Vittorio Tondelli, who published particularly positive reviews.[27]

At the time when Raffaello Sanzio was gaining recognition, modern Italian theatre was dominated by two distinct tendencies, generally described as *postavanguardia* (post-avant-garde) and *nuova spettacolarità* (new spectacle).[28] The problem with the work of Raffaello Sanzio, however, was that its viewpoint and aesthetics could not be subsumed under either of these categories, as it seemed to evade any tendency, current or 'school'. Consequently, the members of the group felt the need to highlight to what extent their practice deviated from other types of theatre, articulating their approach and poetic principles in various theoretical writings and manifestos. These reflections are of almost equal importance with their stage creations. Even a simple browsing of these invaluable texts demonstrates that this theorization of artistic creation is the result of a painful process of study, research, reflection and confrontation with complex literature from different academic disciplines, such as philosophy, history, theology, politics and history of art.[29]

> We arrived at the theatre talking ten to the dozen. Thought is the foundation of all our theatrical work. We have always transcribed our theatrical meditations into theoretical texts (often rather complicated); we work on the premise that one cannot do superficial or pleasurable things within the logic of the digestible ... We must do something that has impact, which transforms.[30]

After *Persia-Mondo 1a1*, Raffaello Sanzio created *Popolo zuppo* (A drenched people), which premiered in Bologna in May 1982 and was shown afterwards at the Metateatro (Metatheatre) in Rome, a space for avant-gardist performing arts. Through a variety of allusions to the visual arts,

FIGURE 3.1 *Romeo Castellucci performing in* Persia-Mondo 1a1, *1981. Courtesy of the Societas Raffaello Sanzio.*

accompanied by the stringent sounds of the avant-garde music and artistic group the 'Residents', the piece was presented as an 'Italian picnic'.[31] It more specifically centred around popular illustrations, consumer products of mass culture and 'all dominant figures that are not there to inhabit the naïve folk saga of the intellectuals, but to stand still, unhooked from their brains that think of nothing but improvement'.[32] The protagonist of the performance is a painter, played by Romeo Castellucci, who described the piece as follows:

> We like to incorporate in our performances the element of illustration, framed by hackneyed verses and citations, whose naïve form may cause embarrassment, but eventually misleads only those who are unable to break with yesterday.[33]

Later in 1982, Romeo Castellucci and the other members of Raffaello Sanzio staged for a single time the performance *Maiali anziani e malandati* (Pigs Old and Shabby), a 'harsh and enthralling piece'[34] they would eventually renounce and delete from their official list of performances. For Romeo Castellucci, the piece belonged to a rather dark period in which he seriously began to doubt the meaningfulness of his experiments with theatre. Perhaps because of these doubts, the next piece of the group struck an entirely different note, as it evoked the lighter genre of the 'commedia pastorale' (pastoral comedy) and was described by the members themselves as their 'primo spettacolo calmo' (first calm spectacle).[35] *I fuoriclasse della bontà* (The Champions of Goodness) is a Sardinian-Tyrolean elegy depicting a group of shepherds wearing kilts and breeding cow atoms. The Arcadian dimension of the piece and its atmosphere of serenity were strongly indebted to the correspondence between Romeo Castellucci and the composer Hans-Joachim Roedelius,[36] 'the only European able to make the music of the future alpine civilization'.[37] According to the group, the piece was an 'early symptom of psychedelic theatre', as they intended to show how 'the brain, over-satiated, explodes'.[38]

In retrospect, *I fuoriclasse della bontà* marks a decisive point in Romeo Castellucci's artistic career, as his interest for theatre starts to wane, while his earlier engagement with the visual arts reignites. More and more, he became convinced that the theatrical milieu was extremely uninteresting and the level of criticism common and boring. Artists and critics working in the domain of the visual arts, on the other hand, proved to be much more inspiring, which also explains why he turned away from the stage and began to explore more intensively than ever before other formats of artistic expression, such as exhibitions, short films or oratorios.[39]

Despite – or perhaps thanks to – these sidesteps into other artistic areas beyond the theatre, Castellucci became decided to take his stage language in another direction. While the archive of Socìetas Raffaello Sanzio contains various documents that demonstrate how the group had always been interested in finding new linguistic codes, their intention to invent and experiment with alternative modes of expression and communication begins in earnest at the end of 1983, when Romeo and Claudia Castellucci developed the so-called *Lingua Generalissima* (General Language). In this fictive linguistic system, they reduced a set of 800 senses to four hierarchically structured levels: *agone, apotema, meteora, blok* (race, stock, meteor, block).[40] 'The language of the future will reduce the verb to the bone', Claudia explains, 'like a cancer: the brain must contain more symbols and less words'[41]

The *Lingua Generalissima* was for the first time tried onstage with the piece *Kaputt Necropolis*, which was presented at the Venice Biennale in 1984 and described by the members of the company as 'a gigantic and encyclopaedic spectacle where nothing alive exists (so everything is dead)'.[42] In the play, in a dazzling universe illuminated by neon lights, Romeo Pilota converses with Paolo Virus, two roles interpreted by Romeo Castellucci and Paolo Guidi, using the *Generalissima* in all successive levels, ending by speaking using only four terms.

Thirty years later, in 2015, Romeo Castellucci would return to the *Lingua Generalissima* in his performance *Uso umano di esseri umani* (Human Use of Human Beings), which reinterprets the biblical story of Lazarus according to the principles set forth by Claudia Castellucci. However, while the interest of Socìetas Raffaello Sanzio in the mechanisms of linguistic communication remains a constant thread throughout its oeuvre, it is primarily their iconoclastic approach to the pervasive presence of the image in Western culture that dominates the works they created from the late 1980s onwards.

From iconoclasm to the revelation of the unique image

In *Santa Sofia. Teatro Khmer* (1985), the stage is dominated by an enormous Byzantine icon of the Pantocrator Christ, whose piercing gaze seems to be staring at the audience. Under his glaring eye, the figure of Leo III Isaurus appears. During the first century AD, he was the emperor of Constantinople and is characterized by the members of the company as the 'greatest iconoclast of the contemporary age',[43] since he summoned the eradication of images of worship. The other protagonist is Pol Pot, who became the leader of the Cambodian communist Khmer Rouge in 1963 and ordered his soldiers to destroy all possible contaminations that came from the despicable West.[44] Socìetas Raffaello Sanzio presents Pol Pot in a catatonic stage, lying sick and motionless in bed throughout the entire performance, introducing the concept of 'theatrical paralysis', which was further developed in the company's subsequent productions, *I Miserabili* (The Miserables, 1987)[45] and *Alla bellezza tanto antica* (In Praise of Such Ancient Beauty, 1988). Next to these two figures, *Santa Sofia* features a child to be sacrificed and two stylite monks holding machine guns.

Santa Sofia is a seminal performance in various ways. For Romeo Castellucci, the piece was a decisive moment primarily because of the manifesto his sister Claudia wrote for this production. Remembering the sensation it caused when he first read it, he says, 'At that moment, I realized that I belong definitely to the domain of theatre'[46] Claudia Castellucci's manifesto shows how *Santa Sofia* was meant to inaugurate the rebirth of theatre as nothing less than a new religion. Drawing on the tumultuous history of the Hagia Sophia, the basilica in Constantinople that was one of the first sites subjected to Byzantine iconoclasm under the auspices of Leo III Isaurus, the manifesto proclaims a similar revolt for Western theatre:

> You shall not enter the church of Saint Sophia in Constantinople without a revolution.
>
> Move aside, theatregoer, there are no images for you here. There is nothing to view and comment on aesthetically. Move aside, common man, this is not the place of traditional biographic-style analyses.
>
> Come, you, who wants to fight against the fact that you were born, and the fact that you are here, and the fact that you can use the tools you find here.
>
> This is the theatre that denies representations (it is only when there are no representations at all that true representations emerge – not my words). This is the theatre of the new religion, so come only you, you who wish to become a follower of the road of the Unreal.[47]

This passage from Claudia Castellucci's manifesto demonstrates how *Santa Sofia* was important for both Romeo Castellucci and Socìetas Raffaello Sanzio in that it marks the beginning of the iconoclasm for which their work would become notorious. *Santa Sofia* was a highly polemical piece, both for its aesthetics and the figures it presented (such as 'negative' characters, war atmosphere, references to bloodstained political events, violent religious rituals, the elements of burning and destruction), while it also turned the theatre into a kind of civilian weapon: 'Like a sharp scythe, it mows down realism of any style and culls the harvest of narrativity. Like an anti-nihilist shovel it digs pits for the planting of the truth that has been plundered from our memory.' Bound by an 'iconoclast curse', Hagia Sophia, through the paradox of stage conventions, 'brings back theatre as the only place where super-reality can be realized'.[48]

To broach this alleged 'super-reality', Socìetas Raffaello Sanzio pursues an iconoclasm that is not only geared towards destruction, but which should also inspire new modes of creation.[49] As Claudia Castellucci explains, 'the iconoclast orientation endows the artist with two hands: one for drawing images, and one iconoclastic. One is Abel's and the other Cain's, and that is the hand who acts last, because it destroys the archetype which lives in it'.[50] The reference to Cain and Abel makes clear how the artists of Socìetas

Raffaello Sanzio found a fruitful way of communication in the religious genre of the parable, which seems to provide a format to make comprehensible that which cannot be expressed directly. At the same time, Claudia Castellucci's reading of the parable of Cain and Abel readily indicates what, for her and the company, is at stake in this tale. The fact that Cain murdered Abel, but was nevertheless permitted by God to continue his life, exemplifies one of the founding doctrines that inform the theatre of Socìetas Raffaello Sanzio: the idea that destruction is the way towards genuine creation. In this sense, the notion of 'iconoclasm' as propounded by the Italian artists does not entail a non-pictorial theatre, but rather a representation of images in a wilfully different way. It is, in other words, a theatre that negates the pre-existing imagery of tradition in order to create new and hitherto unseen images.[51]

The performance in which the act of iconoclasm is most literally visualized is probably Romeo Castellucci's *Sul concetto di volto nel figlio di Dio* (On the Concept of the Face Regarding the Son of God, 2010). The scenery of the piece resembles the one of *Santa Sofia*, as in both productions an enormous projection of the face of Christ make it seem as if he overlooks the entire stage. The performance begins with a private scene between a father and his son, under the gaze of Jesus, as depicted in the painting *The Savior of the World* (1465–75) by the Renaissance artist Antonello da Messina.

The fact that the figure of Christ returns various times in Castellucci's work, albeit primarily as an image, indicates how the pictorial tradition of religion was an important influence for him as an artist. While Castellucci had received a Catholic education, he was not particularly religious, but his first encounter with the visual arts did take place in church. He remembers how much he was impressed, as a child, by the sculpted and painted decorations in churches, magnetized by the holy icons and depictions of passion, martyrdom or naked bodies. Even if the liturgy itself remained inaccessible at first, Castellucci gradually discovered something fascinating in the aesthetics of the ritual, which would leave its mark on his artistic work:

> It was the *distance* from form which attracted me, just like those times when I was a child in the country and attended mass in Latin, so dark and so mysterious, with the priest making all these incomprehensible gestures with his back turned, like an insect buzzing over my bed when I was ill with fever.[52]

Even though 'the distance from form' is what attracted Castellucci in the event of the mass, he did choose to integrate one of the most recognizable images of the Christian tradition in both *Santa Sofia* and *On the Concept of the Face Regarding the Son of God*. As the face and body of Jesus have been abundantly pictured throughout the entire history of Western art, the figure of Christ has become part of our collective imagination, even if the accuracy of his representation is contested. In both performances, spectators direct their gaze to the face of Christ, but as he simultaneously seems to look back, they also become the subject of another's gaze. Especially the title of *On the Concept of the Face …* indicates how the entire dramatic structure and staging of this production are organized around the face, but even more so around the eyes of Christ. His face overwhelms us and draws us into his own orbit, absorbing our minds through space and time. Faced with this iconic image, we travel to the core of Western civilization, while also discovering an individual time, that of our personal history.[53] The piece ostentatiously refers to the religious tradition of Christianity, but not without wanting to overthrow or even to undermine its pervasive influence.[54]

In the second scene of the performance, children enter the stage and perform a blatantly iconoclastic act, as they start throwing grenades at the face of Jesus. Castellucci attempts to turn the at once most innocent and most violent gaze to the audience, which is that of the children. According to the Christian view, no one has the right to judge their fellow man, or rather the Son of God, since no one is sinless: 'He who is without sin among you, let him cast the first stone.'[55] Who could then judge God? A child who does not possess life experiences is beyond any judgement. In the Bible children are also referred as lambs: 'Look at the Lamb of God who takes away the sin of the world.'[56] Therefore, only their innocent presence may judge the judgement of God. The symbolic destruction of an emblematic image of Western civilization does not signify an act of blasphemy, but rather a questioning of its old, inherited, pre-packaged interpretation.[57]

The iconoclasm in the theatre of Socìetas Raffaello Sanzio not only comprises a radical revision of persistent traditions in Western culture, such as Christianity, but it also ought to initiate the probably more constructive process of revealing the one, unique image.[58] This idea of the birth of the unique image is closely linked to the notion of femininity. In *Go down, Moses* (2015), a performance evoking the platonic exit from the cave, we are offered the spectacle of the human descent into the dark cavern, where a feminine hand forms the first hand-print, the image-matrix in the history of mankind and conceives the 'first image', the original staging of the world. In this performance, the Mother constitutes the central figure, as in the second scene we actually witness a realistically performed birth on stage, a forced exit of a baby from the body of a woman in a public toilet. The baby represents Moses, who is considered to be the first iconoclast who broke the fake idols. In contrast to the patriarchal viewpoint of the Old Testament, according to which Moses represents the Father, Romeo Castellucci proposes a reverse, feminine, reading of the biblical *Exodus*, highlighting the primeval primary bond between mother and body, a body born or a body decomposed – these are all images we see in the last part of the performance.[59]

Another hint can be found in the first episode of the *Tragedia Endogonidia, C.#01 Cesena* (2002),[60] where we are confronted with a woman, who is played by a male actor sitting on stage with his/her legs spread apart, as if we are about to see the conception and birth of the world. The image of the mother takes first place on the stage and embodies the beginning of everything. She is the ultimate expression of *matter*.[61] With this scene, Castellucci draws on the notion of matter that Aristotle introduces in his *Metaphysics*, equating femininity with receptive material. More specifically, he conceives of the female as the locus and receptacle of birth, as a place from which the dead emerge at birth and to which they return after death. The archetypical role of the mother constitutes, in this regard, the representation of pure *matter*, which is ultimately devoid of shape and remains unchanged even after the dissolution of life. Thus, woman is figured like a field consisting of 'matter' (ὕλη) from which 'shape' or 'species' (εἶδος) is created and to which it ultimately will return.[62] Further research in Romeo Castellucci's personal library revealed that the intertextual provenance of the notion of matter was Johann Jakob Bachofen's monograph *Das Mutterrecht* (The Matriarchy),[63] an 1861 treatise on ancient ceremonies, especially the Eleusinian Mysteries, which Castellucci had been reading assiduously before and during the creation of *Gilgamesh* (1990), which I will discuss later on.

In the *Cesena #01* episode, Romeo Castellucci endeavours to re-conceptualize the image of the world by setting new rules. He himself is the guardian of a special memory of the future, which negates the position of violence before it takes place. It is a sort of parthenogenesis, a conception taking place within woman, without outside interference. The image, organized in advance, reveals its morbid attachment to the mother, to a distant part, which, as time passes, we are bound to meet again in the future.[64] The image has no father, it is unique, without reference to the womb which produced it. An 'image-womb'.[65] It is within the walls of the virgin mother's womb that the *Tragedia Endogonidia* is created. Her belly will become a place of gestation for a different conception of tragedy: an incubator of unique images.

The issue of the unique, revealing image is a central topic in Romeo Castellucci's theoretical texts 'La riconquista della visione' (The Reconquest of Vision) and 'Epopteia'.[66] *Epopteia*, the ultimate mystic vision of the Eleusinian Mysteries was a representation in the *telestērion* (initiation hall) of Eleusis. It was not considered a necessary and prerequisite stage for the completion of the celebration of the ceremonies, but was open to those who aspired to reach a higher level of understanding and fulfilment. During the *epopteia*, the initiates were supposed to witness a revelation, an epiphany.[67] *Epopteia* constitutes a fundamental element of Castellucci's theatre, as it poses the question of the unique image, a non-reproducible image to be generated by each spectator individually.[68] The artist opposes the practice according to which theatre is viewed as a ready-made product. On the contrary, he believes that a performance is a complex process which demands the full participation of the spectator if something creative is to be the result.

According to Aristotle, the initiates of the Eleusinian Mysteries were not supposed to learn anything, but to be affected in a certain way and to be put in a certain mindset.[69] They were not forced to accept any doctrine or teaching, nor was any thought or idea imposed on them. No dogmatic teaching was offered to them, no interpretation was given, neither for words (λεγόμενα) nor for actions (δρώμενα).[70] Instead, the hierophants, the priests who led the ceremony, showed them holy objects, which the initiates could not see elsewhere and were revealed to them during the ritual. All participants were free to give their own interpretation, depending on the impression made on them by what they saw, heard and underwent.

Romeo Castellucci similarly rejects dogmatism and didacticism in theatre, opposing any kind of theatrical practice that presents a self-enclosed product ready to be consumed. Instead, Castellucci believes that a performance is a complex process that requires the full engagement of the audience and which generates an experience that belongs utterly to the spectator. The director, like an ancient hierophant, initiates a revelation in front of the spectator, but does not provide any further interpretation or comment. Just as the initiates of the Eleusinian Mysteries should see the hidden things that cannot be described with words, so too is the spectator not expected to explain or to connect notions and codes, but, drawing from the burden of his or her experiences and feelings, to create his/her own spectacle. For Romeo Castellucci, the *epopteia* can be seen as a poetic power of the gaze that has the ability to create the object represented.[71] 'Theatre', Castellucci claims, 'is a revelation, a vision'[72]

In 'The Reconquest of Vision', Castellucci refers to Aeschylus, who was put to trial because in one of his tragedies (a text that has not been handed down to us), he showed on stage certain symbolic objects of the Eleusinian Mysteries, thus exposing what Castellucci describes as the one, unique image. Revealing the mystery was considered a crime against the highest law of the rite and also forbidden for its initiates. For Castellucci, the case of Aeschylus marks 'the beginning of re-production', or the moment when the pervasive influence of mimetic representation takes off.[73] By highlighting this inaugural moment, Castellucci wishes to oppose any easy acceptance of the contemporary circulation of infinitely reproduced and reproducible images that govern not only the mass media, but also modern art. In our current visual culture, both significant and trivial images are disseminated without hardly any kind of differentiation, enticing audiences to a passive consumption of a seemingly limitless abundance of alluring resources.[74] According to Romeo Castellucci, theatre should serve as an interruption in this flow of readily digestible images.[75] After all, the role of the artist has always been to impel spectators to rediscover the gaze and to refine the ability to see as such. Accordingly, Castellucci seeks to reactivate the spectator's gaze through bewilderment and confusion, inventing a dramaturgy that thrives on the uniquenesss of the image, rather than on its reproducibility.

The theatre of Castellucci always aimed to lead the spectator to discover the gaze, the ability to see. After all, Greek tragedy revealed to us that the gaze is never innocent. In this age of global unrest and polarized communities, the politics of the gaze acquire great significance. The space of this politics invades our consciousness and intercepts our very being.[76] For Romeo Castellucci, the awakening of consciousness entails an awakening of the gaze, in other words: a detachment from the world of mass communication and unambiguous images, and a transition to a different kind of state or *παθεῖν καὶ διατεθῆναι* (be affected and be put into a frame of mind).[77] Inevitably our thoughts flow to Plato's views on the effect of revealing sacred objects to the eyes of the initiates, when he describes 'the shivering, sweating and prickling induced by a beautiful *prosōpon* (face) in a man who has recently experienced the Eleusinian Mysteries'.[78] What we note is 'the importance of context in determining how and what we see'.[79]

Words, myths and parallel stories

As mentioned, the mechanisms of language and linguistic representation have always been a central concern of the members of Socìetas Raffaello Sanzio, not least Romeo Castellucci. In his attempt to invent a new theatrical language and means of communication, Castellucci investigates the etymology and the history of words, while at the same time elaborating their meaning. He seeks the limits of words, he delights in coining anagrams, such as PALCO-COLPA (stage-guilt) in *Masoch*.[80] He studies and uses rare and ancient terms, such as 'τοῖς ξενετοῖσι δεικτικῶς' (with evidence for those who know) which appeared in *Gilgamesh, Amleto* and *Oratoria n. 6*, while he also includes everyday vocabulary, as indicated by the title of his 2007 piece *Hey, Girl!* Even though Castellucci refuses to conform to the commercialized style of the modern era, he does speak about and to his own era. Nevertheless, he engages with notions that have acquired a diachronic value; each word he chooses seems to have travelled a long way through the ages.

The etymology of words is considered part of the dramaturgy itself, as for example the double meaning of the word 'Lucifer' (lux-fer or light-bearing) in *Genesi: From the Museum of Sleep* (Genesis, 1999), which incorporates a fundamental contrast: on the one side genesis and creation, and on the other genocide and destruction. This double meaning is also reflected in the piece itself. In the first part of the performance, we witness the act of creation, which Castellucci equates with the discovery of radioactivity. In his version, genesis starts with us, in the modern era. The opening scene shows the laboratory of Marie Curie with gladiate radium, followed by scientists who continue studying and working on it with the aim of using radioactivity to rule people's lives one day. Suddenly, Lucifer appears, uttering the first words of Genesis in Hebrew – the words that gave birth to the world, along with Good and Evil. In the next scene, Lucifer places a book on a small table in Marie Curie's office and a radium rock in her drawer. As radium emits its own light, it comes mysteriously close to the etymology of the word 'Lucifer'. Matter, thanks to the power of radioactivity, becomes equal to

God. It is a power with both positive and negative aspects, just as light has darkness as its opposite.[81] Light is also connected to the name of Lucifer, as it brings good and evil, light and death, creation and destruction.

Besides exemplifying Castellucci's interest in excavating the etymological roots of words and names, *Genesi* also shows how he is not interested in faithfully representing the content of a given book or story on stage. This does not mean, however, that Castellucci disregards the importance of text or narrative as a source of inspiration. On the contrary, his creative process usually includes intensive stages of reading, analysing, elaborating and commenting on existing texts. During this process, Castellucci keeps daily notes in a small notebook, jotting down impressions, words and ideas, or drawing figures and cryptic symbols. These notebooks contain the raw material of the work to follow. The deliberate disorder of this vast accumulation of seemingly disparate notes helps the director sink into chaos. Yet eventually, when Castellucci rereads his notebooks, certain structures – or what he calls 'tiny constellations' – start to emerge within this chaos, thus providing the foundations for the performance that will develop out of these collections of primary inspirations.[82] As soon as this preparatory work has been completed, the director wilfully moves against the text, in order to extract new material. In his own words, 'theatre must come from a painful birth, from the carcass of the text'.[83] Comparing his work to that of a blacksmith, he claims that the text is in need of a merciless and even violent treatment to open up its hidden meanings:

FIGURE 3.2 Genesi, *first act, 1999. Courtesy of the Socìetas Raffaello Sanzio.*

I hammer at the text, I hammer, I hammer it, until I make it disperse: It must be tempered through the 'hammering' of reading. This hammering opens new ways, which would not have opened with a simple first reading, or even with a specialist's reading, with a cerebral reading.[84]

In order to go beyond conventional interpretations of a given text, Romeo Castellucci breaks it up, attempting to find new meanings in the cracks that emerge from a heretical attitude towards the written word and from the ardent refusal to show stories in their original form on stage. Words are transformed into ideas and visions that contain the spirit and viewpoint of the director. Processing the text is, above all, a first step towards developing new ideas that eventually solidify and incite other ideas. These incipient intuitions constitute what Castellucci calls a 'dark matter' that acts as a canvas on which 'constellations' slowly start to surface.[85] He will then carve out further these clusters of material, until he comes up with a general name, such as 'inferno', that captures the spirit, atmosphere or intention of the eventual piece. In this manner, the individual inductive elements and the connections between them crystallize into a single word.

'The title is the façade of the building', Castellucci says, 'One must be a geometrician'.[86] Invoking Truffaut who once said that film already starts with the title,[87] Castellucci maintains that the title elicits a specific tone and thereby indicates a dramaturgic direction. In his view, the title should have a resonance like bronze and have a clear sound.[88] When the title sounds right to the ear of the artist, then the stage of structuring the ideas begins together with the philological and etymological research this entails. One must discover the roots of a word 'in order to be able to cut them', as Castellucci states.[89]

After finding the work's title, Castellucci continues to appropriate the material that provoked his first inspirations, trying to forge alternative directions to reach a new level of theatrical expression. This subsequent step of reincorporation is poignantly visualized, for instance, in the opening scene of his 2008 performance *Inferno*. It is Romeo Castellucci himself who appears on stage, firmly declaring 'My name is Romeo Castellucci' After uttering these words, three dogs enter, who viciously attack Castellucci and throw him to the ground. As the scene resonates with the title of the piece, *Inferno*, the intrusion of the dogs might remind spectators of the opening of Dante Alighieri's *Divine Comedy* (1306–21), where the poet, who is the protagonist in his own work, lost in the forest, meets three animals, a she-wolf, a wildcat and a lion. However, it is the simple but meaningful gesture of Romeo Castellucci stating his own name that indicates what is at stake in this particular scene. It more specifically suggests how Castellucci, just as Dante, places himself in the centre of the work, 'transforms himself' into Dante to the extent that he imagines his own hell, while he nevertheless undergoes this transformation without assuming the role of Dante Alighieri himself, as a personality, without wearing his mask.

The fact that the spectator is faced with a radically different way of representing a canonical text, such as Dante's *Divine Comedy*, does not entail that either direct references or indirect allusions to the original material or author are absent, as the dogs in *Inferno*'s opening scene make clear. But there is no doubt that, in Castellucci's theatre, the work must be told as if it had never been written and narrated before.[90] It is also Castellucci's desire to link this legacy of founding narratives of Western culture to our contemporary times that forces him to diverge from well-known paths. In *Inferno*, for example, Castellucci does not chose Virgil as his companion for his journey into the unknown (as in Dante's story), but Andy Warhol, wishing to showcase the hell of his own era. Andy Warhol in his characteristic look and outfits is interpreted by a performer dressed as him.

Castellucci usually prefers to work with classic as well as religious texts, because they contain a universal resonance that, at least for most Western audiences, is immediately recognizable. The power of these texts derives from their mythical nature, which makes them at once open to various interpretations and rigid in terms of structure. Familiarity with the archetypical figures featured in these stories, such as Adam, Eve, Jesus Christ or Oedipus, makes them reverberate more deeply, almost esoterically, making their impact felt in a direct and spontaneous way, as they already exist in the darkness of our body, in the depths of the spectator's thoughts. In *Arbeit am Mythos* (Work on Myth), the German philosopher Hans Blumenberg distinguishes myths from legends, epic poetry or high literature, defining the genre as one that contains legendary or dramatic elements of everyday life and fairy tales.[91] Beginning from myth as a starting point, Castellucci considers anonymity as a condition of existence that surpasses any mythology. In his view, mythology always depends on the power and function of the name, as for example in Greek tragedy: Oedipus, Clytemnestra, Medea, Antigone etc. In a modern dimension, we are all anonymous.[92] As Castellucci states:

> Mythology isn't something connected to the past, myths are generated every day. Walk down the street and you can recognize certain mythologies that persist. Mythology is an attitude on life, it is not solely something academic, dusty: just the opposite. Whoever is capable of creating myths, and also reading them, has an additional tool to interpret reality.[93]

The multi-dimensional nature of myth creates a personal space, which calls to the spectator with his own name. Consequently, any spectator can potentially be a central figure of Castellucci's works, such as the First or the Second Star in *Purgatory*, the son or the father in *On the Concept*, or even Eurydice in *Orpheus and Eurydice*. This is 'the mirror effect',[94] just as ancient Greek drama seems to be rooted in social reality, which does not necessarily mean that it provides an accurate reflection of reality. Myth rather functions like a prism with many surfaces. In a fragment of a broken mirror we may see ourselves and others in a dimension which is at once private and collective. If tragedy is a mirror of the πόλις, the city, it is a broken mirror.[95] It is like placing an object in front of the mirror and moving it constantly. Myth feeds the present. Tragedy, also nourished by myth, places the new in the old and allows the spectator to speculate on their relationship. Myth is dispersed and diffused within us, in the anonymous crowd, and is addressed to each one of us individually. In this way, the spectator approaches many facets of reality, which theatre, as an art of live representation, allows him to do:

> Greek theatre represents the scene of error. It is always the wrong place. But what then is the origin of its song, that so profoundly touches my pain, and that of the species? And why do these two things seem to me to be mixed up, pulled by the opposite ends of the same moral chain of being? What is the origin of these tears of mine, now, devoid as they are of content? Clytemnestra's weeping, that belongs to me – Electra's weeping, that belongs to me – Orestes' doubt, that belongs to me. Am I still myself?[96]

In his work with classical literature, which is burdened with the weight of innumerable exegetic analyses as well as other theatrical interpretations, Castellucci follows his own pathway by choosing strategies such as the reduction of myths, allegorical stories and parables. He combines myths, fairy tales, philosophical texts and scientific studies, but only to invent

FIGURE 3.3 *Paolo Tonti performing in* Amleto. La veemente esteriorità della morte di un mollusco, *1992. Courtesy of the Socìetas Raffaello Sanzio.*

new stories that, instead of being told from beginning to end in a standard narrative format and clichéd imagery, are evoked in often quaint dramatic scenes and radical theatrical aesthetics. This parallel pathway, which I will explain later on, helps him to approach the work and the dramatis personae in a detached, yet simultaneously clear and original way.[97] In *Amleto. La veemente esteriorità della morte di un mollusco* (Hamlet. The Vehement Exteriority of the Death of a Mollusc, 1992), for example, he discovers a parallel pathway through the book *The Empty Fortress: Infantile Autism and the Birth of the Self* by Bruno Bettelheim, a psychoanalytical study on the role of the emotional bond with the mother in causing autism.[98] The main character in *Amleto* was presented as an autistic child, framed in a closed circuit consisting of battery devices, electrical turbines, compressors and children's toys. Castellucci created a hyper-icon of theatrical mimesis, setting the performer and his actions in the very centre of the stage. As he explains:

> Hamlet follows a course which leads him back to the original situation. He follows his thought and by deconstructing it he returns to the source of the scandal, his mother's loins. Even though his doubts lead him there, it is not just a return to childhood or even to the womb. Hamlet ends up in negation, regressing up to the folding up in fetal position.[99]

He will later follow up on this idea of parallel pathways by inventing a new dramaturgy in the *Orestea (una commedia organica?)* (Oresteia [an organic comedy?], 1995), where he brings Aeschylus's tragic trilogy together with *Alice's Adventures in Wonderland* (1865) by Lewis Carroll (1832–98) and the translation of Carroll's poem 'Jabberwocky' by Antonin Artaud.[100] The idea of representing the ancient trilogy through a fairy tale had first come to him when he was reading a book by Vladimir Propp, *Oedipus in the Light of Folklore*, in which Propp draws connections between folklore, primitive culture and tragedy.[101] Another impetus came from the trilingual series 'Scritture tradotti da scrittori', which published a volume with Carroll's original text, its translation by Artaud and the Italian version by Guido Almansi and Giuliana Pozzo.[102] By linking an archetypical tragedy to a children's fairy tale, 'the *Oresteia* passes through the looking glass',[103] Castellucci says. As such, it reflects the notion of 'reverse reality',[104] a technique that is implemented in the *Oresteia* by introducing Carroll's figures into Greek tragedy.

Seeking so-called parallel pathways thus allows Castellucci to put literary, religious or other types of text into new and often unprecedented perspectives, leaving his own artistic mark on textual resources that, due to the interpretative history clinging to them, are often recalcitrant subjects for reinvention. In Castellucci's *Orestea*, however, there is an additional reason for his deliberate choice to juxtapose – or perhaps 'infect' is a better term – Aeschylus' trilogy with Carroll's 'Jabberwocky' and Artaud's translation. This reason, as we shall see, stems from his ardent desire to transcend the confines of language, even if text is, without a doubt, a crucial source of inspiration as well as an important medium of expression in his artistic practice.[105]

The descent to the core of language: Sense, non-sense, silence

So far we have seen how language is a driving force in Castellucci's quest for radically new theatrical aesthetics, as the etymology of words and the mythological appeal of canonical texts ignites his artistic imagination and enables him to forge his way through the so-called 'dark matter' of primordial intuitions. At the same time, language also provides an entrance to a deeper dimension that, once we reach it, takes us beyond the grasp of linguistic and discursive expression. This double-sided perspective that sees language as an incipient opening as well as a restrictive limitation to the depths of our inner passions underpins what Castellucci calls the 'theatre of descent'. The term is explained in a text published on the occasion of *La discesa di Inanna* (The Descent of Inanna), the 1989 performance in which the central heroine, the Sumerian goddess Inanna, descends into the underworld where animals and total silence reign. In this work, the movement of descent, or κατάβασις (*katabasis*), involves language and symbolizes a trajectory that leads to the 'passionate dissolution of linguistic meaning'[106] until silence is reached.

In Castellucci's 2014 piece *Uso umano di esseri umani* (Human Use of Human Beings), the audience can almost literally witness the descent of language, which in this case is equated with the descent of Jesus to the grave. Together with him, spectators, who are not seated but who literally follow the action, descend to a place where they will watch the contest of words between Lazarus and Jesus on four levels, where they will be transported through the *Lingua Generalissima*. Carved on a circular millstone, the *Generalissima* functions as a gravestone on Lazarus' grave and as Jesus' coffin. The grave becomes the place of symbolic rest for *logos*. The death of Jesus and the fact that he never resurrects symbolizes the final dissolution of recited speech and its replacement by subterranean sounds of wind instruments and lungs, which seem to come from the bowels of the earth. It is an allusion to the underworld, the result of an eternal coming and an eternal loss: an endless movement between opposite poles.[107]

The equation of the extra-linguistic dimension with the mythological underworld also recurs in a text Castellucci wrote for the performance *Gilgamesh* (1990). In his efforts to give a glimpse of his own descent into the world of the unutterable, Castellucci chooses as his companion an emblematic figure of the Eleusinian Mysteries, Eubulus. As he writes, 'Eubulus allows me to become a visionary of the unsayable'.[108] In Greek mythology, Eubulus is known as the swineherd from the town of Eleusis, who witnessed the abduction of young Persephone, daughter of Demeter, by Hades, the god of the underworld. When the earth opens, he and his pigs are borne up on a whirlwind, along with the chariot of Hades and are swallowed up by the darkness of the underworld. The movement of descent opens a crack in the narrative trammel of the world. The order of things is overturned. It is the opposite movement, which presupposes a theatre of descent. Eubulus, in his descent to the underworld, is left speechless; faced with a total loss of language, he reverts to childhood.[109]

Castellucci's encounter with Eubulus indicates that, in his view, the notion of descent is to be discovered in the domain of the pre-tragic, rather than in tragedy as such. In contrast to tragedy, which puts into a reasonable form that which is essentially unreasonable or even unspeakable, the pre-tragic designates the realm of rituals, archaic enactments and mysteries, which embraces the unutterable and silence. For Castellucci, the actual core of tragedy is therefore not tragic, but pre-tragic.[110] It is also for this reason that his unorthodox staging of the *Oresteia* complements Aeschylus' tragic trilogy with Lewis Carroll's *Alice in Wonderland* and Artaud's translation of 'Jabberwocky'. While it might seem curious to align Carroll and Artaud with the pre-tragic core that interests Castellucci, both their predilection for disrupting common sense and logical reason allows him to add a distinct nonsensical layer to Aeschylus's founding story.[111]

In Castellucci's *Oresteia*, the primary figure to import irrational talk into the overall piece is the Coryphaeus. Whereas in Greek ancient drama the Coryphaeus is the leader of the chorus, Castellucci stages him as a white rabbit, obviously to emphasize how he reads Aeschylus' trilogy through the looking glass of Carroll. It is the rabbit-Coryphaeus indeed who during the piece recites 'Jabberwocky' from the first chapter of *Through the Looking Glass*, a poem that Alice sees inverted and can only read through a mirror. What follows is an intricate game of sense and non-sense between the texts of Aeschylus, Carroll and Artaud.[112]

The rabbit-Coryphaeus is aware that he is declaiming the text of another author. 'Antonin, the rabbit begs your pardon', he says, asking forgiveness for his apparent plagiarism. The sentence thus becomes meaningful when knowing that Artaud himself had accused Lewis Carroll of plagiarizing him. He claimed that the ideas for not only 'Jabberwocky' but also for a poem on little fishes (which both appear in 'Humpty Dumpty', the sixth chapter in Carroll's *Through the Looking Glass*) were actually invented by him. In a letter to Henri Parisot, Artaud fiercely wrote about 'Jabberwocky' that it 'is nothing but a sugar-coated and lifeless plagiarism of a work written by me, which has been spirited away so successfully that I myself hardly know what is in it'.[113] Artaud's accusation can be regarded as an instance of so-called 'plagiarism by anticipation', which holds that an incipient idea by a given author can be later picked up and reworked by another author, resulting in a preposterous line of influence that can be interpreted as an unwitting act of plagiarism.[114]

FIGURE 3.4 *Paolo Guidi as Rabbit-Coryphaeus in* Orestea (una commedia organica?), *1995. Courtesy of the Socìetas Raffaello Sanzio.*

In the context of Castellucci's theatrical oeuvre, however, it is not so much Artaud's reclaiming of authorship that is most significant, but rather the way in which his reappropriation of existing material leads to a shifting of authorial identities. Just as it becomes impossible to decide if 'Jabberwocky' is the sole invention of whether Carroll or Artaud, so too does Castellucci's own reworking of textual resources complicate the singularity of his artistic signature. In this respect, it might be that the rabbit asking for forgiveness should also be understood as Castellucci's own mocking 'apology' for his radical usurpation of other author's writings.

Besides the tangled issue of authorship, the choice to put the words of 'Jabberwocky' into the rabbit's mouth is also meaningful because it introduces a non-language into the discursive construct of Aeschylus' *Oresteia*. 'NEANT OMO NOTAR NEMO/Jurigastri – Solargultri/Gabar Uli – Barangoumti/Oltar Ufi – Sarangmumpti/' – these are some of the phrases the rabbit-Coryphaeus recites from Artaud's 'unintelligible' translation of Carroll's poem.[115] In *La Logique du Sens* (*The Logic of Sense*), Gilles Deleuze devotes an entire chapter to Artaud's translations and his letters written at the Rodez asylum. In his reading of 'Jabberwocky', Deleuze realizes that language slips into a central and creative collapse which leads us into another world, another language. This reveals the distance separating Carroll's language, emitted at the surface and Artaud's language, carved into the depth of bodies. Artaud was the only one to represent absolute depth in literature, and to discover a vital body – and the prodigious language of this body – through his own personal suffering. As Deleuze writes, 'he explored the infra-sense', meaning he penetrated to the core of the language.[116]

The text gradually loses its meaning. The non-sense is expressed through hermetic and portmanteau words (blends), which diffuse the meaning in two different directions, ascension and descent, at the same time. 'Not only is there no sense any more, there is no grammar or syntax either, and in fact not even structured syllabic, graphematic or phonetic elements.'[117] In this way, the portmanteau words offer the possibility for countless open interpretations, which can be analysed on many levels. Guided this time not by Eubulus, but by the rabbit-Coryphaeus and Antonin Artaud, Castellucci attempts to go beyond the surface, to descend into the domain of the unutterable and of silence.[118]

Silent bodies and penetrating gazes

For Romeo Castellucci, each body projects a meaning – even more so in the domain of silence that lies beyond language. This explains why Castellucci not only collaborates with professional actors, but frequently also with non-professionals, among them people who had never been to the theatre before. Occasionally, he chooses to work with very young children, aged actors, or people with a deviant body-type or even with an obvious disease. Indeed,

Castellucci's reputation as one of the most radical directors in twentieth-century theatre has much to do with the fact that his work confronts spectators with obese, emaciated or maimed bodies, which in everyday life are marginalized and kept out of sight. For Romeo Castellucci, the body is inextricably linked to dramaturgy. He develops a whole dramaturgy of these bodies-signs; the bodies employed reflect exclusively the notion-meaning they bear. The body is a grave, σῶμα-σῆμα (body-grave but also body-sign), as Gorgias puts it.[119]

Form is superior for Castellucci, since form is the condition through which the body's corporeality expresses itself. As form affects signification, it also changes the meaning of the body. One of Castellucci's hallmarks as a director has become his ability to draw multiple connections between a performer's physical appearance and the meaning of the fictional character. In *Genesi: From the Museum of Sleep* (1999), for example, the part of Eve is played by a woman who has undergone a mastectomy and whose amputated breast clearly symbolizes how she has lost one of her children, Abel. Eve's other son, Cain, is figured in the piece with an atrophied arm, as if to emphasize his inability to touch freedom after the murder of his brother. For his unorthodox staging of Shakespeare's *Julius Caesar* (1997), Castellucci made the remarkable and much debated choice to cast a young actress who suffers from anorexia for the role of Brutus. The deprivation that marks her body seems to turn her into a weightless appearance on stage, thus contributing to the overall 'fasting' and weakening of the text.[120]

These bodies are meaningful, even if – or perhaps precisely because – they do not communicate through words. Their physical appearance tells a story of its own, adding another interpretative layer to the text framing the performance. This potential of communicating with and through the body is even exacerbated in Castellucci's staging of Gluck's opera *Orpheus and Eurydice* (2014), in which the very ability to communicate at all becomes the thematic hinge of the piece. Placing the actual performance of the opera against the background of a live documentary, projected full size at the back of the stage, Castellucci likens the kingdom of shadows – as the underworld is called in *Orpheus and Eurydice* – to a neurological clinic. The image shows a young woman lying in a hospital bed and we see how her life radically changed after she was diagnosed with the locked-in syndrome.[121] Castellucci's Eurydice is locked inside her body. She cannot move any of her limbs, or speak, but communicates only with her gaze.[122] Her body is the authentic image, the quintessence of absolute truth on stage. With her participation in the show all notion of acting is undone, since stage power is inscribed in her unique presence, without speech and movement, tearing through the surface of the performance.

The absence of speech and movement that lies at the heart of Castellucci's *Orpheus and Eurydice* is a continuation of the early experiments with bodily stillness, which the members of the company had been exploring from the 1980s onwards and which they described as the 'technique of stage paralysis'.[123] We have already encountered this 'technique' in *Santa Sophia*, in which Pol Pot is presented in a catatonic state in order to establish a strong contrast with his *logorrhoea*, or his irrepressible speech. Socìetas Raffaello Sanzio pursues this strategy further in their next production, *I Miserabili* (The Miserables, 1987), where a standing herald remains motionless and almost speechless for the entire duration of the show, breaking the stage into four hyper-symmetrical parts. This apparent immobility seems to attenuate, if not abolish, any appeal to individual subjectivity, drawing attention instead to the body as organic matter. This then becomes the symbol of voicelessness, immobilization and invariance, contrasting with the empire of speech, which requires a constant change. If the core of acting traditionally consists of breathing life into a text through the conjunction of speech and movement, Socìetas Raffaello Sanzio's *I Miserabili* clearly intended to disrupt this convention and, by extension, to break with the dominant theatre practice of their time.

Romeo Castellucci's *Orpheus and Eurydice* differs from these early productions to the extent that the paralytic state presented in the former is not the result of an artistic technique, but a real condition from which an actual human being suffers. His choice for a real-life ASL patient standing in for the mythological Eurydice not only brings the perhaps unknown illness from darkness to light and into the centre of the audience's attention, but it also effectuates a two-way communication between the ancient myth, on the one hand, and the reality of the outside world, on the other. That is, while the fictional story becomes a carrier for a palpable and irrefutable truth, the myth itself is also reframed by infusing it with a concrete corporeality that, at first sight, might seem to stand outside it. After further thought, however, one realizes that Castellucci discloses a body that was enclosed in the hospital, not unlike the manner in which Eurydice was imprisoned in the Elysium fields, whereas Orpheus' love also corresponds to the care of family, doctors or nurses, who attempt to relieve Eurydice's 'imprisonment' on a daily basis.[124]

Even though Castellucci often stages bodies that, through their outward physical appearance speak directly to spectators, he also works with bodily transformations in order to maximize the expressive power of the piece. In this respect, it is interesting to note the stark contrast between the lived reality of Eurydice's body and the superficially perfect social body of the figure of the Father in *Purgatorio* (Purgatory, 2008). His pathology is hidden behind his smart figure and calm face, which obscure the scandalous act to which he commits himself by abusing his son. While Castellucci initially traps the spectator with the illusion of realism, he eventually resorts to a strategy of amplified bodily expression, using form to penetrate the dramatic hero's inner soul. The revelation of this secret interiority comes after the suggestive rape of the child and is inscribed as much in the body of the father as in that of the son, as we are faced with a simultaneous transformation of corporal images. The body of the child, interpreted now by an adult actor, grows bigger than that of the father, whereas the father's hands become deformed. As if to transgress the limits of reality and to surpass the act itself, they both start a sort of epileptic dance, allowing them to enter into an ecstatic dimension. The body suffers, but it changes and is reborn.[125]

From the late 1980s, Romeo Castellucci expanded his interest in the dramatic potential of the bodily presence by introducing animals on stage, thus infusing his performances with an even more vigorous kind of physicality that defies psychologization. The presence of animals imparts an organic quality to the performance and is related to Castellucci's quest for the unique image, which – as we have seen – operates in a mode of presence rather than belonging to the domain of representation. Various examples could be mentioned here: in *Alla bellezza tanto antica* (In Praise of Such an Ancient Beauty, 1988), pythons evoke the matriarchal shapes as they can be seen in Minoan figurines, while the sheep which appears during the piece seems to have come straight out of one of Caravaggio's paintings. In *Iside e Osiride* (Isis and Osiris, 1990), six baboons and pigs appear on stage in order to assert their power and to deregulate social and stage order. In the extravagant children's show *Le favole di Esopo* (Aesop's Fables, 1992), the Comandini Theatre is transformed into a stable for no less than 300 animals; in *Inferno* (2008), a white horse is painted red by the blood of humanity's victims; Tiresias is played by a blind dog in *Hyperion. Letters of a Terrorist* (2013), while a large ox dominates the stage in *Ahura Mazda* (1991) as well as the recent staging of Schoenberg's opera *Moses und Aaron* (2015).[126]

By including animals in his work, Castellucci returns to the pre-tragic roots of theatre, to the era when speech did not yet prevail and animals were granted a central role in archaic rituals and celebrations related to the cult of Dionysus. In these ancient times, the animal did not appear as the counterpart of humanity, but stood beside man, on an equal level or was united with him, as symbolized by hybrid creatures such as the satyrs, which are half-human and half-animal.[127] Worshippers believed that divine figures, such as Dionysus, were incarnated in the body of animals, whose meat they would eat to share in their sanctity. The eventual removal of the gods from the stage marked the birth of traditional Western theatre, placing man at the centre of creation and ousting the animals to the margins.[128] Instead of committing himself to the alleged contemporaneity of theatre, Romeo Castellucci wants to retrieve the lost spirit of those archaic days by reinstating the animal, along with all of its characteristics, to the venerable position it once enjoyed. This reinstatement is literally visualized in *Gilgamesh* (1990), where the eponymous hero, moving on all fours like an animal, goes towards a group of dogs and sets them free from their chains. Receding to the background, the actor leaves the centre of the stage to the animals. By untying the ropes that bind the dogs to the wall, the actor unleashes the energy that will defeat the human presence on stage.

Aiming to undo the predominance of mimetic representation, Castellucci aspires to discover a genuine and strongly affecting stage presence, one which calls into question the very game of theatrical convention. Since animals do not act or pretend, they are closer to truth than actors, establishing a more direct, instead of mimetic, relationship to the world outside the theatre. Unlike human actors, animals possess the organs of speech, but not speech itself. 'What fascinates me', Castellucci says, 'is that "woof", which contains the unsayable and shows it without actually saying it'[129] The gaze of the animals is almost paralleled with 'perfect pleasure' when the director himself, upon entering the stage at the start of the performance *Inferno*, surrenders himself to the attack of three dogs.[130] Due to the unpredictability of their behaviour and reactions, the presence of animals on stage is fraught with danger, creating a continuous tension that they might interrupt the planned performance. When a dog appears on stage, it is charged with powerful, raw feeling, presenting the intense effect of the animal's stage presence on the human body. Castellucci has stated: 'When I go on stage and I have an ape next to me, I feel an earthquake in my blood and I hear bells tolling. He, the ape, I feel that he is looking at my interior, and insists on being with me on stage.'[131]

Because of their unfeigned presence, animals also establish a different relationship with spectators, often making them feel uneasy, even provoked.[132] In the *R. #07 Rome* episode of the *Tragedia Endogonidia*, for instance, a chimpanzee appears alone on stage, like a powerful ruler who is granted a momentary governance of the entire performance, as the animal can be on stage as long as it wants, twelve minutes, a quarter of an hour, twenty minutes, seemingly free and not trained to perform a prescribed act. As the chimpanzee stares at the audience, spectators start to feel as if they are the objects of viewing, while the smouldering danger of unpredictability looms over the performance. The chimpanzee seems to extend his gaze beyond the frame of the stage, piercing through the limits of representation and disrupting the boundaries of the theatrical setting. Only this gaze proves capable of judging form and reading the surface, since it does not become prey to thought. The animal, in other words, constitutes *being* on stage.[133]

Castellucci's quest for the real, unique image resulted not only in the inclusion of animals or deviant body types, but it has also impelled him to explore the affective impact of putting young children on stage. Both the child and the animal share a complete ignorance of the stage, language or plot. As Castellucci writes about children and animals:

They are what they are: creatures devoid of reason and speech. Absolute dynamic, immobile and total presence. They are not actors, because they do not know what theatre is. We are dealing with a kind of optical inversion. Poetry in motion. Bodies who do not answer. Only living creatures. I believe that this is the enigma they bear: life. The sphinx of life, who, as we know, is stranger than death.[134]

The presence of infants expresses the absence of speech and acting. Not coincidentally, the Latin word *infans* means the one who cannot speak. Before acquiring language, a child stands outside the predetermined structures through which human beings eventually come to read the world.[135] This idea of childhood as a prelinguistic but powerful being in the world is one of the core themes in Castellucci's version of the *Oresteia*, even if the piece does not feature actual children. Electra is presented as a small girl, Orestes is cast as a white, hairless adolescent lying in a small crib, while his friend Pylades has no voice. All three figures represent a children's fantasy world, turning against the world of the adults. In this respect, Castellucci's *Oresteia* evokes Walter Benjamin's description of childhood as the area where the spirit of time meets in every generation with the myth-creating force or with the weakness absent from the language of adults.[136]

The speech of children is their body and their gaze. Their gaze turns to the spectator, transfixing him and judging him, as in the *Concept of the Face Regarding the Son of God* or in the Brussels episode *BR.#04* of the *Tragedia Endogonidia* (2003). When the curtain opens, the audience sees a baby of only a few months playing in blissful ignorance on an empty marble stage that is reminiscent of a mausoleum. As Socìetas Raffaello Sanzio writes in a description of the piece, 'It is the power of a mute presence, unselfconscious, white and microscopic, inside a white, macroscopic space'.[137]

In *Inferno* (2008), small children are encased in an enormous glass cube, yet they are laughing and playing nonchalantly. Their space seems safe and protected, an area of insouciance, cut off from the rest of the world. The children bring to mind the unbaptized babies that Dante encounters in the first cycle of *Hell* in his *Divine Comedy*. As innocent souls, they are remnants of human beings who were lost at an early age and who, being in limbo, cannot know heaven or hell anymore. In Castellucci's *Inferno*, adults stand before the glass and observe the children, as if they are watching their own spectral reflection travelling through history and time. Spectators are left to wonder whether hell is inside or outside the glass casing, which a little while later is covered by a large black cloth. At that point, the inexpressive faces of the actors turn their gaze directly towards the audience. Yet some spectators might have realized that the performers had actually been gazing at the audience the whole time through the reflection of their faces in the glass of the cube. Its surface thus became a mirror for an intricate exchange of gazes between the actors, spectators, as well as the children captured inside the glass box. This exchange disrupts any distance the audience might want to retain towards the piece, insofar as the gaze enacts an immediate recognition of the spectator's presence that simultaneously pierces through the theatrical universe Castellucci creates on stage.[138]

The mirror always reflects our image neutrally: that is why it is so irritating, so dense, so intense. The power of the gaze is thus revealed. With a look we may kill but a look may also kill us. The phenomenon of gaze reversal takes place. We watch yet we are being watched, a concept that evokes the visual dimension of theatre or the dramatic side of painting, hence Diego Velázquez's, *Las Meniñas*, where We are You. The presence of children tears through the surface of the performance. It creates a black hole, in which the performance collapses and all fiction is shed.

'While to my shame I see'[139]

In this chapter, I have uncovered some of the roots of Romeo Castellucci's artistic practice that, despite the growing discourse on his theatre, are not always fully accounted for, while I have also singled out several formal and thematic aspects that impregnate his directorial signature. Even though it is generally acknowledged that Romeo Castellucci is one of the most significant directors who have set new frontiers for twentieth-century theatre, his uncompromising aesthetics have left many wondering how to make sense out of his primarily sensual theatrical practice. The bewilderment that spectators often experience when watching Romeo Castellucci's theatre stems from the deeply paradoxical nature of his theatrical poetics and his aspiration to visualize what can be described as *a theatre of the non-representable*.

Already the early iconoclast stance towards both traditional theatre and visual cultures, has led Castellucci to embark on a quest for the one, unique image that tries to restore the religious, mythical and ritual dimensions of theatre, which he would later on intensify through his fascination with the expressive power of bodies, animals and children. By breaking through the limits of representation that continue to delimitate Western theatre – in terms of both conventions and architectural setting – Castellucci strives to bring us face to face with a deeper reality that underlies the images he creates on stage. At the same time, even though Castellucci's theatre can be described as a theatre of revelation, it is only through shame and by averting our gaze that we might be able to achieve this. As Castellucci claims:

> It is a shameful theatre. A theatre of shame. Shame as a higher kind of feeling. Inalienable. A state of being. A mask of truth. Acoustic of the soul. A theatre which should be worth the shame, capable of it; in which a final fitting into one's own destiny should be possible. The shame is the essential bond of exposure.[140]

Once again we are faced with a perhaps impossible paradox. Our desire to see and to penetrate into apocryphal areas of human existence is enabled by the gaze that pierces through the outer layers of the world, but also compromised by the sight of the forbidden or repressed reality that one might find there. If shame is a driving force in Romeo Castellucci's theatre, then the gesture of a shameful gaze peeking through the fingers of one's hand becomes emblematic for the spectator's position in this unsettling theatrical universe that touches upon taboo and the margins of human life. How are we to bear the sight of the seemingly helpless old father in *On the Concept of the Face Regarding the Son of God*, who is subjected to violent acts of 'care' by his son on whose help he depends? How can we endure the image of an immobilized Eurydice, who is physically bedridden but mentally resilient? Why do these scenes, excruciating as they may be, still evoke a sense of engagement and agency? Why do we ardently desire to look and, at the same time, to shut our eyes?

Medusa is the figure Castellucci invokes when explaining the double-sided act of watching at the core of his theatre: 'holding one's gaze on a representation would be like not wanting to detach one's eyes from Medusa. The monster is not a person, is not an equation: the monster is this, the performance itself'.[141] The sometimes monstrous aesthetics of Castellucci's theatre ought to act like the mythological Medusa, whose gaze attracts but also transfixes the onlooker. The revelation of the ultimate image can only take place through a confrontation of gazes and by moving across both the human and the non-human. This is what, deep down, the theatre of Romeo Castellucci wishes to demonstrate. To distance ourselves from the human, in order to be able to conceive its fragile existence, full of questions.

4

The Transgressive Theatre of Romeo Castellucci

Thomas Crombez

Dividing an artist's oeuvre into different periods is always a somewhat precarious endeavour, due to the risk of reducing the singularity of individual works to the neat categories of an overarching scheme. From a historiographical point of view, however, the articulation of larger patterns can provide insight into the major directions a body of work has taken over the course of various years. Even in the case of Romeo Castellucci and his company Socìetas Raffaello Sanzio, whose theatre practice has been the subject of continuous reinvention ever since its beginnings in the early 1980s, it is possible to discern several distinct stages that mark the most decisive stepping stones in the maturation of his theatrical poetics. It is, in fact, only against the background of this larger picture that one might be able to uncover what I will describe as the *theatrical structures* in his work and which comprise the artistic strategies as well as the thematic concerns that underlie his directorial signature.

In order to excavate these deeper dynamics that steer Castellucci's theatre, I want to begin this chapter by briefly surveying the evolution his work has undergone from the 1980s up until the early 2000s, singling out four consecutive stages. This will allow me, in a second movement, to consider which contemporary notions can be used to analyse how his work functions and to understand the peculiar impact it generates on audiences and critics all over the world. Relating Castellucci's artistic authorship to larger debates on post-dramatic and post-modern theatre will subsequently lead me to a discussion of how the alleged impression of 'illegibility' often produced by Castellucci's work is to be understood, while it also requires me to investigate his relationship with the historical avant-garde. In this respect, it is with the benefit of hindsight that this chapter intends to provide insight into Romeo Castellucci's theatre of transgression.[1]

Tracing Romeo Castellucci's theatre trajectory

The theatrical productions Romeo Castellucci and the SRS created during the first ten years after the company's founding (1981–91) may be seen as an exploration of visual theatre, or as a 'theatre of the unreal' in the words of the makers.[2] Its impact depended strongly on illogical yet powerful connections between very diverse topics. A key piece they produced during this period is *Santa Sofia. Teatro Khmer* (1985), a performance that explicitly referred to very recent political events as it focused on the Cambodian dictator Pol Pot. When Pot seized power in 1975, he proclaimed that this date was the new year zero. His army evicted city people from their houses to find 'salvation' in an agrarian communist state. The operation would take the lives of almost 2 million people. Only a few years after the genocide, in the 'manifesto that was given in custody in the theatre', Claudia Castellucci appropriated the bloody creativity of the Khmer Rouge for the 'unreal' theatre of the Socìetas Raffaello Sanzio: 'This is the Khmer theatre, we say it loud and clear: it is about doing tabula rasa with the whole world.'[3]

Even while the SRS was drawing on the reality of politics to launch their aesthetic credentials, they clearly refused to work in the vein of the prominent political theatre companies of the 1970s. There is an enormous difference between the 'iconoclast' performance of *Santa Sofia*, and other contemporary theatre productions that were inspired by the recent history of Cambodia, such as *L'Histoire terrible mais inachevée de Norodom Sihanouk, roi de Cambodge* (The Terrible but Unfinished Story of Norodom Sihanouk, King of Cambodia), a text of Hélène Cixous performed by the Théâtre du Soleil and directed by Ariane Mnouchkine (1985) [see **Volume 7**].[4] In Cixous's play, more than fifty-five characters were brought to the stage (including members of the royal court of Cambodia and American politicians and generals) to provide a detailed historical tableau of recent events. Mnouchkine's staging of Cixous's text stands in stark contrast to SRS's depiction of the same subject matter, which takes only isolated images from the contemporary setting, but does not attempt in any way to give a broad, coherent picture of the political and military developments.

In the second stage of the Socìetas' development (1991–2001), the canonical texts of Western culture played a central role. Although the company based its productions on either great texts from the dramatic tradition (Shakespeare's *Hamlet* and *Julius Caesar*) or from other literary or religious traditions (Louis-Ferdinand Céline's *Voyage au bout de la nuit* [Journey to the End of the Night], Charles Perrault's collection of fairy tales, the biblical Book of Genesis), it was clear that the dramaturgical treatment of the text was highly untraditional. For *Journey to the End of the Night* (1999), for example, fragments of Céline's novel were treated as a 'score' for a vocal performance by four members of the company. In *Orestea (una commedia organica?)* (1995), the figurative weight of Clytemnestra in Aeschylus's play was translated literally into body weight, as it featured an obese woman in the role of the trilogy's most formidable female character. The importance of rhetoric in the play *Giulio Cesare* (1997), exemplified by Marc Antony's speech at the burial of Caesar, was underlined by letting the actor place a surgical camera in his throat, and projecting the movements of his vocal chords while he said the speech.[5]

The third stage consists entirely of the *Tragedia Endogonidia*, a cycle of eleven productions created over a three-year period (2002–4). The *Tragedia* clearly signals a movement away from textual dramaturgy and into the domain of a purely visual dramaturgy. According to Romeo Castellucci, the title is an 'oxymoron', since it combines two seemingly incommensurable categories.[6] While *tragedia* refers to the Western tradition of the tragic in which the heroic death of the protagonists is a recurring theme, the biological term *endogonidia* refers to unicellular organisms that contain the genitalia of both sexes and which are therefore capable of virtually endless self-reproduction. Thus, by putting both notions together, absolute human mortality is contrasted with the blind immortality of the microscopic animal.

FIGURE 4.1 Orestea (una commedia organica?), *1995. Courtesy of the Socìetas Raffaello Sanzio.*

Interestingly, the *Tragedia Endogonidia* was also itself a living being or, more specifically, 'un organisme in stato di fuga' (an organism in a state of flight, or on the run) – as described in the programme of the first episode.[7] From January 2002 to December 2004, it passed through ten cities in six European countries. The company always emphasized the intimate relationship between the performances and the place where they were produced. Sometimes this relationship was visualized through an explicit reference, by quoting elements of the urban setting on stage. The Paris episode (subtitled *P.#06*), for example, featured the French national flag and an actor dressed up as General de Gaulle. In Brussels (*Br.#04*), various actors wore uniforms of the Belgian gendarmerie. In some cases, the real-life details were even perceived as naturalistic, such as when an actual combat tank entered on stage in the Strasbourg episode (*S.#08*).

While it often remained unclear why exactly a particular visual detail had been chosen, the effect on the audience was invariably uncanny. After all, these instantly recognizable items brought something familiar to a production that, in its entirety, was quite hard to interpret. The performances contained virtually no spoken dialogue, but consisted of a range of highly visual scenes, accompanied by a soundtrack of electronic sounds and concrete music (composed by Scott Gibbons). It was simply impossible to extract a coherent set of meanings from the scenes of the *Tragedia*. How to understand, for instance, the scene in *P.#06* in which French police officers wash their uniforms in laundry machines and then re-enact the sacrifice of Isaac? Moreover, as if to intensify the abstract and distanced nature of these actions, they were often partially obscured by a fine-meshed gauze or by sophisticated lighting effects.

Even though this aesthetic has become the trademark of the Socìetas ever since the company was founded, the *Tragedia* marks the stage when they no longer start from a dramatic or literary text as the source of a piece. For spectators, this also meant that the only orientation consisted of several enigmatic statements about ancient Greek tragedy in the programme. However, while the work of Romeo Castellucci and SRS might seem cryptic, or even illegible, I will show later in this chapter how the *Tragedia Endogonidia* allows the extraction of at least three metaphors that provide insight into the theatrical structures of Castellucci's visual dramaturgy.

The method first demonstrated in the *Tragedia* is continued in the fourth (and ongoing) stage of Castellucci's work, which started in 2006 when an organizational change took place. From then on, the core members of the Socìetas Raffaello Sanzio (Romeo Castellucci, his sister Claudia Castellucci and Chiara Guidi) chose to follow separate artistic paths. In the productions Castellucci created afterwards, such as the *Divine Comedy* trilogy (2008–9) and *Sul concetto di volto nel figlio di Dio* (On the Concept of the Face, Regarding the Son of God, 2011), he often strikes a more personal tone. A typical detail is the opening scene of the performance *Inferno* (2008), in which Romeo Castellucci himself takes the stage, speaks the words 'My name is Romeo Castellucci', and is attacked by police dogs.

Despite the distinct stages one might discern in Romeo Castellucci's theatrical trajectory, one thread that seems to run throughout his entire oeuvre is the difficulty spectators, critics and scholars experience in acquiring a reasonable understanding of his work. In this respect, the main problem is not even that his performances remain devoid of any narrative storyline (even though the titles of some pieces might suggest otherwise), since one can assume that contemporary spectators are increasingly familiar with this type of theatre. It is rather the unprecedented theatrical aesthetics with which Castellucci confronts his audience which cause considerable confusion and pose specific interpretative challenges.

From a multiplicity of meanings to illegibility

The most obvious labels to apply to Castellucci's work are *post-dramatic* and *postmodern* theatre. The former term was introduced by German theatre scholar Hans-Thies Lehmann in his eponymous 1999 book *Postdramatisches Theater*. Lehmann's voluminous work provides a sort of 'encyclopaedia' of contemporary theatre as it developed from the 1970s onwards. He primarily focuses on experimental and avant-garde theatre in Western Europe and North America. The book discusses companies and directors such as Klaus Michael Grüber and Peter Stein (Germany), Maatschappij Discordia and Dood Paard (the Netherlands), Guy Cassiers, Jan Fabre and Jan Lauwers (Belgium), and Robert Wilson, the Wooster Group and Robert Lepage (North America).

In post-dramatic theatre, as the name implies, drama (in both senses of the word: play-text and action) no longer takes the central role. This theatre abandons its previous concern with the realistic depiction of people who engage in certain actions and play out a conflict through social interaction and dialogue. Even though the enactment of lifelike events may have been theatre's core terrain for various decades, this quality has been usurped by the emergence of film, which inaugurated a new mode of representation excelling at realism. As Lehmann writes, 'what until then had been the inherent domain of theatre, the representation of acting people in motion, is taken over by motion pictures which in this respect soon surpass theatre'.[8] At the dawn of the post-dramatic era, then, theatre is faced with the challenge to reinvent itself. Accordingly, Lehmann's book aims to draw up a taxonomy of the myriad methods used to meet that challenge.

Post-dramatic Theatre frequently refers to the work of Romeo Castellucci and the Socìetas Raffaello Sanzio.[9] In particular, the anomalous bodies in their early work (emaciated by anorexia, or obese and bloated) and the live animals appearing in *Giulio Cesare* and *Genesi*, serve to illustrate the new 'postdramatic bodies' that populate the contemporary stage. According to Lehmann, the extreme physicality of Castellucci's theatre exemplifies a 'return of the body as an incomprehensible and simultaneously unbearable reality', which uses the body for its sculptural qualities rather than as a bearer of semiotic meaning.[10]

Next to post-dramatic, the concept of post-modernism is equally applicable, especially if we consider post-modernist theatre from the vantage point of philosophical deconstruction. Outlining how deconstructionist theory found its entrance into theatre, Gerald Rabkin has argued that its influence made itself primarily felt in the mechanism of polysemy or the continued refusal to settle for one interpretation of a text or stage event.[11] Following Rabkin's suggestion, we may posit that a deconstructed theatre can be understood as an ambiguous theatre, which renounces text and allocates a central role to non-linguistic signs (visual, physical, ceremonial...). Yet it also implies a reflection on a meta-level about the dogmas of the modern theatrical tradition: logocentrism, the status of the text and the predominance of dialogue over non-linguistic signs.

From the speculations of Lehmann and Rabkin several characteristics can be derived that apply remarkably well to the work of Castellucci and the Socìetas. Most notably, post-dramatic theatre privileges the theatrical *event* and the act of *experiencing* a production over the timeless theatrical 'masterpiece', traditionally identified as the drama text.[12] Text disappears as the central signifier or, in Lehmann's words, as 'a comprehensible narrative and/or mental totality'.[13] The narrative, but also the characters, the conflict and even the thematic unity of a play start to fall apart. These technical concepts previously guaranteed the philosophical coherence of the theatre.

FIGURE 4.2 Giulio Cesare, *1997. Courtesy of the Socìetas Raffaello Sanzio.*

The thought-structure of the play was generally characterized by causality, teleology and clarity. From the moment these principles are left behind, spectators are increasingly confronted with polysemy or polylogy (multiple, intermingling worlds of thought or logic), an emphasis on physicality and a deliberate play with the physical presence of the performers – often through technological mediation.

However, even though post-dramatic theatre emphasizes the impact of 'breath, rhythm and the present actuality of the body's visceral presence', it does not focus exclusively on stage events without words.[14] Indeed, text is still often used, but it no longer serves a fictional narration nor does it appear only in the format of a comprehensible dialogue or monologue. In a scene from Jan Fabre's *De macht der theaterlijke dwaasheden* (The Power of Theatrical Madness, 1984), for example, the performers mechanically recite a list of great names, works and dates from avant-garde theatre history. An actress is barred access to the stage because she cannot connect the right event to a specific date given to her. Language has become the instrument of power, while also delivering a meta-theatrical criticism of the rapid canonization of the avant-garde.

In Castellucci's work, the decomposition of human language goes even further, as it demonstrates what Lehmann calls a 'phonetic materiality', a soundscape or a 'textscape'.[15] One of the few instances of dialogue in the *Tragedia Endogonidia* concerns a baffling conversation about a piece of rope and a well between two Mormon-like characters in the Marseille episode (*M.#10*, 2004). When interviewed about the meaning of the scene, Castellucci offered the following rebuttal:

> What does that mean, 'text'? For me, there was no text in Marseille. There was only a black cloud of words, without beginning or end. Perhaps it had a great degree of coherence, but it was no text, no dialogue, no narration.[16]

The fragmented text, which in some cases is even reduced to a mere succession of letters or sounds, forces spectators to seek refuge elsewhere in their attempt to make sense out of the piece. From the side of the performers, the radical rejection of the text's previous status as the pivot of the work gives them an unprecedented freedom in uttering and enacting these linguistic expressions. In Castellucci's oeuvre, this playful juggling with words and textual elements was perhaps most beautifully exemplified in the adaptation of Céline's novel *Voyage au bout de la nuit* into a score for whispers, screams and grating vocal sounds. It should, however, be added that Castellucci's most recent productions, from 2016 onwards, increasingly feature dialogue. One clear example is his March 2017 production titled *Democracy in America.*

Various other characteristics of Lehmann's post-dramatic theatre can be found in the work of the Sòcietas, including, most notably, the interest in dream images (*Traumbilder*) as a dramaturgical principle, the exploration of scenic simultaneity through the juxtaposition or layering of different actions or theatrical parameters and the heightened emphasis on visual dramaturgy.[17] The latter term may cause some confusion, since visual dramaturgy clearly suggests a parallel to textual dramaturgy. Hence, it implies that what is communicated through dialogue (and other forms of textual narration) in conventional dramatic theatre can apparently be translated into other, purely visual media in post-dramatic theatre. Obviously, this is rarely the case in a literal fashion. Post-dramatic theatre does not 'translate' a fictional narration in the manner of a cartoon film or a comic strip. On the contrary, post-dramatic visual dramaturgy often *refuses* the legibility of the events on stage, begging the question as to how the spectator's involvement in this type of work is redefined from the moment any straightforward understanding is corrupted. This question seems to be particularly relevant in the case of Castellucci, insofar as his theatre is often considered to be obscure and enigmatic.

Characteristic of Romeo Castellucci's specific brand of visual dramaturgy is indeed that it leads to a tenacious form of illegibility. In this respect, the theatre of Castellucci and the Socìetas Raffaello Sanzio may be usefully compared to a palimpsest: when the original content of a material carrier of information becomes damaged and overwritten, the text – or a theatrical event – becomes hard to read. In the case of Castellucci, the effect of illegibility is a deliberate aesthetic choice. How to explain that choice? Why would an artist want to make his work intentionally unreadable?

The assumption that a theatrical production should be legible has its roots in the predominance of the dramatic text in the Western tradition. Since the inception of theatre studies in 1920, the dramatic text was the main subject of scholarly attention.[18] One reason that explains this privileging of text as the most important parameter of theatrical practice is, of course, the more esteemed status of literature and literary studies within academia. More importantly, however, is that the dramatic script also made it possible to examine a performance long after the players had disappeared from the stage. It also served as a tool to acquire knowledge of productions that had been performed in different countries.[19]

Roughly after the Second World War, theatre studies began to emancipate itself from its literary pendant, and even while the predominance of the dramatic text was questioned, the textual paradigm remained in place. Despite the recognition of the theatre performance as a medium of artistic expression in its own right, it was systematically considered to be a performance *text*. Semiotics, a new and highly successful approach to cultural phenomena and products, provided the framework. Building on the advances in linguistics by Ferdinand de Saussure, C.S. Peirce and Roman Jakobson, theatre semiotics was premised on the idea that acting, set design, dancing, lighting and sound design could be regarded as just as many readable layers of theatrical signs. Along with the linguistic utterances, these constituted a complex and immense performance text.[20] According to the German theatre scholar Erika Fischer-Lichte, theatre installed a 'theatrical code', which reproduced all common signs that can be found in society and everyday life.[21] The semiotics of spoken language, clothing, interior design, body language or etiquette were quoted, so to speak, by the actors on stage.

From this semiotic perspective, however, theatre studies could only understand those aspects of performance that it could read, whereas various other dimensions of the theatrical event – such as experience or corporeality – seemed to escape the framework of the theatrical code. Interestingly, it was exactly the semiotic study of the body that brought the limits of this approach to our attention. If the body were to be considered as merely one sign among many others, how could one account, then, for the materiality of this living flesh as well as for the affective responses it might provoke on the side of spectators? Did the performer's body and voice not constitute a hyperparticular sign, irreducible to any general code?[22]

poststructuralist thinkers have tried to tackle these questions by insisting on the inerasable materiality of the sign.[23] Likewise, the conspicuous presence of anomalous bodies in the theatrical language of Castellucci appears to be an artistic response to the same set of issues. This is a body of work that is profoundly hostile to a semiotic approach. It is, however, not only the provocative reality of seeing such disfigured bodies on stage that baffles spectators, but also – and more importantly – Castellucci's radical choice to create a theatrical world that seems to be devoid of any rational sense or logic. While his theatre might give the impression of being built with elements that, in themselves, could be interpreted as 'signs' (be it actors, light, costumes, or music), it is his unique way of combining these different layers that thwarts any attempt to subsume them into a singular, overarching interpretative framework.

At this point, we can begin to understand where the alleged illegibility of Castellucci's theatre stems from. One of the seminal insights, not only of linguistics but also information science, is that processes of signification depend on at least two criteria: on the one hand, selected signs must be symbolically coherent (coming from one particular alphabet, and not from a random combination of alphabets), while, on the other hand, they must be syntactically well formed. A sentence in which a small number of errors or random combinations occur, may still be relatively readable. Yet when all linguistic differentiations have been jumbled, the result is unstructured complexity, pure randomness, or illegibility. This dynamic by which semiotic clarity is disrupted can, as we shall see, also be regarded as a constitutive working principle of Castellucci's theatrical poetics.

The theatrical structures of Castellucci's visual dramaturgy

Just as silence, illegibility is an antithetical concept that may hide multiple meanings. When someone is silent, he does not speak. But *what* he does not say one cannot know. Similarly, while it is certain that the artists of the

Socìetas deliberately made their productions unreadable, it remains unclear which underlying meanings were erased.

This is revealed in the interpretations that several commentators, including members of the Socìetas, have given of individual scenes of their work. The theatre cycle *Tragedia Endogonidia* was accompanied by a series of publications, titled *Idioma Clima Crono* (Idiom Climate Time). The contributions in these cahiers, written by critics, scholars and Socìetas members, are full of expressions that emphasize the necessarily limited nature of their interpretations, due to the stubbornly enigmatic character of the scenes. Joe Kelleher, for example, avows that the productions are using 'a language we barely know how to play with yet'.[24] Céline Astrié asks: 'What is the *seeing* of a sign if it does not provide us with any signification?'[25] And Nicholas Ridout affirms that the cycle constitutes 'an organism in the form of an enigma'.[26]

Perhaps these bewildered voices are best summed up in the phrase with which Romeo Castellucci invariably begins his own explanation of a scene: 'I only have a hypothesis.'[27] This statement should not be mistaken for an easy recourse to deliberately cryptic explanations. On the contrary, Castellucci is highly consistent regarding what he sees as the fundamentally unfathomable nature of the *Tragedia Endogonidia*. Every interpreter, including the artist, attempts to penetrate the enigma and, through that gesture, to replace the primarily visual language of the image with the verbal language of description. In this sense, the enigmatic nature of the theatrical aesthetics presented by the Socìetas implies a hermeneutic problem, since it confronts us with the question of how to make sense out of something that appears to be devoid of meaning.

Still, the productions of the SRS do not present the spectator with *random* enigmas. There are structural similarities in the visual dramaturgy used throughout Castellucci's entire career. To uncover these structural characteristics, I will introduce three metaphors that help to explain the perceived illegibility of Castellucci's and SRS's visual language. These metaphors derive from the idea that there are at least three levels at which the performances alienate the spectator: the spatial (scenic) structure of the productions, their temporal structure and the treatment of language.

The Wunderkammer

Regarding the spatial design of Castellucci's productions, the stage is often dominated by a single visual element. Well-known examples include the huge reproduction of Antonello da Messina's portrait of Jesus for *On the Concept of the Face, Regarding the Son of God* (2011) or the dual circle-shaped projection screens and the mounted horse cadaver in *Voyage au bout de la nuit* (1999). Yet the perhaps most intriguing examples can be found in the *Tragedia Endogonidia*.

In most episodes of the cycle, the stage is entirely occupied by a monumental and claustrophobic cube, open only on the side that faces the public. The golden mirror room in the Cesena and Avignon performances is, just like the marble cube in Brussels, a box that forces the spectator to look inside. This appeal to the gaze of the audience is sometimes emphasized through lighting effects (for example, with bare neon lamps), or hindered by veiling the stage with various kinds of translucent gauze, or even a full-length sheet of acrylic glass (as in the Rome episode). In the Brussels production, *BR.#04*, the open side of the cube was closed after each scene with thick white curtains, accompanied by loud electronic noise. This served to remind spectators that their view of the event was not gratuitous, but only made possible through the generosity of the theatrical space itself.

In the case of *BR.#04*, the five hermetically sealed walls of the cube are reminiscent of a Baroque *Wunderkammer*, which offers an opening – literally and figuratively – to understand how Castellucci's stage functions as a true exhibition space. Such cabinets of curiosities were the early modern predecessors of the museum and became popular from the sixteenth century onwards. They were designed to surprise, delight and confuse the visitor. The walls and cabinets of a *Wunderkammer* were filled with objects as diverse as ostrich eggs, Roman coins, the horn of a unicorn, a stuffed crocodile, a gun, coral, agate, marble, complex astronomical instruments, precious books, deformed babies or animals, and so on. In a *Wunderkammer*, the visitor was confronted with all sorts of curiosities that were placed close together to maximize the heterogeneity of the collection as well as to reinforce the wondrous nature of each object. Glancing at the tightly packed sets of items, visitors could go from one surprise to the next, struck by the seemingly endless succession of astounding things.[28]

Not unlike the Wunderkammer, the *Tragedia Endogonidia* also creates a space that organizes the amazement of the audience. It amasses as many diverse characters, costumes and icons as possible in one place. One scene in the marble room of *BR.#04*, for example, shows an old man, wearing a colourful bikini. He starts to put on several layers of clothes, beginning with a white fabric inscribed with Hebrew characters, until he is dressed in what appears to be a rabbi costume. But once he is finished and fully looks like a rabbi, he starts to put on a new costume above it. Now, he transforms into a Belgian policeman. Another bewildering masquerade took place in the Bergen episode (*BN.#05*). A masked male figure wearing a nineteenth-century, Gothic-like costume, sheds his suit and reveals that he is actually a naked woman in lace underwear. Moments later, the 'woman' puts her underwear into her vagina and strips off her skin. Under the flesh-coloured woman's suit is a naked boy.

Castellucci's theatre is a theatre of wonder that gives its enigmas free rein. In this respect, his work differs strongly from other genres, primarily popular in film, that want to produce a sense of wonder or shock, such as the fantasy film, science fiction or thrillers. While these genres expose the viewer to visions, hallucinations and wonders, the narrative structure of the film ultimately keeps the miraculous nature of the depicted events at a distance. Ample dramaturgical hints are provided in order to integrate the possibly unimaginable situations into a coherent storyline. In contrast, productions such as *Tragedia Endogonidia* purposefully dismiss the spectator's possibilities for narrative integration. The *Wunderkammer*-like architecture offers no relief from the confusion the bizarre accumulation of images might provoke, creating instead an airtight intimacy between the spectator and this stage of wonders.

The dream

Comparing the work of Romeo Castellucci to the genre of the fantastic film also indicates at which point the spatial metaphor of the *Wunderkammer* falls short. Castellucci's productions offer a series of wonderful scenes within a kind of exhibition space. But, contrary to the more enduring nature of both film and the *Wunderkammer*, Castellucci's cabinet of curiosities is anything but permanent. The parallel world he wants to create on stage evaporates when the show is finished. Moreover, as if to emphasize this ephemeral quality, the temporal structure of Castellucci's pieces often seems disordered, just as a nocturnal dream might confound the chronological succession of events. More specifically, throughout his oeuvre, Castellucci clearly shows an interest in playing with the condensation, acceleration and reversibility of time.

The rhythmic alternation between stillness and speed becomes evident when putting together various scenes from the early productions as well as from the *Tragedia Endogonidia*. Most obviously, theatrical time takes on another dimension in those pieces that feature live animals, such as monkeys in the final part of *Orestea* (1995), the scene with the chimpanzee that opens the Rome episode (*R.#05*), the buck in Bergen or the horses in Paris and Cesena. The animals show little theatrical awareness. Due to the long duration of such scenes, as well as the absence of any dramatic development, the experience of witnessing such scenes tends to be long and drawn out. The same holds for the controversial start of the Brussels episode, where a baby is sitting all alone in the marble cube, looking around for minutes long (or, on other nights, loudly screaming). The temporal experience of other scenes is diametrically opposed to these examples. There is, for instance, the stroboscopic film in the Cesena episode (*C.#01*), or the violent outbursts of alien machines (a machine that shoots arrows, a robotic doll that mimics epileptic behaviour, cars falling from the sky). Spectacular interventions such as these intensify the pace of the piece and often interrupt the more sustained tempo of the preceding scenes.

Besides stillness and acceleration, the course of time in the *Tragedia Endogonidia* is also marked by inversion. Just before the compelling scene of *BR.#04* in which a policeman is beaten up by two other performers, the perpetrators had already poured out fake blood on the floor and marked the crime scene with letter signs. The Bergen episode, *BN.#05*, begins with an old woman who is covered under a sheepskin. In the next scene, when she comes from underneath the blanket, she is miraculously transformed into a little girl, while at the end of the play, she will complete her reversed cycle of life by going through a birthing scene.

The extension, contraction and confusion of time guide spectators into a dreamlike world, where temporality follows a different logic than in everyday life. Once more, their search for an overarching framework in which causal relations could be drawn between different events is frustrated by the oneiric sequence of scenes. This otherworldly atmosphere is further amplified by the ingenious light design and the use of gauzes, which blur one's gaze and make it seem as if the events we see unfolding are both real and unreal at the same time.

One must be wary, however, of identifying Castellucci's theatre unequivocally as a dream art, despite the apparent dreamlike aesthetics that permeates his work.[29] While the notion of the dream offers a good *structural* analogy for describing his theatrical poetics, there are also limitations to the term. Taking into account that the dream has been used as a general label for characterizing a broad oneiric tradition in both the performing arts and film, it might have the unwarranted effect of effacing the singularity of the oeuvres that could be ranged under this strand of artistic production.[30] Both *Endgame* by Samuel Beckett (1957) and Jodorowsky's *El Topo* (The Mole, 1970) may be termed oneiric on account of their dramatic structure, but that conceals the profound differences between those works.

In addition, the very idea of a 'dream theatre' inevitably refers to psychoanalysis and dream interpretation, which is another infelicitous association. In relation to the theories of Sigmund Freud, the work of Castellucci can only be defined negatively. That is, in contrast to the

FIGURE 4.3 Tragedia Endogonidia. *Courtesy of the Societas Raffaello Sanzio.*

psychoanalytic aspiration to *read* dreams to uncover hidden or repressed truths, Castellucci's theatre stubbornly adheres to the enigma of the images presented on stage. There is no 'information' to be uncovered here. Castellucci emphatically distances himself from the idea of legibility that is always presupposed in psychoanalysis. The productions are an invitation to interpret their bizarre, often iconoclastic, theatrical language. However, the dream ultimately always insists that its images were not exhausted by this or that interpretation. Even though this may remind one of Umberto Eco's famous notion of the 'open work' (*opera aperta*),[31] which always remains open to new interpretations, it is a frustrating experience. Castellucci himself gives the following explanation:

> Just like in a dream, some small narrative elements are provided in this theatre, but without any context. It's like reading a book with your nose too close to the paper. You can see the details very well, but the general context has disappeared. The story is made available to the spectator, but that openness is also a trap in which to lose yourself … In the dream, there is always a lacuna. There is insufficient information. You cannot understand everything. And just like in a dream, you know that you must go searching exactly there where the lacuna is.[32]

The dream thus repeats in temporal terms what the *Wunderkammer* had achieved in spatial terms: producing wonder. Within the structure of the dream offered by the *Tragedia Endogonidia*, each of the images is a new 'chunk' of meaning that excites wonder and invites interpretation. But this openness of the work is no gratuitous semiotic legibility. On the contrary, as Castellucci states, it is also 'a trap' for the spectator.

The Golden Record aboard the Voyager

Next to space and time, Castellucci also contorts language in the *Tragedia Endogonidia*. While there is very little dialogue, speech and language are almost continuously present on stage. In one scene of the Bergen episode (*BN.#05*), a split-flap display (as familiar from older train stations) was lowered. But the device produced gibberish, filled with obscure references to a particular etymology of the word 'tragedy', which derives the word from the song (*ôidé*) intoned when a goat (*tragos*) is sacrificed: 'It's me – the goat – speaking. Now I will start to speak. My own language.'

In the Brussels performance, a metal plate appears after the opening scene with the infant baby.[33] A mechanical mouth and eyes open, repeating the five vowels of the alphabet. Later in the piece, a policeman undresses and is attacked by his former colleagues. Then, covered with blood, he is placed on a chair in the middle of the stage. His tormentors put a microphone in front of him. He remains silent. Only after he has been dressed in a grey garbage bag and deprived of his face, he begins to stammer the Hail Mary in French and in Dutch.

To capture the effect of linguistic alienation in the *Tragedia Endogonidia*, one image is particularly useful. Its importance was also suggested by the artists themselves, as it was not only the very first image that was projected in the first episode (*C.#01*), but it was also included on the front of each programme issued during the cycle. The image was taken from the golden phonograph records NASA placed on board Voyager 1 and Voyager 2, the two spacecraft that were launched in 1977 to explore interstellar space. The discs contain sounds and images that ought to give a description of life on earth for any intelligent extra-terrestrial beings that might come across them. The images include: a symbolic representation of the spin transition in a hydrogen atom; a (naked) man and woman; a silhouette of the spacecraft drawn to scale of the human figures to communicate their dimensions; and a schematic representation of the planets in the solar system to clarify from where the spacecraft originates.[34]

For Castellucci, the Golden Record aboard the Voyager, sent into space for a completely unknown and even unimaginable audience, is a metaphor for his *Tragedia Endogonidia*. Like the interstellar 'message in a bottle', the productions can be viewed as a communication that is adrift. His own explanation captures a positive side of the purposefully unreadable images:

> The Voyager was sent adrift into space, towards strangers. The record says: 'this is who we are'. ... The *Tragedia* project is also adrift. Only in this way are major discoveries possible. This image from the Voyager is not about a trip, or a route which is known in advance. It is the experience of *aporia*. A road whose destination you cannot know. Like the Voyager record, the destination of your journey is unknown.[35]

The Golden Record can be interpreted as the dreamy image of a future inter-galactic encounter. Castellucci's interpretation, however, emphasizes the immense tension present in this seemingly naive vision. The phonograph's inscriptions project a perpetual dream of a communication that will never happen, and yet has already started. Human speech, images and music are whirling around somewhere in space, unseen and unheard. The language of the Voyager record cannot actually communicate, since there is (as far as we know) no receiver for its message, yet it constantly speaks its message to the silent darkness of the universe.

The three metaphors I have presented here help to understand the theatrical structures of Castellucci's work in terms of space, time and language. The bewildering density of the *Wunderkammer*, the disjointed temporality of the dream and the pseudo-communicative aspirations of the Voyager Record clarify the underlying mechanisms that produce the illegibility that, to a certain extent, stands at the core of Castellucci's visual dramaturgy. The question that remains, however, is why the Socìetas deliberately wants to defy the understanding of the spectator. What is the purpose or programme behind this overt desire to complicate any straightforward interpretation of their work? To account for these issues, it is useful to situate the poetics of Castellucci and the Socìetas against the larger background of the historical avant-garde, given their common interest in transgressing the boundaries of art.

A theatre of transgression

In a 2001 book that looked back on their work from the 1990s, the members of the Socìetas included a chapter titled 'The Transgressive Manifestoes'.[36] This self-avowed interest in transgression is undoubtedly a constitutive feature of their theatre. Both aesthetically and morally, boundaries are transgressed and audience expectations are confounded. The vocabulary of transgression suggests a direct connection with the (historical) avant-garde. For Futurism, Dadaism and Surrealism, provocation and shock were deliberately employed as strategies to bring home their new aesthetic principles and the new functions they ascribed to art. One of the names from the history of avant-garde theatre that repeatedly turns up in Castellucci's discourse (and in the critical discourse about his work) is that of the French director and essayist Antonin Artaud (1896–1946).[37]

In a superficial sense, the relationship between a historical innovator such as Artaud and a contemporary post-dramatic director such as Castellucci is obvious. In his writings, Artaud called for 'a physical, tangible stage language', to escape from the dominant theatrical practice in which 'everything that is not contained in dialogue … has been left in the background'.[38] This seems like a fitting description for the visual dramaturgy which developed much later in post-dramatic theatre. Yet, to borrow a phrase from Jerzy Grotowski, Artaud's writings were prophetic, rather than programmatic: they were inspirational but did not constitute a sound methodology for the reform of Western theatre.[39] The call for a physical stage language could just as well apply to the ritualistic theatre project of Jerzy Grotowski [see **Volume 5**] or The Living Theatre.

On a deeper level, the relationship between Castellucci and Artaud is anything but obvious and even fairly opaque. Whereas Castellucci explicitly admits that Artaud is a name which he 'cannot name' and even actively tries to avoid,[40] there is no other name that returns so persistently in the texts of Castellucci as Artaud's. Moreover, Artaud even seems to deserve his place on stage. In the second act of *Genesi: From the museum of sleep* (1999), the soundtrack features an excerpt from Artaud's 1948 radio play *Pour en finir avec le jugement de dieu* (To Have Done with the Judgement of God). It is the passage in which he imitates a conversation with his psychiatrist.[41]

The fascination of Castellucci for Artaud follows the lines of Jacques Derrida, who emphasized the philosophical importance of Artaud as the nemesis of all representational thinking.[42] He is revered by Castellucci as a symbolic figure of radical self-creation. It is the Artaudian body of flesh and more specifically the *voice* ('the sexual throat of Artaud') that would make it possible to create oneself anew from scratch.[43] A prime example of this ambition is the translation Artaud produced during his internment of a chapter from Lewis Carroll's *Through the Looking-Glass and what Alice Found There* (1871). As Castellucci sees it, Artaud's translation is an example of 'cruelty' because he dares to invent a new language.[44] In Castellucci's own words:

> Every day, Artaud, my Artaud (not my Artaud because he belongs to me but my Artaud because I cannot write it otherwise) tears from his skin this sentence: The theatre is the Genesis of the creative act.[45]

Clearly, it is not solely the destructive impulse behind Artaud's self-creation that is of interest to Romeo Castellucci and the Socìetas. The subtitle of the company's first book significantly emphasizes how they are pursuing a transition 'From the iconoclastic theatre to the super-icon'.[46] This super-iconized world is a completely new universe and the theatre might be the only place where one may create it. Precisely this dialectic between destruction and creation is what Romeo Castellucci derives from Artaud's ideas.[47] Even if performance has a limited time span, it allows for the creation of a parallel world in which time, space and language are broken in two, only to be reinvented.

The fact that Antonin Artaud is one of the primary sources of inspiration for Romeo Castellucci signals how his theatre aims to continue the avant-gardist aspirations that Artaud ardently voiced, but which – due to their inexorable radicality – can, in fact, never be achieved. However, while the figure of Artaud helps to understand Castellucci's philosophy of the theatre, it is primarily the avant-garde's programmatic principle of transgression that informs his aesthetics and which provides further insight into what is actually happening on stage. To elucidate this, I focus again on the eleven episodes of the *Tragedia Endogonidia*, not least because the cycle abounds in transgressive scenes. A few examples will suffice to illustrate this.

In the fourth episode, *BR.#04*, a puddle of fake blood is poured out on the white marble floor by a policeman. Another policeman undresses and lies down in the puddle, where he is beaten by his (former) colleagues. The blows of their batons are accompanied by extremely loud bangs on the soundtrack (a split second out of sync with the actors' actions). He is smirched by the fake blood that was already there.

The sixth episode, which premiered in Paris, shows a re-enactment of the sacrifice of Isaac by Abraham. The scene is more reminiscent of slapstick than of the original story from the Old Testament. Isaac is laid on a washing machine in order to be sacrificed, and looks not very biblical in his black shorts with his fake moustache. Although a (divine?) sign seems to come from the wings, he is still killed by the knife of Abraham. The whole act seems to be a parody. But why parody the biblical story in the first place?

The seventh episode (in Rome) contains an abstract, yet humiliating scene featuring the Italian actress Francesca Proia. Naked, only dressed in high heels, she walks around in a blindingly white space. The audience cannot precisely see what is happening because the stage is closed off by a giant sheet of acrylic glass that is not completely transparent. She performs an unreadable 'pantomime' act. With her back to the audience, she takes off her left shoe, places it on a chair, stares just above the chair as if a shopping rack were there, eventually discovers her shoe again, puts it in a shopping cart, takes it to the checkout, and pays. All the while, she is limping rhythmically because she only wears one high-heeled shoe. Then she softly sings a song. There is a dramatic change in the stage lighting. It switches from twilight to hard neon light, and back. The woman is now with her back against the sheet of glass, and tries to look over her shoulder at those who spy on her – the audience. A loud, anonymous voice coming from the loudspeakers punishes her: *non guardare* (do not look). She tries two more times, and is punished again. The voice further admonishes her: *sedere* (sit); *fatti vedere* (show yourself); *voltati* (turn around). Anxiously she obeys the voice.

At the end of the Paris episode, a remarkably violent scene is acted out. During the performance, the audience is presented with two remarkable characters: a man dressed in a loincloth (referring to Christ as well as to Oedipus), and an elderly, somewhat shabby woman wearing a cap. This grandmother-like character is suggested to be the mother of Oedipus-Christ. She prepares a cot for him and lures him there with cookies. Finally, she bares her breasts and starts squeezing them (which again is accompanied by loud sounds on the soundtrack). At a later point in the piece, French policemen collect urine or semen from the Oedipus-Christ figure in a glass tube. The tube is inserted into the side wall of the theatre space. The final scene begins with a Chinese dragon dance. At least twenty dancers carry the head of the dragon and the fabric which forms his body. Then, the dancers lift the middle of the dragon's body, and present a large red shaft to the group of French policemen. The officers collect the glass tube from the wall and insert it into the red 'phallus' of the dragon. When the red phallus is shown to her, the grandmother-like figure is shocked and faints. She is taken to the centre of the stage and laid down with spread legs, while the immense dragon's head is placed on its side, staring into the audience space. The granny is now ritualistically 'raped' with the phallus of the dragon, which is handled by the policemen.

These four scenes are obviously transgressions mimed on stage. They appear to be scenes about police violence, human sacrifice, humiliation and rape. The actions represent violations of moral values and legal regulations of human society, but they are also peculiar transgressions of *dramatic* conventions. First of all, there is no narrative to prepare the audience for the violence they are about to witness. Dialogue (or any other form of narration) is absent from almost the entire *Tragedia Endogonidia*. Characters are not named, and often only appear in a single or a few scenes. The scenes create strong visual images that are connected only by an extremely loose structure, with no causal links. Each episode as a whole reminds one of the sequences of images and sounds during a dream or of a strange ceremony of an unknown community. There is no question of poetic justice nor of other dramatic mechanisms which generally allow authors and directors to couple a violent act to an interpretation. In Castellucci's work, it is impossible to recognize such motifs as the hero's noble sacrifice for a greater cause, the innocent victim, or the rightful vengeance, or any other stereotype of dramatic storytelling.

To interpret the violence in the productions of Castellucci and especially in the *Tragedia Endogonidia*, the spectator completely relies on the sparse information each scene contains. At most, it is supplemented with associations from previous scenes. This reveals the second peculiarity of the transgressive scenes: never is the audience presented with a conventional theatrical representation of a violent incident nor with a neutral representation, such as in a documentary. The transgressive scenes of Socìetas Raffaello Sanzio refrain from getting a clear grip on the actions they appear to present, as they seem to have no core or comprehensible subject. Moreover, by adding a level of highly theatrical artifice – such as outlandish costumes, a reversed chronology, a soundtrack that is slightly out of sync – the alienation one might feel from the actions is amplified. At all times, the moral and legal transgressions depicted in these scenes (police violence, human sacrifice, humiliation, rape) are accompanied by transgressions of the formal laws of the theatre. Hence, a transgression in the *content* of the stage action is always combined with a theatrical transgression. The least one can say is that the spectators are stunned and shocked by the events they are witnessing.

The question of the avant-garde

The transgressions in Castellucci's theatre rarely happen in the context of a generalized transgression, as was the case with various avant-garde movements or figures such as Artaud. Castellucci does not use the theatrical resources at his disposal to nullify the art of theatre itself, but to create an *unreadable* theatre. This theatre encourages its audience to engage incessantly in interpretation, but time and again forces it to face the very impossibility of doing so. In essence, Castellucci's work not only wants to produce enigmas, but also aspires to remain enigmatic in itself. In this respect, scenic transgression is a steering principle that, in some cases, is visualized in a literal way. In an exemplary scene from the Rome episode of the *Tragedia Endogonidia*, one of the main characters had to make his way to the stage from below, using a battering ram to crash the wooden boards of the stage floor. In the same vein, the Oedipus-Christ figure in Paris had to open a window in the back wall of the theatre before appearing on stage. These actions of literally breaking through a theatre's architecture reflect Castellucci's overarching aim to overturn the spectator's theatrical experience.

Understood as aesthetic transgression, the deliberately enigmatic nature of Castellucci's theatre can carry different meanings. It is not difficult to interpret his work according to an anti-aesthetic programme, fully in line with the dozens of innovations that avant-garde theatre has introduced. In the second part of the Marseille episode *M.#10*, for example, there are almost no performers on the stage. Behind different types of gauzes of varying thickness and translucence, objects and colour surfaces appear and disappear for almost sixty minutes, accompanied by a sophisticated lighting and sound score. Is the scenic imagery thus created not a contemporary instantiation of the ideas of theatre reformers such as Edward Gordon Craig, Adolphe Appia, or the Futurists? In their vision, humans had to disappear completely from the stage. Craig wanted to neutralize the element of chance that always affects the presence of human actors, dreaming instead of a theatre of light, movement, sound and scenography. Similarly, is not the title F.T. Marinetti gave to a futuristic manifesto from 1924 – 'Anti-psychological abstract theatre of pure forms and tactility' – the perfect description of Castellucci's project?

There is, however, a problem with the idea that avant-garde intentions from art history could be 'realized' by younger artists at a later date, under profoundly changed circumstances, such as technological progress and a broader public receptivity. The actual historical sting of the programme has disappeared. 'Anti-psychological' did not mean the same to Marinetti as it does today. Each 'anti' implies a polemical stance and, as times change, so too does the establishment against which one reacts. Phrased otherwise, in an era of post-dramatic theatre, the overruling of dramatic conventions takes on a different impact than the bewilderment the innovations of the historical avant-garde might have caused. Furthermore, even while influences from the avant-garde can be traced in Castellucci's work, there is no similar oppositional programme behind his oeuvre. On the contrary, he is profoundly hostile towards any attempt at founding anything like a Castelluccian school or style.[48] Thus, the innovations he pursues are solely for their own sake and cannot be situated within a broader aesthetic school or programme.

This inward orientation is illustrated by the ambiguous effects of the semi-transparent gauzes that became one of Castellucci's signature features. From a historical point of view, Castellucci's use of gauze evokes strong, anti-theatrical sentiments. As the French theatre sociologist Jean Duvignaud recounts, theatre in eighteenth-century Paris was dominated by a duopoly of two companies: the Comédie-Française and the Comédie-Italienne. Any attempt to found a new theatre was punished by sabotage and harassment. The new company was either served a writ against public speaking or was obliged to install a semi-transparent gauze between the stage and the audience.[49] With the French Revolution, however, everything was overturned and so too in the theatre. When the storming of the Bastille was announced, the actor Plancher Valcour was performing behind such a gauze. The moment of the announcement, he drew his (theatre) sword and tore apart the gauze with the cry: 'Vive la liberté' ('Long live freedom'). It was more than a pathetic echo of the Revolution on stage: in 1791, the right to found a theatre company was decreed by the National Assembly.

From this perspective, when Castellucci once more installs the gauze, he is actually forging a symbolic regression in the modern theatre. He wants to question the well-oiled theatrical machinery that developed during the nineteenth century, and which contributed to the rise of today's society of the spectacle. Just like the reactionary groups of eighteenth-century Paris, his critical project is not a frontal attack on the institutionalized system of theatre, but rather attempts to disrupt it from within by confounding the spectator's experience through a radically irrational aesthetic which puts any interpretative framework under pressure. No explosives are placed in the theatre. The show must go on. But it is made unreadable behind the semi-transparent gauze.

A surrealist Wonderland

Even though Romeo Castellucci does not want to explode the theatre and destroy all remnants from the dramatic tradition, his work undoubtedly carries out a theatrical bombardment of the audience's senses. Spectators are alienated from their habitual perceptual environment as well as from any system of artistic conventions, and have to resort to other modes of watching in order to engage with the work. But rather than leaving the audience with nothing in hand, Castellucci is seeking to lead them into a parallel reality that functions as an otherworldly Wonderland. Castellucci describes this intention as follows:

> The present mass culture does not permit a worthy antagonism, there is no worthy enemy. Taking an attitude towards mass culture therefore calls for a catastrophe. That is indifference, but not in the sense of political neutrality. It is an indifference that is able to open a parallel world and to break the course of time. ... The theatre proves that it is possible to suspend the world for an hour, to suspend language and time. It's like a switch. The theatre is the proof that a parallel world exists ... Communication today has become the fundamental ideology of power. The task of the *Tragedia Endogonidia*, or even of theatre itself – if such a 'task' exists – is to interrupt the communication, and instead give a form of revelation.[50]

This citation finally elucidates the avant-garde intentions of Castellucci's programme. The deliberate illegibility of the productions and the ensuing opacity of meaning go against the grain of the information and communication society, which professes to thrive on the uninterrupted flow of knowledge. Amidst the proliferation of images in our current digital and networked culture, Castellucci's artistic imagery takes up a singular position. Lehmann has termed this a strategy of refusal:

> In the face of our everyday bombardment with signs, postdramatic theatre works with a strategy of refusal. It practises an economy in its use of signs that can be seen as asceticism; it emphasizes a *formalism* that reduces the plethora of signs through repetition and duration; and it demonstrates a tendency to *graphism* and writing that seems to defend itself against optical opulence and redundancy.[51]

If Castellucci explicitly takes a stand against the ideology of constant communication, to which alternative does his work refer? Is there a utopian undercurrent present in his work? While Castellucci emphatically refuses to be labelled as a Surrealist, it is the avant-garde programme that best seems to describe his productions.[52] Is Surrealism not the ideal name for a theatre that wants to open a parallel world, above or next to this world, a *surréalité*?

Castellucci wishes to avoid such associations with Surrealism, because it appeals to chance to produce its artworks. In contrast, he emphasizes the profound necessity and accuracy of the images he produces. There is, however, a common ground that connects these seemingly oppositional stances that revolve around whether the worshipping of coincidence or the idea of artistic urgency and precision. Both views ultimately spring from a deeper criticism (shared by the Surrealists as well as by Castellucci) of the romantic cult of the artist's personality.

According to the surrealist leader André Breton, the crucial ambition was to let as few conscious interventions or literary techniques as possible come between 'le fonctionnement *réel* de la pensée' ('the true functioning of thought') and its expression. The writer is no more than a recording device for what is happening in his (and the collective) subconscious.[53] The results are the well-known surrealist genres of text, such as automatic writing, the dream narrative, the *cadavre exquis* (exquisite corpse) and nonsensical dialogue. In the early manifestos of Surrealism, Breton committed himself to the radically democratic striving of 'bringing mechanic writing within reach of everyone'.[54]

Castellucci, by contrast, does not seem to foster such ambitions. Utopian thinking and the ideal of a generalized cultural democracy are never so tangibly present in his work as it was in the case of the Surrealists. At the same time, Castellucci does appear to provide a peculiar update of the surrealist aspiration to arrive at 'the true functioning of thought'.

One of the Socìetas' favourite references in interviews and essays is the German art historian Aby Warburg (1866–1929).[55] On the occasion of the London episode of the *Tragedia Endogonidia*, the company even installed an

'Atlas Room', which showed a collage of clippings from the creative process. Visitors could complement the collection with their own images. Castellucci thus made a connection between his project and Warburg's most famous work, his research library (which, in 1933, was transferred to the Warburg Institute in London, where it still is). According to Claudia Schmölders, Warburg regarded his library no longer as a spatial structure, but as a temporal one. Hence the bewilderment of new employees of Warburg when they noticed the bizarre arrangement of the books, which were also often rearranged by the historian, depending on the changed relationships he had discovered between them.[56]

The 'Image-Atlas Mnemosyne' is the most famous result of Warburg's eccentric method.[57] To support his hypothesis that specific visual elements, or 'pathos formulas' (*Pathosformeln*), had literally been transplanted from Greek and Roman art into the Renaissance, he placed reproductions, diagrams and text documents from entirely different contexts side-by-side on large panels. Following Castellucci, Warburg's 'collage' method demonstrates that certain eternal artistic forms manifest themselves through history.[58] With this reference in mind, it is extremely tempting to explain his works as being driven by a surrealist poetics. For even if Warburg's pathos formulas cannot be considered coincidental juxtapositions of seemingly random elements, they do seem to offer a visual instantiation of the 'real functioning of thought' that Breton had wanted to bring to light.

However, no matter how tempting the parallels, Castellucci must be taken seriously when he dismisses the relevance of the avant-garde programme to his work. The work of the Surrealists was built on an ardent belief in the liberating power of chance events and the creative force of the subconscious. The suppression by the authorities of 'father, fatherland, and patron' involved not only a physical but also a spiritual exploitation.[59] Hence their admiration for works by psychiatric patients, for *objets trouvés* (found objects), and for works from non-Western cultures. The surrealist techniques do not matter so much in themselves, as they primarily serve as instruments in a much larger struggle for emancipation.

Castellucci does share a certain religious vocabulary with the avant-garde, but not their utopian, often eschatological desire for an entirely different world and the concomitant demand to annihilate reality as it exists. He speaks about art as a 'revelation' that should go against the omnipresent flow of information in our current communication society. Indeed, he believes theatre installs a specific kind of intimacy.

Castellucci's oeuvre can be read as an extension of the theatrical avant-gardes of the past, insofar as his radical aesthetics as well as the apparent illegibility of his work are reminiscent of the typically avant-gardist intention to shake both the art world and society to its roots. Nevertheless, following Castellucci's persistent disavowal that his art continues the avant-garde project, it does become clear that, even though the theatrical structures of his visual dramaturgy are both innovative and transgressive, they are not aimed at founding an entirely new future of the theatre by simply erasing the classical dramatic tradition. The innovations he pursues rather function as flies that are caught in amber: they appear to be alive, but their flight is without destination. While the poetics of Castellucci and the Socìetas is reminiscent of the religious dimension of the avant-garde's utopian project, the crucial difference is that the very idea of a possible utopia has been resolutely removed. All that rests is, at most, a 'disenchanted religiosity'.

Resisting interpretation

If the analysis of Castellucci's theatre offered in the paragraphs above has brought something to light, it certainly is the resistance his work to a final interpretation. This theatre is illegible and wishes to be so. Any interpretative act must, inevitably, end in failure. The only potential in trying to 'read' Castellucci's work might reside in highlighting the theatrical structures by which it makes itself deliberately opaque. Metaphors such as the *Wunderkammer*, the dream and the Golden Voyager Record provide entrances into the quaint aesthetics that seems impervious to rational thought and appeals to other, more sensorial modes of spectatorial commitment.

The Socìetas starts from the premise that 'art is not pure'.[60] Or, as Castellucci claims:

> The work of the artist is a work that does not exist, a ridiculous work, a work of nothing. The work of art is a forgery. It is not something that saves the soul. It is not an end. I think the work of art stands in relation to evil. Even Giotto stands in relation to evil.[61]

Castellucci's enigmatic statement only deepens the perplexity one might feel when watching his theatre on stage. How to interpret a work of which the artist denies its very existence? How to deal with the nihilistic alignment of art with forgery and evil, and the implicit refusal of any kind of relief or even redemption?

Trying to find yet another entrance to gain insight into Castellucci's poetics, I have probed the relationship between his theatre and the historical avant-garde. The radical nature of his work seems to invite this perspective quite immediately, even if Castellucci himself rejects any direct association with the legacy of the avant-garde. On further thought, we have seen indeed how Castellucci does not partake in the same antagonistic project that drives the avant-garde and which, in general terms, is aimed at overthrowing established systems of thinking and living in light of the utopian dream of an entirely new world. For all its unconventionality, there is no categorical 'anti' in Castellucci's work. He explicitly states that he does not work against, but *outside* the domain of communication.[62] In this sense, the moral underpinnings that can be discerned in the historical avant-garde are absent, if not dismantled, in Castellucci's artistic oeuvre. His work might even turn out to be as obscene or vicious as the ideology it attempts to escape from.

The amoral pretences that seem to pervade Castellucci's theatrical practice may help to explain why his relationship to classical theatre and especially tragedy is so crucial and yet so complicated. Even in productions that explicitly refer to classical tragedy (such as *Amleto, Orestea*, the *Tragedia Endogonidia*), there is no question of a tragic dilemma, a heroic protagonist or the calamitous workings of fate. One could say that Castellucci's theatre is in lack of tragic *substance*, as it seems to appeal to the same kind of universality while deliberately refusing to fill in the blanks. This is exemplified by the fact that Castellucci's tragic theatre is populated by nameless figures, whereas in Greek antiquity, the protagonists were crucially defined by their *name*. The figure of 'Antigone', for instance, came to symbolize the insoluble conflict of the heroine torn between divine and worldly laws, demonstrating how narrative content was meant to uncover universal structures of living. None of this factual information is present in Castellucci's theatrical universe. Even in pieces such as *Orestea* (1995) or *Giulio Cesare* (1997), in which the performers are still linked to characters that have a name, their often aberrant corporeality drowns out the fictional world to which they might refer. In the *Tragedia Endogonidia*, the hoods or balaclavas the 'butchers' wear and the 'victims' receive only aggravate the anonymity that, in Castellucci's view, seem to be the ineluctable condition of today's tragic hero.

It is not a coincidence that the programme of the *Tragedia*'s first episode included the famous news photograph of Carlo Giuliani, the Italian student who was shot in Genoa during demonstrations against the G8 meeting in July 2001. During the performance, the event was also 're-enacted' by a little boy. For Castellucci, Giuliani stands as an emblem for today's tragic hero:

> Carlo Giuliani was not a terrorist. It was someone like you or me. He did not put a balaclava on his head in order to commit terrorist attacks. He did it simply to hide his identity. Anonymity has become the contemporary condition of the hero. In classical tragedy, the name was important. That name has disappeared. Anyone can be the tragic hero. The battle with power will always take place. That power may take the form of the police or of the ruling class, but that is not necessary: it can also be the law of Moses. But always there is someone who must be crushed.[63]

Tragedy today, Castellucci claims, has become a generalized condition, rather than an extraordinary course of events in which a handful of privileged figures might take part. The tragic corollary of this generalization is that the alleged 'heroes' are destined to anonymity if they want to play their role. Mimicking this mechanism, Castellucci's theatre features figures that, even though they are summoned to appear on stage, must remain unknowable. Any shelter the representational machinery of the stage might offer implies that it hides something from sight. Any scene is always already ob-scene, taking place behind, next or beyond what we might perceive at first sight. Even while Castellucci opposes the incessant circulation of images in our information society with his own singular imagery, he does not offer any 'authentic' or anti-obscene tragedy. On the contrary, he leads us into a universe that is both illegible and more than obscene. Any interpretative attempt to get a firm grip on this world is therefore corrupted from the very start. It nevertheless holds the promise of expanding the spectator's horizon, even beyond the confines of the theatre.

Jan Fabre

5

Becoming Something Else: The Transformative Aesthetics of Jan Fabre

Luk Van den Dries

The aesthetic universe of Jan Fabre has always been driven by the power of the imagination and metamorphosis. In his drawings and sculptures, one can see how he exploits his fascination with transformation, conjuring up all kinds of hybrid beings that sit squarely between the animal and the human, the vertebrate and the invertebrate, object and insect. At the age of twenty-one, he created a performative installation in his parents' garden, observing insects and transforming them through his peculiar imagination in drawings and small sculptures. *De neus. (Project voor nachtelijk grondgebied)* (The Nose. [Project for Nocturnal Territory], 1978–9), for example, is an odour tent arranged like a boy's laboratory, where he burrowed into the soil, using a magnifying glass to observe minuscule details imperceptible to the naked eye. Piercing through to the world of eggs, larvae and writhing insects, Fabre remoulded these creatures by drawing or sculpting surreal assemblages of new life forms: scarabs have bizarre tails or the head of a fountain pen, while spiders become winged insects that seem to fly off the paper or are held captive into eternity by being chained to a bath plug.

Theatre has been a part of Fabre's nascent artistry from the very beginning. This interest first manifested itself in the form of plays in which his true or feigned family members feature as the characters of often brutal tragedies. He was only eighteen years old when he wrote one of his first plays, *Een familietragedie* (A Family Tragedy, 1976). The title of the piece shows immediately to which genre he wants to return: the Attic tragedy, which seems to provide Fabre with an entrance to the foundations of Western theatre. Fabre adopted the primary ingredients and refurnished them into his own. In addition, tragedy is to Fabre like a garden in which he can indulge in the delights of transformation. It continued to be a source of incessant inspiration, culminating in his creation of *Mount Olympus: To Glorify the Cult of Tragedy* (2015), one of the highlights of his near-forty-year career.

An even stronger influence than tragedy that steers the young artist at the inception of his artistic quest is performance art, as it had developed in Europe and America from the early 1960s. Specifically, the principle of 'real time/real action' that typifies this art movement inspired Fabre to seek out actions that explore the borders between fiction and reality.[1] Seminal performance artists such as Carolee Schneemann, Chris Burden and Gina Pane wilfully exposed their body to pain, endurance and aggression in order to question power structures or to uncover the expressive force of the ordinary. Often, spectators are also drawn into these transgressive experiments, as artists deliberately defy the audience's predominantly passive and distanced position by inviting them into a certain kind of interaction.[2] Touching upon the extreme to broach the unstable zone of liminality equally typifies the actions that Fabre will bring about, most of the time within the territory that he knows best: the city of Antwerp, located in northern Belgium, where he was born and raised and where he still lives and works today. In these early years, Fabre preferred to operate in public spaces, choosing several different locations in the city for his performative interventions. During a nocturnal action in 1978, for instance, he followed the trajectory of tramline two with his nose between the tram tracks, which took him no less than four hours, thirty-six minutes and twelve seconds;[3] he let slugs, decorated with the colours of the Belgian flag, slip and glide across his naked body in the window of a shop on a busy shopping street (*Window Performance*, 1977); and, dressed in a white doctor's coat, he gave a speech on a balcony in the Ommeganck street (*Doctor Fabre Will Cure You*, 1980).[4]

The territory of the city has always been an important topos in Fabre's oeuvre and Antwerp remains a crucial source of inspiration as a home base and working space. The city is a metaphor for the jungle in which he grew up, not only because of its architectural maze of streets and alleys, but also because it functions as an impenetrable secret that, like a magnet, both repels and attracts. In Fabre's perception, the city has no centre; it is a labyrinth in which one can only get lost. There are neat lanes with polished houses but there are also cracks in the streets and sidewalks that lead to a subterranean network of sewers and drains. There is the daily life that moves to the rhythm of labour and a timeless nightlife in which one can vanish like a ghost. There are places filled with history, such as museums, forts and cemeteries, but also blank wastelands that invite new inscriptions of meaning and allow for a rewriting of the past they seem to have shed.

But the city also has a distinct graphic quality. There are cobblestones, pavements, kerbs, grids of water pipes and sewer systems. There are the linear patterns of drains and gutters. There is the rhythmic succession of shop windows with their glaring colours and lights. There is the iconography of street names and traffic signs. And there are the tram tracks cutting through streets and connecting the different areas of the town. In his early performances, Fabre appropriated some of the graphic elements one can find throughout a city. During yet another nocturnal raid in Antwerp, for instance, he changed the name of the Lange Beeldekens street where his parental house stands into 'Jan Fabre street' (1977). One year later, he hung a sign onto the façade of his house, saying 'Here lived and worked Jan Fabre'. It is a copy of the commemorative plaque attached to one of the houses in the same street which read: 'Here lived and worked Vincent Van Gogh from the end of November 1883 until the end of February 1886'.[5]

These last actions show another important element typical of his performances: they are not merely inscribed in the architecture of a city, but also and very literally in their artistic and historic context, as Fabre playfully demands a place for himself in the history of art. In the *Weckworld* project (1979–81), performed in many public museums, for instance, he will leave empty glass canning jars in the work of other artists, such as in *The Beanery*, an installation by the American artist Edward Kienholz in the Stedelijk museum of Amsterdam or in *De grote ammoniet* (The Giant Ammonite), a sculpture by Rik Poot in the Middelheim museum in Antwerp. The canning jar is a strange, incongruous object that functions as an infectious body intruding into and contaminating another artist's work. Fabre's intention, however, is neither to comment on these works nor to undermine them, but rather to play around with the often sacrosanct objects that populate the visual art world. It is a jocular intervention of someone who takes art very seriously, albeit always with a wink.

This inscription into the history of art also happens in a different fashion, by literally overwriting it. For the performance *Ilad of the Bic Art/The Bic Art Room* (1981), Fabre locked himself up in a completely blank space for seventy-eight hours, patiently covering all sides of the room with lines, drawings and inscriptions, using a blue 'Bic' ballpoint pen.[6] He applied the same action to a series of small reproductions of famous paintings. Drawing fine blue lines on the masterpieces of Rembrandt, Botticelli, Lautrec, Van Gogh and Cézanne, he appropriates and literally defaces the historical tradition with his deft and defiant hand. It is a typical expression of what Emil Hrvatin calls an 'accumulative dramaturgy': 'by adding elements, Fabre arrives at an ultimate gesture; usually an installation or its destruction'.[7] His blue lines rewrite the existing work and create a sort of palimpsest between different layers of time.

Fabre not only hijacks existing art, he also explicitly questions the conditions that frame art *as* art. He seems to circle around the artwork as if to highlight its framework. Walking the chalk line that separates art from non-art, he explores this porous border, only to wipe it out again. In his three 'money performances', for example, which Fabre performed in Antwerp (1979), Ghent (1980) and Milwaukee (1980), he used the banknotes of his audience's entrance money as the basic material of the performance. The financial transactions that accompany the purchase of art thus become the focus of the performance. After making a collage with the money of his audience, Fabre cuts the banknotes into pieces, burns them and uses the ashes to write words such as 'art' and 'culture', which he then wipes out again. It is a form of actional and linguistic affirmation that demonstrates how money becomes art/culture from the second it is used inside a specific circuit. The money is literally transformed into different matter and it is the framework around it that grants the artistic product its identity and added value.

The title of the second 'money performance', *The Rea(dy)Make of the Money Performance*, is another obvious reference to Marcel Duchamp and his legendary use of the 'ready-made'. It exemplifies how Fabre leans heavily on Duchamp's legacy and continues to position artwork in the conceptual tradition, which no longer defines art in terms of aesthetics, but as a reflection on the nature and constitution of the arts. It is, more specifically, the spectator's perception that becomes the focal point: how do we look at things? To what degree does the framing of art as art determine our viewing habits? How do our ways of looking change when concerning art? Such questions revolve around the contract between the spectator and the work of art, shattering the tacit agreement that underpins the inclusion of the work in the art circuit by turning the very act of framing into the subject of the work itself. These issues continued to be examined in various other performances Fabre created during the 1980s. With *Sea Salt of the Fields* (1980), he wants to honour Duchamp's importance for art, as indicated by the title which is a literal English translation of 'Mar'-'cel' 'Du'-'champ'. In this performance, Fabre uses salt to write several word combinations (sun, sea, salt, sex), while he also performs actions as a tribute to Duchamp. In *Art as a Gamble/Gamble as Art* (1981), which he presented at the School of Visual Arts in New York, Fabre turns the relationship between artist and critic on its head: he records a number of art critics' observations on magnetic tape, while directing them like an orchestra conductor. Each of these early performances can be read as a statement about art and at the same time as a reflection upon the way in which artists can relate to art itself. Just like his inspirational example Duchamp, Fabre wants to seek out controversy, even though he is fully aware that any undermining gesture in art can be reintegrated and affirmed as an artistic deed.

While performance art clearly exerts a strong appeal for Fabre in these early years, he never stops experimenting with other art forms and different media: besides theatre plays, performances, drawings and sculptures, he also creates installations and explores photography and film. These experiments are almost always driven by a compulsive obsession: Fabre loves to work in series and to exhaust a specific kind of material by engaging with it in incessant repetition. Whereas the materials he works with can be very diverse, including – for instance – his own body fluids (blood, sperm, tears, sweat, saliva), in the course of his career as a visual artist, the blue ballpoint pen drawings and the sculptures with jewel beetles have made the greatest impact. At the same time, the different art forms that Fabre works with continuously inspire one another. Fascinations jump from one art piece to another, slipping from one medium to the next. At the start of his career, it is hard to distinguish between the genres and media that constituted his practice. He seems to create his own artistic laboratory in which he constantly concocts new experiments using different materials and forms of expression. Freeing himself from any limitations, he tests out his own imagination by materializing his self-conceived universe while also exploring its boundaries.

During these early years, his area within the art scene is still undefined; he presented his work in galleries, public spaces, university auditoriums or an occasional theatre. Gradually, however, two more or less separate circuits started to form: one for visual art and one for theatre. This eventually also led Fabre to establish two organizational structures to support his work: he set up a non-profit organization for his performing arts (Troubleyn) and a production company for his visual art (Angelos). In both disciplines, Fabre maintained astonishing levels of productivity, building an international reputation as a multidisciplinary artist whose exhibitions are featured in museums and galleries all over the world; his theatre work is also shown in many different countries. Obviously, there are various parallels and overlaps between both oeuvres, but given the focus of the present volume on theatre directors, I will restrict myself to his performance work and will only occasionally refer to his fine art.

What is real and what is unreal?

To be able to situate and apprehend Fabre's theatre oeuvre precisely, his actions and performances at the beginning of his career are crucial. Out of these largely conceptual interventions he also developed his theatrical language. For the most part, this is based upon the extreme physicality and often very raw and real ingredients that characterize performance art. This is also the hypothesis that performance historian Rose Lee Goldberg puts forward:

> By the mid '80s, visual theatre groups were flourishing in nearby Antwerp, led by the wildly imaginative Jan Fabre, who also took his inspiration from the complex and cathartic endurance pieces of Marina Abramović and Hermann Nitsch ... It was as though, by the end of the '90s, the seeds planted some twenty years earlier by performance artists in Europe and the USA, concerning time, motion, space, imagery, the body, and sound, had at last come to marvellous fruition.[8]

Fabre knew all about endurance. He had himself locked up inside a gallery for three days in *Ilad of the Bic Art/The Bic Art Room*, just as Joseph Beuys had done for *I Like America and America Likes Me* (1974). He also experimented with razor blades and made blood drawings (*My Body, My Blood, My Landscape*, 1978). These early works showed how he drew inspiration from the leading performance artists of and before his time, who had caused great commotion with their extreme actions during the 1960s and 1970s.[9] But the true inspiration for Fabre's radical physical performances came primarily from the paintings of the classic Flemish primitives, such as Gerard David (*c.* 1450–1523) whose *Het oordeel van Cambyses* (*The Judgement of Cambyses*) very explicitly depicts incisions on the body. Fabre was deeply familiar with the history of art, having studied at the Academy of Fine Arts in Antwerp, and repeatedly referred to the old Flemish masters, who, in his view, had established a canon of pictorial motives and painting techniques.

As well as performance art and the fine arts, Fabre also knew the theatre from the inside out. Between May 1978 and November 1980, he worked on six productions at the NVT (Nieuw Vlaams Theater, New Flemish Theatre), as a set and costume designer. The NVT was a small experimental theatre in Antwerp 'where different styles and genres from various authors could be tried out'.[10] This first immersion in the workings of Flemish theatre was, for Fabre, above all an example of how *not* to go about things. After yet another premiere that, in his opinion, had failed, he wrote in his diary: 'The piece *In de naam van Oranje* (In the Name of Orange) of Paul Koeck might be saved! There's only one solution. Sack all the actors and the director.'[11] The remedy for the false realism he sees everywhere in the theatre around him is evident: 'The theatre is in need of the mentality of performance art. This mentality will erode the border between illusion and reality. A graze will open and with pleasure I will strew salt in it.'[12]

When Fabre made these notes, he was already rehearsing his first theatre production, *Theater geschreven met een K is een kater* (Theatre Written with a K is a Tomcat, 1980). Centre stage is the figure of a writer who sits behind a table with thin and stretched legs; during the entire performance he is hammering his lines into a typewriter, as if possessed by some evil demon.[13] Beneath him on stage, three actors perform actions as dictated by the writer's imaginary world. Fictional characters are still vaguely discernible: the man, the woman and the beast. In turn, they begin something that resembles a family role play which features the daughter, son and their grandparents. Yet more important than the remnants of a tragedy about guilt and frustration are the actions the actors are performing: these are at the same time completely banal (making dinner, looking in the mirror, arguing) and disconcertingly brutal. Daily props – such as bread, knife and fork, shaving cream, a bottle of milk or a walking cane – become tools of torture the actors use to attack one another as if it were real. Instead of classic plot development, there is a series of scenes in which the escalation of violence and rushes of adrenaline build to a climax. But after each cruel assault, the actors calmly pick up the pieces and clean up the whole mess.

In his very first theatre production, Fabre explored the basic conditions of the theatrical setting: what is real and what is unreal about theatre? Is the actor pretending? How far does the lie of theatre go? Especially in the light of the next two productions I discuss, the question of theatricality and its common alignment with fictionality occupies a central position in this first theatre performance. This is also recognized by Bart Verschaffel who, after the scripts of Fabre's first three theatre plays had been published in 2009 together with the recordings of their original staging, writes that:[14]

> In *Theatre (written) with a K* ... Fabre uses the 'exceptional condition' of the theatre, defined by the possibility to prescribe an act to the players and the way in which something is being shown and looked at is controlled and manipulated, in order to thematize and try out this condition and to present the 'reality' of the theatrical situation as the *truth* of the theatre.[15]

This programmatic attention to the unique position and essence of theatre, which hovers between the reality of the stage and the manipulation of the theatrical machinery, make up both the content and form of *Theatre Written with a K is a Tomcat*. This is also evident in the somewhat bizarre title of the piece, which is difficult to translate in English without losing some of its resonance. In its original Flemish version, the title plays with the rhyme and meanings of the words 'theater' and 'kater', which is the Flemish word for hangover or tomcat. Many scenes in the piece invoke the holy trinity of 'sex, drugs and alcohol', which suggests how Fabre wants to create a theatre where the affective impact is as real as a severe hangover. The word 'theatre', on the other hand, evokes the Flemish word 'thee', which means 'tea', an ingredient that Fabre uses in various installations and performances.[16] But tea also belongs to the repertory of tricks and lies often employed in the theatre: tea is used to represent whisky during drinking scenes. In his first production, Fabre thus posits that theatre negotiates between lie and truth, between make-believe and a splitting headache. This tension between illusion and reality dominates the piece and is the thread connecting the trilogy Fabre created between 1980 and 1984.

I dwell on this starting phase of Fabre's career, not only because it forms the nucleus of his entire oeuvre, but also because Fabre returned time and again to the rich and diverse materials he excavated during this period. Or, as Verschaffel claims, 'Fabre has always revisited and rearranged his own "beginning"'.[17] In 2012, almost thirty years later, he would restage the two most renowned productions of the trilogy, to bring these seminal works – which, as Roselee Goldberg already indicated, propelled a wave of artistic innovations in both Flemish and international theatre – to a younger and more contemporary audience.

Theatre as a ready-made

Until 1982, Fabre was a marginal artist still making his way in the scene. While he was invited to show his *Theatre Written with a K ...* in America, his breakthrough came with his second production, *Het is theater zoals te verwachten en te voorzien was* (This is Theatre as it was to be Expected and Foreseen, 1982). Fabre took immense risks: after the relatively short *Theatre Written with a K ...* of forty-five minutes, he created a play of no less than eight hours. For this production, Fabre organized auditions and chose a couple of people without any experience in acting and who would join him for excruciatingly intensive rehearsals during the next four months. Fabre borrowed the working budget – a mere €3,750 – from his costume designer Pol Engels, the only money at his disposal, as he made the piece without any additional governmental subsidy. The scenery consisted of only a few standing lights, bought in a cheap bric-a-brac shop. The actors performed for the money spectators paid to see the piece: in reality, this meant they had to divide a half-empty cash register between the eight of them.

The conditions were rather dire, but in retrospect it seemed that the right people showed up for the premiere at the Stalker theatre in Brussels on 16 October 1982. After seeing the piece, Hugo de Greef decided to include the production in the next edition of the Kaaitheater festival (1983), together with the premiere of, among others, *Rosas danst Rosas* (Rosas Dances Rosas) by Anne Teresa De Keersmaeker and *Route 1 and 9* by The Wooster Group.[18] Ritsaert ten Cate, director of the legendary Mickery theatre in Amsterdam, was intrigued by Fabre's production and immediately wanted to book six shows. Jan Fabre noted in his diary: 'Ritsaert ten Cate, *The Big Boss* of the avant-garde theatre in Europe, writes and publishes everywhere he can that *This is Theatre as it was to be Expected and Foreseen* is a shock and is historically as important as *Deafman Glance* (1971) by Bob Wilson.'[19] Indeed, after its performances at Kaaitheater and the Mickery, various programmers were waiting in line to book the production. Over the next few years, the performance was invited to all the major theatre festivals and has developed into a cult event.

With his eight-hour show *This is Theatre...*, Fabre immediately and definitively established himself as a leading figure in the theatre landscape of his era. The 'shock' that Ritsaert ten Cate refers to has something to do with that: with this production Fabre created a kind of theatre that was not easily pushed into existing categories; it is right off the map, but at the same time tremendously fascinating in its own right. The piece contains various references to the work of Robert Wilson, but other than its minimalism, the power of repetition and duration, there is little the two have in common. When we consider this production from the vantage point of Fabre's early experiments with performance art as well as his *Theatre Written with a K...*, it is primarily the link with Marcel Duchamp, Dadaist and self-declared 'an-artist',[20] that once again becomes pertinent. Duchamp's oeuvre is time and again at play with the borderlines of what defines art, further stretching the notion of art itself in an unorthodox and radical-anarchistic way. This is exactly what Fabre was aiming for in his first theatre pieces, but was probably most explosively and poignantly arrived at in *This is Theatre as it was to be Expected and Foreseen.*

The title itself already challenges the spectator to test expectations that are subsequently torpedoed one by one in a theatre performance that balances installation and performance art, but still stubbornly clings to its tautological self-definition of 'theatre' as articulated explicitly in the title. One could also interpret the piece as a theatrical elaboration of Duchamp's notion of the *ready-made*: recycling various everyday objects, Duchamp astutely aimed to change their nature by imposing his own artistic signature on them or by placing them into an institutional setting. Fabre, too, starts from very simple *ready-made actions* during the eight-hour performance, such as dressing and undressing, looking at oneself in the mirror, putting on lotion, and licking up yoghurt from the floor. But even while all these everyday actions are recognizable for virtually every spectator, Fabre makes lucid use of both the theatrical stage and the mechanism of repetition to estrange the action from itself. At regular intervals, the performance is interrupted by quotes from an audio interview with Marcel Duchamp about art and *ready-mades*,[21] enforcing the connection with Duchamp even more. As mentioned before, Fabre is always provoking a dialogue with the tradition of art, which in this production is manifest in the references to not only the work of Marcel Duchamp, but also of Jannis Kounelllis (1936–2017),

FIGURE 5.1 This is Theatre as it was to be Expected and Foreseen, *1982 (Patrick T. Sellitto).*

Marcel Broodthaers (1924–76) and Ben d'Armagnac (1940–78). About this Fabre says: 'As a base to create a theatrical concept, I use my knowledge of the modern history of art. In this way I am always involved with the phenomenon "art about art", showing my position as a visual artist and/or theatre maker'.[22]

It was clear to all that a visual artist was making his way into the theatre, someone fascinated by lines, shapes and canvas. From the ceiling of the stage hangs a rectangular pattern of meat hooks, changing into a perfect circle when sand bags or a series of chairs with burning candles are attached to it. Fabre had also recorded 8mm movies from his own physical performances, which are projected upon the bare backs of the performers, as if he is tattooing his own self-portrait onto his actors. But still, in the midst of this predominant geometrical absoluteness, coincidence reigns: while two turtles with a burning candle on their shell follow their own uncontrollable route, the exhaustion of the performers continuously destabilizes the ostensible containment of posture and action. The most gripping part of this production is without a doubt the presence of the performers, all but one without any experience in the theatrical field. Dressed in similar costumes, but also often naked, they have to rely on body language, for barely a word is spoken during the eight hours. These bodies are thrown into a fierce fight in which boundaries of physical endurance are tested: two actors run each on a fixed spot; someone else jumps up and down until they reach the point of complete exhaustion. Jumping, falling, running – the performers engage in these simple tasks as if their life depends on it. Without a hint of pose or theatricality, they merely carry out these actions. Even the frequently brutal and depleting acts seem to leave them unaffected, as they remain present by simply displaying their being. This goes most definitely for the penultimate scene in which all of the actors take a seat at the front of the stage. Their real name is called out, their real profession is stated, and they stand up from their chairs and let themselves fall forward, like a bow sliding off into a fall. This scene is repeated endlessly, until, somewhere beyond the physical, self-representation becomes theatrical again.

Fabre's theatre is first and foremost a theatre of the body, the blood, the sweat. About this extreme physicality Fabre wrote in his diary:

> Theatre should most passionately go further than language, than the condition of our mouth. If not, theatre renounces instinct, intuition and the intelligence of the body. We should talk theatre out of all the cracks and holes of our body.[23]

Fabre deploys the body of his performers always in a twofold manner: it is the body making itself known again as a body that is marked by sweat, exhaustion, red stains of a beating, but at the same time it is presented in a carefully crafted image that uses bodies, scenery and space to construe a living drawing. Hans-Thies Lehmann summarizes this powerfully: 'He creates a connection between cruelty and geometry that is often difficult to bear, an intense concentration of tormenting physicality and at the same time a functionalization of the body within the elements of a spatial geometry'.[24]

Theatricality and iconography

The conjunction of physicality and visuality that characterizes Fabre's work is even more present in the last part of the trilogy, *De Macht der Theaterlijke Dwaasheden* (The Power of Theatrical Madness, 1984), which is conceived as a dialogue between iconographic tradition and scenic deconstruction. Typical for the post-dramatic nature of this piece is that it does not seem to have a centre, a fixed point that structures the entire performance. This becomes particularly evident in the eclectic mix of media and genres Fabre uses in this production. The text is construed as a list of all the crucial theatre, ballet and opera performances since Richard Wagner's 1876 premiere of *Der Ring des Nibelungen*. The music is a compilation of minimalistic scores, composed specifically for this production by Wim Mertens, together with several phrases and cadenzas from opera history: Liebestod from *Tristan und Isolde* (Wagner, 1875), *Penthisilea* (Othmar Schoeck, 1927), *Carmen* (George Bizet, 1875), *Salome* (Richard Strauss, 1905) and *Elektra* (Richard Strauss, 1909). The scenic action is based upon the fairy tales *The Emperor's New Clothes* by Hans Christian Andersen and *The Frog King or Iron Henry* by the Brothers Grimm. And the immense backcloth shows projected slides of paintings in traditions stretching from Michelangelo to the Mannerists.

One of the many frictions in this monumental production arise between the projected images and the scenic action. During the piece, the performers constantly enact reminiscences of the backcloth projections. In this manner, Fabre spreads out a complex memory structure for the spectator. Actor and image seem to respond to one another, but always in a fragmented time lapse, shifting and altering meanings in a multi-layered process. To Fabre, it is about a diametrical collision between two conceptions of time: the coagulated time of the painting versus the processual time of the theatrical scene. The continual friction between both temporal dimensions causes them to adopt features of each other. While some of the scenes are interrupted by momentarily freezing into a fixed pose that refers to an iconographic momentum, mixing the paintings with scenic actions also attributes a progressive development to the otherwise still images.

Fabre plays a cunning game with theatricality and iconography, the two major modes of expression he merges in this early key production. By infusing the theatre with visual art and vice versa, he wants to rediscover and redefine both disciplines by subjecting each to the mirroring gaze of the other. During the second scene of the piece, for instance, he projects the upper part of Louis Le Nain's painting *L'allégorie de la Victoire* (The Allegory of the Victory, 1635), which shows a winged woman baring her right breast. A few minutes earlier, one of the actresses opened up her shirt, supporting her breast with one hand. This gesture attains a very different meaning when the painting is projected, since both depictions of the same pose refer back and forth to one another. Only in the penultimate scene, almost four hours later, do we get to see the rest of the painting. The woman with bared breast appears to be standing on a conquered and slain body, as the allegory of victory.

Sometimes the references are easier to grasp, especially when the images are drawn from widely known iconic paintings, such as Michelangelo's famous fresco *The Creation of Adam* in the Sistine Chapel (*c.* 1612). Just as Michelangelo pictured God reaching out to Adam, Fabre has two actor-emperors literally repeating the same gesture on stage. But he also uses the projections to recontextualize certain poses enacted on stage. When a couple of male actors raise their right arm to three-quarter shoulder height, their gesture unmistakably evokes a fascistic past, causing momentary confusion and perplexity. It acquires an entirely different content, however, when quite a while later the painting *Le serment des Horaces* (Oath of the Horatii, 1784) of the French painter Jacques-Louis David is projected, which shows three brother-soldiers raising their arms to swear an oath to their father who is handing them their swords. Also the projection of Bernardino Luini's painting *Salome with the Head of Saint John the Baptist* (1527), with the horrifying image of John's severed head served on a platter to the vindictive Salome, lends a completely different meaning to what happens on the proscenium. Walking across the edge of the stage, a blindfolded baritone is singing Wagner's *Liebestod*, holding a large, sharp knife in his hand. When he meets another blindfolded actor, he slashes through the air with his knife, while the other hastily stoops or shies away just in time.

With Luini's painting on the background, spectators might begin to wonder to what extent the threat of cutting a throat is real. A similar confusion about the assumed realness of the actions on stage has already occurred at the very start of the piece. Carrying living frogs on a white plate, the actors release them, but after they have freely explored the stage for a short while, the performers catch the frogs again with their white shirts and squash them. Is this happening for real or is it a part of the theatrical fiction? This question is at stake in the third part of Fabre's trilogy, which again questions the theatre itself in its title. The piece aims to expose 'the power of theatrical madness' through countless scenes that mimic – but also mock – the glory and splendour of the lie of the theatre. As an audience, we ardently want to believe that frogs can transform into heroic princes who honour their princesses. Through endless repetition and gradual but incessant acceleration, these heroes and princesses end up being mere sweating, heavy bodies, just as a very gracious and slow ballet pose repeated tirelessly during forty minutes changes into a wobbling choreography. In this manner, the duration of real time undermines the lie of fiction.

The mysteries of the blue hour

After his radical deconstruction of the theatre, Fabre starts exploring new territories in the performing arts by turning towards dance and opera. During the eighth edition of *Documenta* in Kassel (1987), Fabre premiered his first choreographic piece, *The Dance Sections*, as a part of what, in 1990, would become the opera trilogy *The Minds of Helena Troubleyn*. He was also invited by William Forsythe to create a dance piece with the Ballet Frankfurt, *The Sound of One Hand Clapping* (1990). In addition, Fabre staged a range of theatre monologues with some of his favourite actors: Marc 'Moon' Overmeir, Els Deceukelier and Dirk Roofthooft.

What is remarkable about this period in Fabre's oeuvre is that he draws his inspiration completely from the technique of the blue ballpoint drawing, which at that moment made up the core of his visual art practice. In 1987, *The Hour Blue* opened in the De Selby gallery in Amsterdam, a first retrospective exhibition of his blue ballpoint drawings.[25] What started as the scratching of objects by means of a simple blue ballpoint pen slowly swelled into the creation of an entirely distinct universe. This development effectuates an interesting reversal. At first, Fabre used the blue ballpoint technique to seize something else, such as reproductions of masterpieces or various objects and materials, with the blue lines functioning as the signature of the artist Jan Fabre. The reversal happens from the moment the drawing disappears and there is no longer any sense of signature, just blue lines starting to stand on their own. The scratching, often carried out by several people working on large surfaces with dozens of blue Bic ballpoints, results in a patchwork of innumerable lines and through a chemic interaction of the blue ballpoint with paper, canvas or another kind of material, creating a world of its own. The amorphous mass of blue lines overtakes the initiative of those who drew them. Their hand becomes invisible behind the shapelessness of the endlessly variegated game of blue lines that, ultimately, determines the shape in a seemingly autonomous fashion.

The underlying motive behind these 'drawings' is Fabre's desire to create a separate cosmos in which he can disappear. This longing is closely related to his fascination with the blue hour, the short moment between day and night when the blue of the sky is so immense, so mysterious and quiet that it seems to neutralize all contradictions. He will apply this principle to his visual art and his theatre, in an attempt to capture and elongate the momentum. Probably the best-known example is *The Castle Tivoli* (1990), which refers to a real castle near Mechelen (Belgium) that Fabre covers with immense cloths that are entirely ballpointed in blue. The sight of this fairy tale building and especially its mirroring in the nearby pond brings about an almost hallucinogenic effect; it seems to belong to a different world. Fabre also introduced the 'Blue Hour' in his opera and theatre pieces of this period, by dressing the performers in blue ballpointed costumes or by hanging large cloths on the back of the stage, which seem to drain every notion of perspective into a 'black' hole. In *Prometheus Landschaft 1* (Prometheus Landscape 1, 1988), this aesthetic is exploited to the fullest: not merely on a spatial level, as the entire space from floor to ceiling is coloured ballpoint blue, but also in terms of time, as the piece is performed during that short blue hour, that mysterious transition from day to night.

But the desire to disappear completely as a subject by merging with a world transcending ours is not merely restricted to the blue hour. Fabre's dramatic oeuvre testifies to a similar drive. In the monologue *De Keizer van het Verlies* (The Emperor of Loss, 1996), for example, the main figure, played by Dirk Roofthooft, expresses how he wants to fuse with the tree he had been drawing. 'I did not draw a tree', he says, 'I became a tree. My skin became bark.'[26] This longing is once again echoed in the monologue *De dienaar van de schoonheid* (The Servant of Beauty, 2010), in which the protagonist, who plays the role of a puppeteer, claims: 'I will become immaterial. Invisible.'[27] This drive for ecstatic unification should not be misunderstood as striving after a harmonious experience, but rather continues the tradition to which both Hölderlin and Artaud belong, who saw pain and violence as necessary conditions to reach beyond one's own boundaries.[28]

As this pain is mainly expressed through the body of the performer, it becomes most tangible in Fabre's choreographies. Also for his dance pieces, Fabre adopts a deconstructionist stance, uncovering the basic mechanisms of classical ballet:

> He reduces the movement schemes present in his choreography to elementary positions and orientations of the body of the dancers: *écarté, tendu, port de bras, ronde jambe à terre*, etc ... One could think of the whole choreographic system of *The Dance Sections* as a juxtaposition of different preparatory movements, traditionally considered to be secondary, subordinated to primary jumps, figures and poses in ballet, which are themselves more complex.[29]

Fabre has his dancers repeat and slow down these 'secondary' warm-up exercises, in order to make visible the disciplining of the body as a basic condition of classical ballet. As the dancers do not perform any extraordinary figures, it is not the lightness of the ballet but the training of each muscle that Fabre shows, by means of a sequence of ballet poses that are repeated endlessly. Consequently, while at first these basic exercises are performed in unison by a *corps de ballet*, emotionless and seemingly without effort, real time will eventually catch up with these trained bodies and show itself through fatigue, quivering muscles or audible breath. Gradually, real bodies emerge out of the choreography, in much the same way as in Fabre's theatre trilogy.

Fabre's unfolding of the mechanisms of disciplinization is clearly inspired by the ideas Foucault developed in *Discipline and Punish: The Birth of the Prison*.[30] In Foucault's analysis, power is a perfidious mechanism that tries to instrumentalize the body through sophisticated strategies in order to make it subservient to ideologically conditioned production processes. All bodies pass, for that purpose, through a phase of adapting to an almost invisible system of norms, which the body eventually internalizes and makes it acceptable to the societal standards of normality and conditions of optimization. This standardization process, with all the disciplining violence that coincides with it, is the crux of Fabre's ballet as well as of his early theatre work. To illustrate this, one may recall an iconic scene from *The Power of Theatrical Madness,* a scene that through its duration and repetition made a great impact on the audience and poignantly shows the extreme, internalized violence Foucault talks about. Fabre's fetish actress Els Deceukelier is allowed on stage only if she knows the answer to the question '1876?', which is endlessly repeated by another actor. She is brutally pushed and pulled off stage, subjected to a physical violence that becomes ever more real as it does not seem to stop. The extreme duration, endurance and repetition makes the sadistic scene almost unbearable to watch. When she finally gives the right answer ('Ring des Nibelungen, Richard Wagner, Bayreuth'), she is granted access to the stage and adapts to the prevailing body regulations and restrictions. She bends to the order of the normative discourse that disciplines bodies. She surrenders willingly to the gaze of power. When Michel Foucault died on 25 June 1984, Fabre dedicated the piece to him.

This kind of systemic disciplinization not only applies to the body (I shall be dealing with how Fabre works with his performers later in this chapter), but also to the organization of the theatrical space. As Emil Hrvatin points out in his discussion of Fabre's choreographies:

> The isolation of the body in space implies the reorganization of space into a 'disciplinary space' in *The Dance Sections* ... Because the space is perceived in function of the distribution of bodies and because the shaping of movement is nothing else than the affirmation of this distribution, we call Fabre's choreography *topography*. The partition of individuals in space merges with the partition of space itself.[31]

This distribution of space is predominantly symmetrical, as Fabre likes to cleave or, to use his own terminology, 'to split' the space. To Fabre, performers are playmakers of energy, and to possess insight into what a space needs or can bear is crucial for this. In this respect, the splitting of the space always results from the intention to distribute that energy better across the playing field, to permit greater depth, or more breadth, or to enlarge a diagonal. In the period of the 'Blue Hour', there is often one central point structuring the space and 'splitting' it into symmetrical patterns. In *The Sound of One Hand Clapping*, for example, Els Deceukelier lies down in the middle of the stage. As the central focal point, Deceukelier not only steers the perspective of the audience, but also structures the parallel or V-formations of the *corps de ballet*.

Symmetry is, of course, the spatial expression *par excellence* of the desire for extreme order and discipline. At some point during his career, Fabre even had plans to build a theatre in the shape of a triangular piece of cheese, which would optimize the symmetry of the theatrical architecture and give the audience a grandstand view of the symmetrical proportions on stage. As Fabre explains, 'they are all king and if they want to, they can watch from a separate royal space, made by themselves. Seated in the central axis. Symmetrical. So they can look at and experience my stagings from the right perspective'.[32] Unavoidably, this quest for the ultimate symmetry, or the supreme perfection in performing a repetitive *port de bras* in unison, is haunted by its counterpart, as the slightest failure or disintegration immediately leads to a collapsing of the symmetrical purity. But failure is also typical of Fabre's work in this period:

> His work is particularly interesting in its manner of handling symmetry, and in the impossibility of achieving perfection in movement and in the construction of space. Fabre's work calls into question what it is that constitutes beauty, and draws our attention to the failures that compose it.[33]

If the impossible quest for ultimate beauty is at one end of Fabre's poetical spectrum, at the other end stands his explicit endeavour to undo any form of control and mastery. This becomes most evident in those pieces in which he introduces animals on stage: dying carp in *Het interview dat sterft...* (The Interview that Dies..., 1989), parrots in *Der Palast um vier Uhr morgens ..., A.G.* (The Palace at Four O'Clock in the Morning..., A.G., 1989), stick insects in *Prometheus Landscape 1* (1989), tarantulas in *Zij was en zij is, zelfs* (She was and She is, Even, 1991) or the falcon in the opening scene of the opera *Silent Screams Difficult Dreams* (1992) that noiselessly comes winging down from the highest balconies onto the stage to peck at the flesh of a prone figure. 'These animals are oblivious to discipline', Gilpin notes, 'enacting a dynamism that the performers can only attempt in vain.'[34]

But besides animals, Fabre also wields other scenic means to make the perfect symmetry and extreme awareness of proportional forms implode into an eruption of chaos and disorder. The peaceful, contemplative Fabre forces us to face the other side of the Janus head: madness displaces order. Unity crumbles into innumerable fragments as if a dream falls apart. These fragments should sometimes be taken literally: piles of white plates – which already appear in *The Power of Theatrical Madness* – fall to smithereens in his third dance piece *Da un'altra faccia del tempo* (From Another Side of Time, 1993), or the floor of the stage is littered with shards of plates in *Een doodnormale vrouw* (A Dead Normal Woman, 1995). It belongs to the typical binary character of the 'Blue Hour': quietude always leads to restlessness, order leads to chaos. It is 'a dream world of twofold similarity. Its two-facedness perceives traces of the day world, while on the other side, night looms in which all differences subside.'[35] In other words, the pure beauty that Fabre pursues, or the sublime dream world of the 'Blue Hour' in which the borders between self and world are dissolved, is always already poisoned:

> I call this the aesthetics of poison. An image of beauty, craving and desire is presented, but with the addition of a disturbing element, a vivid, poisonous green tinge of colour, so to speak. ... Quite rightly, a strain of the baroque has been said to run through Fabre, and in fact Fabre's stage does resemble, at this point, those baroque still lifes where living, blooming fruits are gnawed at by all manner of loathsome beasts, allegorically demonstrating memento mori and vanitas. A theatre of death, calling to mind that it was the apple poisoned by original sin which, along with knowledge, brought about mortality.[36]

But this image of decay, putrefaction and mortality immediately announces another of Fabre's obsessions, which he started to investigate more explicitly at the beginning of the millennium.

The power of metamorphosis

Opposing the terror of disciplinization, Fabre's *As Long as the World Needs a Warrior's Soul* (2000) shows a body that, vehemently and with all its strength, tries to escape from the strangling clutch of normality. The rigid, disciplined bodies are impersonated by a series of Barbie and Ken dolls that display their perfect, impeccable bodies at the beginning of the piece. In contrast, the performers slip into a flowing, almost liquid presence, continuously assuming different shapes. The central ingredients of this performance are nutrients: chocolate paste, jam, ketchup, flour, eggs and butter. The actors not only treat their dolls with these, but they also smear, besmirch and smudge their own bodies. What normally is taken up and digested by the inside of the body is now applied to the outside as a new skin. One of the strongest images in this production is the one in which dancer Lisbeth Gruwez is making love with a lump of butter in her mouth – not as a woman, but as a man. For minutes on end her body rides upon an imagined partner. The ecstatic repetition of the same jerking movement exhausts her, makes her body transform into man, back to woman, and both at once. During this transformation, the butter in her mouth distorts. The prop – or, rather, the torture instrument that rendered her mute – melts to a lubricant. It becomes organic, fluid like the fats in the work of Joseph Beuys. The body also fights against this clump of butter, as it wants to expel it. It is an extremely powerful image that returns in another form in the dance solo *My Movements are Alone like Street Dogs* (2001).

The bodies in these performances draw their life energy from the power of metamorphosis, a crucial motif in Fabre's oeuvre. They are subject to a continuous process of change. Every kind of standstill is strange to them; they even have the potential to change into an animal, to experience the other sex or switch from toddler to elder in a split second. Their elusiveness makes them recalcitrant. Turning everything around, inside out and upside down, they are performing a sort of carnival with their bodies. The debauchery of the body is celebrated once they have wrenched themselves from the order of the normal. The focus no longer lies on the ideal or idealized body, but on the imperfect and disfigured. Only grotesque figures are permitted to this exuberant feast. The sublime steps aside for the grotesque body:

> Against the uniformity of a sanitized society, he places heretic human disorder and the audacious discipline of chaos; against the industrialized beauty of publicity icons, he shows the sublime rebellion of the body in excess; against the diktat of reason, he defends animal intelligence and the mystical quest of a new humanism. But he does not content himself with denouncing them, he undertakes the task to the fullest, until it becomes parody, its denial; he incarnates it until it becomes ridiculous and grotesque.[37]

This grotesque body constantly returns in his work. It questions the ruling order of the body, rebels against normality and especially celebrates the freedom of the opened body. In several productions, he investigates the fluids of the body that guarantee the power of metamorphosis, such as blood in *Je suis sang. Een middeleeuws sprookje* (I am Blood. A Medieval Fairytale, 2001) or sweat, tears and urine in *The Crying Body* (2004) and *L'Histoire des Larmes* (History of Tears, 2005). Fabre puts a viscid and succulent body on stage as an anachronism of our time, in which it is endangered by draught, the denial of nature by excessive reason and control. He rehabilitates the body of grace, which can participate directly in the mystery of the cycle of life and death.

What Geneviève Drouhet writes about *I am Blood* equally applies to each of these pieces: 'The performance progressively picks up its rhythm and organizes the constant transition between representations of the beauty of the human being and the bare display of its animality.'[38] This double-sided bodily being that underpins the transition and transformation of one body into another is also what Eleni Varopulou remarks upon in her analysis of the baroque aesthetics in *The Crying Body*: 'The transition from a *corpus politicum* to a *corpus mysticum* and vice-versa indicates that the theatre of Jan Fabre, all the while delivering sharp critique on our civilization, is at the same time a place where the paradox of sadness lives, it is a place of baroque.'[39]

The body's transformative power is, as mentioned before, intimately linked to the notion of metamorphosis, which is also a key concept in the acting method Jan Fabre has developed throughout his career as a theatre director.[40] In many acting theories, transformation is understood as the actor's task to impersonate a character, using various techniques to get under the skin and inside the psyche of the person to become somebody else. In Fabre's practice, however, the idea of transformation proceeds in an entirely different direction: he does not require the performer to become *somebody* else, but *something* else. Rather than impersonation, it is the change in physical materiality that Fabre is looking for. In this respect, the process of transformation should take place on the level of cellular structures and atomic economy, with substance modifying itself and turning into something that might still be recognizable as a human form, but which has renounced its functionality to bring forth a new 'creature'. This is the genuine essence of Fabre's theatre: transsubstantiation, or becoming something else.

The work of the performer produces the same amazing, almost shocking effect as when a larva metamorphoses into a caterpillar and eventually into a butterfly; or as the heavy armoured beetle popping out of its pupa. The metamorphosis of Fabre's performers is just as unlikely: in a sort of magical tilting of time, they can change their appearance, putting on the guise of an animal and wielding it until a different metamorphosis strikes them as more appropriate to engage in a new action. This metamorphosis is never without effort, but always contains a mixture of violence and beauty. As Fabre himself avows, while beauty is a starting point, metamorphosis is a necessary antidote:

> My theatre speaks about the secret truths of the body's reality. So in my own way, I'm very old-fashioned. I'm always looking for metamorphosis. I'm interested in change, literal change from cocoon and pupa to butterfly. I'm always looking for people that I think are beautiful. That means that they have a beautiful body, charisma, something sexual or something erotic, a strong personality. A then I ask from these people that they become abnormal. To deform their body, or metamorphose into something else: an old person, a woman, a fish, a monster. I believe in metamorphosis, the constant state of change.[41]

From small to monumental size

Besides being an artist who works in various disciplines, Fabre also uses a varied range of formats within each segment of his oeuvre. His visual artwork, for instance, includes small drawings as well as huge surfaces covered with Bic ballpoint blue (*The Road from the Earth to the Stars is not Paved*, 1987). Also in his sculptures Fabre likes to alternate between small and big. *Searching for Utopia* (2003) shows the artist sitting upon a giant turtle, a kind of anti-knight who wants to fight for slowness, freedom and reflection. His most monumental sculpture is without a doubt *Garden of Delight* (2002), a ceiling piece in the Royal Palace in Brussels, which Fabre designed in the tradition of Michelangelo, Tiepolo or Tintoretto as an imposing spectacle of light. To achieve this, he used the shells of millions of jewel beetles, which he glued to the ceiling in a variety of patterns to conjure a play of green and blue light. This work is regarded as 'the apotheosis of the scarab-motif in Fabre's oeuvre'.[42] The scarab is indeed a recurring element in Fabre's visual oeuvre, as he wants to rework the rich symbolic of the insect and return to a tradition that has its roots as far back as the Palaeolithic shamans and ancient Egypt. Yet what fascinates Fabre the most about the scarab is that it bears 'his skeleton on the outside, and by this radically offers himself as the protector of the fragile interior'.[43] These characteristics also underlie the appearance of armour in Fabre's *The Dance Sections* and *I am Blood*: just like the scarab's outer skeleton, these armours are a shield for the performers, wrapping the fragile fluidity of their bodies.

Small and big formats return in Fabre's theatrical work. Throughout his entire career, Fabre has continued to create theatre monologues and dance solos. They are always written specifically for the performers, interweaving motives and fantasies of their own biography with Fabre's obsessions. As such, they are often an ode to the primary 'warriors of beauty' (as Fabre calls his performers).[44] Most solos tour extensively and are kept in the repertoire for several seasons. *Quando l'uomo principale è una donna* (When the First Man is a Woman, 2004), for example, was created for and by Lisbeth Gruwez, but after two seasons and 108 performances, it was taken up by a new dancer, Sung-im Her, for another 63 international performances. The piece experiments with gender roles and the possibility of switching between

FIGURE 5.2 *Lisbeth Gruwez in* Quando l'uomo principale è une donna, *2004 (Wonge Bergmann).*

them: the female dancer constantly plays both male and female identities against each other during which she gradually seems to uncover multiple layers within her own personality and body. This liquidity of her identity reaches its summit when she lets twenty-two bottles of olive oil gush across the scene, drenching herself in the oil until each movement seems to flood into an endless meandering stream.

Fabre's work for opera and musical theatre often results in pieces of a huge format. After the opera triptych *The Minds of Helena Troubleyn,* for which Fabre wrote the libretto and collaborated with composer Eugeniusz Knapik, he was invited by the National Opera of Belgium to stage Richard Wagner's *Tannhäuser* (2004). It was one of those rare occasions when Fabre staged a production outside his own Troubleyn, but the fact that he accepted the invitation is hardly surprising, given his longstanding fascination with the writing, concepts and music of Wagner.[45] In his staging, Fabre discards *Tannhäuser*'s traditional dualism between pious and carnal love. In his version, the opera's female characters play the leading role: Venus, Elisabeth and the Virgin Mary each come to represent the long history of suppression of women by the patriarchy. Fabre puts eight heavily pregnant extras on stage to reinforce the opera's theme of fertility. Even more radical is the way he handles the choir of pilgrims that annually leaves for Rome, a penitential procession as a symbolic purgation in service of the community. Fabre dresses the pilgrims as clowns and gives them their preferred role: the scapegoat, who is ridiculed and expelled by the community of knights. This elementary hostile *gestus* is visualized in Fabre's staging by the symbol of the sword,[46] which returns in nearly every scene: like a multiplied sword of Damocles, hundreds of them are ominously hanging above the scene; the sword also replaces the staff the pilgrims carry on their way to Rome; Fabre includes the iconic image of Maria pierced by swords, symbolizing the seven sorrows; swords are used to evoke a field of tombstones with crosses in remembrance of all those who succumbed under the pervasive German violence dominating the opera.

To glorify the cult of tragedy

Wagner is not the only classical figure from the Western cultural canon to which Fabre is drawn. As mentioned at the beginning of this chapter, he also regularly returns to Attic tragedy as a model and source of inspiration. In 1988, Fabre called upon Aeschylus, the oldest writer of tragedies, to create his *Prometheus Landscape 1.* For the first time, he staged an already existing text, although he completely reworked it: Aeschylus' poetry is emaciated, the performers almost spit out the fragments, the text is materialized into physical sound, while the pain of the verses is squeezed out of the performers' stuttering bodies. Fabre is obsessed with the myth of the 'fire-bringer', leading to the creation of *Prometheus Landscape II* in

FIGURE 5.3 *Andrew Van Ostade in* Mount Olympus, *2015 (Wonge Bergmann).*

2011, Fabre's first collaboration with writer Jeroen Olyslaegers. In eight monologues, the inhabitants of Olympus are given a voice, one by one delivering their view on the mythical story of Prometheus. In this version, Fabre shows how the fire, the preciously cherished gift of civilization that Prometheus had stolen from Olympus, was extinguished by man. In a stream of images and execrating rhetoric, Fabre tells how man traded the Promethean fire for a codex of new religions. Even though fire still might spark someone's interest, at all times a fire extinguisher is on hand to quench the inspiring flames with a bucket of sand, axes or some other kind of equipment.

The fascination with tragedy finds its ultimate completion in Fabre's *Mount Olympus: To Glorify the Cult of Tragedy* (2015), a performance of no less than twenty-four hours that is a challenge to both the performers and the audience. His dream to create a monumental project about the tradition of Greek tragedy and the meaning of catharsis today had lain dormant for many years. Fabre is attracted to the unbridled passions rampant in the oldest surviving plays. To him, tragedy is the primeval core of theatricality; it constitutes the source, the nucleus from which theatre as we know it in the West was born. He also considers tragedy the purest form of theatre, since it is the place where drunkenness and reason meet one another. Tragedy is a form of theatre born out of friction and collision: it has its roots in Dionysian rites in which music, rhythm and dance played a central part, mixing the rigidity of the poetic metre with matters of conflict in which violence, lust, conceit and blindness luxuriate. It is precisely this explosive mixture, this condensation of conflict that enthrals Fabre and which he wants to translate physically, an ambition he has been pursuing during his entire career. He wants to move spectators, to confront them with those dimensions of being that reach far beyond the censoring filters of consciousness. In an interview in 2003, he suggests how the principle of catharsis influences his oeuvre:

> An important principle to me is catharsis. The viewer is confronted with some of the darkest passages from the history of mankind. He's taken along on a journey through extreme pain and horror. By confronting that deep suffering, his mind is cleansed. In my stagings I try to do the same thing. I launch an attack on the audience. I take them on a journey. I show them images of man that they've repressed or forgotten about. I appeal to their violent impulses, to their dreams, their lust. ... I want to have my audience and actors learn through suffering.[47]

Theatre for Fabre is a kind of cleansing ritual, inviting and even instigating a process of change. It is not only about the metamorphosis of the actor, but also of the viewer. In his own words:

> Sometimes I feel like some sort of old-fashioned Greek witch doctor. I know what rituals are for and what refined brews can accomplish. The Greek word 'pharmakon' means both a curing drug and a dangerous poison. That's the ambiguity of my work method and of my performances. To actors, dancers and audience alike, my theatre is an aesthetic of poison that just might cure.[48]

Creative process

To a certain extent, *Mount Olympus* is the culmination of Jan Fabre's theatrical career and the creative process leading up to this production condensed the distinct working method that Fabre has developed throughout the years. As such, it stands as an illustrative example of the creative processes preceding most of his other works. Everything starts with Fabre's own imagination, his dreams and obsessions that have always been the cornerstone of his oeuvre. Without exception, these ideas find their first expression in the form of a drawing, or more precisely, a series of drawings. For all his projects, Fabre makes countless working drawings following where his imagination takes him. Describing the creative process of *Tragedy of a Friendship* (2013), Fabre elucidates the crucial role of drawing as follows:

> It is thinking while drawing and drawing while thinking. My imagination runs away with me and I start to fly in my head and in my hand. It is a form of dancing with the wrists, very erotic actually, I still love to do that. And then things flow out of my hand that have nothing to do with

Wagner, but at times are associative. Then I start doing Wagner on a piece of paper, and on another piece of paper a sculpture is being formed, and then words follow, forming the beginning of a text ... This is the way my brain works, I guess. Ninety per cent of the drawings by the way does not end up in the performance.[49]

Parallel to the free flow of drawings and sketches, Fabre works with his actors in the rehearsal studios of Troubleyn on an exploration of the material. Improvisations are key to this preparatory stage. During the first weeks of the rehearsal period, the performers receive hundreds of improvisational tasks, with the purpose of methodically trawling the subject terrain and to find out which aspects could be used in the production. Fabre and his regular dramaturg Miet Martens give improvisation tasks, formulated in a sentence, a theorem or a question, which are investigated in small groups by all the performers. For these exploratory assignments, the performers are already required to enact them in space and with their bodies, since, to Fabre, veracity on stage can only be achieved when it also has a physical truth. The results of these tasks are immediately shown and in most cases thrown away, but gradually little elements and fragments are retained, which are then further elaborated.

In preparation for *Mount Olympus*, countless improvisations were dedicated to the notion of *sparagmos*, the ripping apart of the hero, the tearing of the flesh. But they also researched what a contemporary Dionysian rite would look like, how a cosmological origin could be envisaged, or how satyrs subject everything within reach to their sexual lust. During these sessions a great deal of material is generated that does not make it to the piece, but it is only through this daily, incessant, patient and insistent concentration that one can discover the entrance to a deeper imaginative world that, like a cave, holds the secrets that Fabre wants to unearth. It is a matter of tracing these subterranean tracks and excavating the energy from the space until it gradually starts to reveal itself. Obviously, one often gets lost in these explorations or promising avenues might turn out to be a dead end. Yet it is crucial to persist in recalibrating the focus and the direction, by asking – in the case of *Mount Olympus* – what the matter of tragedy still has to say to us today and how the substrata that have been broached can interweave into a theatrical form.

It is striking to see how Fabre, at the beginning of the rehearsal period, does not seem to start from fixed concepts or preconceived ideas – which he has, of course, but he is not necessarily sharing these with his team. Before the rehearsals for *Mount Olympus*, a lot of dramaturgical research had already been done and several fundamental choices that would buttress the project had been settled: Fabre wanted to examine how tragedy's heritage can be recast into a radical shape, a performance lasting twenty-four hours in which sleeping and waking are part of the staging. He wanted to bring the different generations of performers that helped him to build his career from early on, together with new and younger performers, in this way passing on the embodied knowledge of his acting method. These fundamental choices, as well as the long and intense preliminary research in preparation of the project,[50] did not prevent Fabre from restarting from square one when the rehearsals begin. He wanted to leave everything as open as possible for his performers, which is closely connected with his obsession to strive for physical transformation: 'Fabre's diversified recourse to improvisational techniques during his creation processes serves to destabilize and expand the limits of both the body and its imagination, in an attempt to expose what the human subject may become instead of reinforcing what it always has been'.[51]

Fabre's working methods result in a strongly collaborative process in which everyone is immersed in the creative laboratory and also responsible for the end result. A specific element of the creative process of *Mount Olympus* was that a couple of performers were asked to search for characters and passages in the great tradition of Greek tragedy that personally moved them. These texts, together with a selection of other extracts were adapted by writer Jeroen Olyslaegers who, just like the actors, would dive daily into this material over the course of a whole year. Halfway through that year, a new and vital layer was added to the already enormous collection of material: the dreaming and sleeping scenes, based on Jan Fabre's own poetical writings. In *Mount Olympus*, Fabre also wanted to explore the power of fatigue and the surrender to sleep. Again the performers threw themselves arduously into new improvisation sessions on dreams, insomnia and nightmares. These scenes, too, were gradually inserted into the immense construction of this performance.

Fabre's signature is, of course, present in all aspects of this creative process. In the morning, he gives body-training classes to his performers, based on his self-developed series of exercises,[52] with the intention to prepare them mentally, vocally and physically for the work on stage. He is the one who selects the usable material, filing and shaping it further until it has the right tension and expressive power. He suggests to the performers how to distribute or occupy the space better or gives instructions concerning timing. Throughout this long and daily creative process, he will design ideas for the scenography, lighting and costumes, which will be worked out by others. In *Mount Olympus*, he collaborates with composer Dag Taeldeman and scent designer Peter De Cupere, who develops several perfumes that will be blown across the audience by ventilators. But the thing that stands out the most, during that long and intense year of rehearsals, is Fabre's inexhaustible energy, his gigantic commitment, his own enormous physical effort, his desire for precision: all these reflect upon the actors, inviting and encouraging them to explore their own boundaries and descend even further into their own imagination, obsessions and taboos. His inseparable companion and dramaturg Miet Martens supports him (and the rest of the team) in this, keeping an overview of the development of the whole performance. Together with Jan Fabre, she will make the eventual montage of the hundreds of separate scenes that have arisen out of improvisation. She helps to structure the complex maze of material, making further divisions into groups and composing larger families and tales.

It is, of course, impossible to describe twenty-four hours of theatre in a couple of sentences, just as it is impossible to capture *Mount Olympus* with any usual terms or categories. Theatre, opera, performance, play, installation, *Gesamtkunstwerk* – it is not, or not completely, any of these. The piece rather has the shape and atmosphere of a rite, sometimes sliding into a bacchanal or a satyr play, while other scenes refer to tragic adventures of defeated heroes of Greek tragedies. Above all, it is the excessive duration that reigns. Time itself is the most important character in this production: *Mount Olympus* is like a maze, a kind of spongy space with holes in which one can suddenly fall, a timeslot in which endurance and fatigue affect the perception of the spectator at its core. As the fictional duration of the performance gradually overtakes real time, the audience ends up floating, somewhere in between sleeping and waking.

With this performance, Fabre wants to address the community – however abstract and even utopic this idea has become in our increasingly individualistic society: for twenty-four hours we are part of a rite, immersing us in mud and blood, but also in flower petals, oil and wine. It shows that, however bloodstained the guilt of humanity may be, there is always the possibility of a new beginning. The white sheets, the only costume of this performance, are covered with all the colours of the rainbow during the show but, in the end, they are an unblemished white again.

6

The Titan of Paradoxes

Hans-Thies Lehmann

If you consider the enormous scope of his achievements as an artist and as a theatre director, if you let pass before the mind's eye the aesthetic as well as intellectual claims that this oeuvre rightly substantiates and add the broad reception, the impact and influence of his work on the contemporary art of theatre since decades, then the obvious must be stated: Jan Fabre is a titan in the field of theatre and art. The protean character of his production has never stopped growing both in width and depth. Fabre is an incredibly energetic worker. He creates as author, director and choreographer, works in sculpture, drawing, painting and as an installation and performance artist. Theoretical writings – in-depth criticism as well as academic enquiry[1] – bear testimony to the impact his work has on how we think what the art of theatre is and can be. For this is the criterion which distinguishes the essential art of a given epoch from the mass of other works which in itself may be excellent, but does not acquire the same status: essential art influences the art making of others and changes the concept of art practice itself. Both are the case with Jan Fabre. The artistic strength and the depth of his work are both a convincing demonstration and proof that theatre can obtain an artistic value of the highest order when it leaves the protective sphere of dramatic conventions and relies solely on its dimension as performance, installation, choreography and on the power of its theatricality. It is essential theatre in the times after the dominating convention of dramatic framework.

Fabre's work is full of contradictions of a profoundly paradoxical nature. He is an *iconoclast* driven by a deep *iconophilia*. He is a *traditionalist* with a deep admiration for the traditions of great painting and art in general – but in all of his truly experimental work he appears as a reckless *innovator* time and again destroying or deconstructing tradition. Fabre's theatre reminds you of the most *ancient times*, of Greek tragedy and the imagery of the middle ages, of the bloody spectacles painted in the sixteenth century, of Bosch and Breughel, of the dwarfs and the deformed in works of Diego Velázquez and of baroque mourning plays and their allegories of melancholy. At the same time, Fabre is an artist who quotes all these precursors on his stage, as his work is replete with references and quotations, placing him in a typically post-modern lineage. This peculiar mixture of contemporaneity fused with references to the past places Fabre in an ambiguous position. While his cutting-edge work seems to honour Arthur Rimbaud's famous saying, 'Il faut être absolument moderne' ('One has to be absolutely modern'), he is also rooted in the most distant past. This quality lends to his productions the strange appeal of being hypermodern *and* archaic at the same time. They remind us of the figures of Giacometti (whose sculpture *The Palace at 4 o'clock in the Morning* was used by Fabre as the title for one of his works).[2] These figures seem to exist likewise in another dimension of time: their often elegant poses are reminders of *archaic* forms, of early Egyptian art, while they simultaneously present a completely *contemporaneous* shape, which speaks a language that immediately appeals to the sensibility of the viewer of today. The contours of these emaciated figures critically resonate with reigning bodily standards, but also draw attention to the very physicality of the sculptures. Not coincidentally, Giacometti's famous sculptural signature corresponds closely to Fabre's highly physical theatre that similarly restages, but also reshapes, dominant body images.

Fabre is a thoroughly *serious* artist with an obvious penchant for the tragic dimension of life. While he paints the contemporary world in rather black colours, time and again humour and the comic aspects of life surface in him and mark him out as a master of *satire*. Even though ancient tragedy was presented seperately from the satyr play that followed the tragic performance, in the spirit of post-modernity Fabre punctuates the tragic theatre with moments of satire.

Equally paradoxical is the relation of this director to the discourse of morality. The actions on Fabre's stage are often placed in a liminal state between real doings and fictive representational acts. The endless jumping and falling scene in *Het is theater zoals te verwachten en te voorzien was* (*This is Theatre as it was to be Expected and Foreseen*, 1982), for example, is an ostentatiously theatrical act that nevertheless creates a tangible level of pain, not only for the performers executing this 'task' but also for the audience exposed to the scene. We call it the 'irruption of the real'[3] when the observer is put into an insecure state, and must try to decide whether what she or he has perceived is to be considered a matter of aesthetic intention (that is, as fictitious) or as a real event – which would entail a different moral reaction.[4] This undecidability is a much stronger reflection of the nature of the live moment of spectating than the certainty that perhaps real pain is inflicted on a performer. Even though theatre (most commonly understood as a representational art form) may integrate elements of performance (which can be defined as 'real doings'), it remains theatre insofar as it cannot escape the framework of the theatrical apparatus together with all the conventions and expectations this brings along. But these conditions ensure, paradoxically, its *real* effectiveness. In other words, raising the question of what it means to be a spectator, constitutes an appeal to consider the responsibility connected to the act of spectating, which is much stronger than any direct moral plea that, because of its very straightforwardness, could be easily brushed aside.

Fabre can be called a *moralist detesting all moralism* of the simplistic kind, which is widespread in politics as well as in aesthetic matters. He is an artist who knows that no great theatre, no great art is possible without a *step beyond* what, in terms of morality, our conscious thinking can accept. Without the risk to hurt or to offend, art remains only a commodity. In the same way that Brecht could affirm that sport, real sport, begins only there where it becomes unhealthy,[5] one is tempted to say that art, real art, begins only where comfortable entertainment ends.

Jan Fabre constantly provokes protest from moralistic enemies of his work. But is he a provocateur? Clearly the answer is no, if you think of provocation as an end in itself. With the exception of some of his early solo-performances,[6] it is impossible to detect in his work any desire to provoke or to attack for the sake of attacking. Let us advance this thesis: morally reprehensible is not theatre containing as a content what may be judged morally unjustifiable, but rather theatre that remains harmless. This moral conviction speaks unmistakably from the work of Fabre: theatre that leaves us content with how we are in our so-called culture is unacceptable. For it is our 'culture' which all too often forgets – and wants to make us forget – the catastrophes befalling so many bodies across the globe. Fabre's art forbids any simple-minded 'yes' to this world of violence and terror, sadness and loss we live in. It is a world that has been abandoned by the gods, and we might encounter ourselves perhaps only at those moments and places where we share with each other the experience of loss, emptiness and mortality. For example, in the theatre.

Image and duration

Like various other leading directors in the Flemish theatre scene, such as Jan Lauwers or Guy Cassiers, Fabre started his career as a visual artist – he had already found recognition for his so-called 'Bic' drawings – before he turned to provocative solo performances and actions in the 1970s.[7] His renown as a visual artist and theatre director came quickly and grew steadily in the 1980s. In his own view, Fabre remains as much, and perhaps even more, a visual artist as a theatre director. His visual talent and the durational aspect of his work soon earned him the name of a new Robert Wilson, but it also became readily clear that he must be interpreted and recognized as a completely original and independent artist whose aesthetics differ deeply from the American's. It can perhaps be said with Stefan Hertmans that performance is something like the 'hard body' of Fabre's work, while visual art and theatre are its two wings.[8] The radicalism that is often aligned with 1960s performance art has always remained a motif in Fabre's theatre work. Since 1980, when his theatre work in the narrower sense of the word began with *Theater met een K is een kater* (*Theatre Written with a K is a Tomcat*), he has followed his path with impressive consistency, merging performance, theatre and dance in a perhaps unprecedented way, creating huge tableaux of theatre and solo performances, many of them with Els Deceukelier, soli which radiated a disconcerting fascination.[9]

One might say that, in the first stage of Fabre's career, exposition, reflection, aggression and 'working through' (in the Freudian sense of the word) were prominent. This certainly counts for his first trilogy[10] that reflects and exposes the nature of theatre, seen from the 'real time/real action'-adagium of early performance art. The dialectic of discipline and chaos in the bodily physical reality of the stage – which culminates, as Emil Hrvatin clearly demonstrates, in Fabre's dance works[11] – lead to a 'concrete theatre', which imposed a new way of spectating concentrating on the formal aspects of space, time, distance and distribution of elements. From the turn of the millennium onwards,[12] it is the reality of the organic body that became a central theme, while the performances grew into a kind of (self-)torturing inspection into vanitas

FIGURE 6.1 Requiem for a Metamorphosis, *2007 (Filip Van Roe).*

and mortality. This feast of the organic body within a decaying and dying temporality reached its climax in *Requiem for a Metamorphosis* (2007), in which professions related to death and rituals revolving around dying went hand-in-hand. But the foundational tension between form and body always remained present. In this respect, it is the *ob-scaena*, the unashamed presentation of the human animal, its naked and vulnerable skin, its liquids and its potential of entrancing beauty and of pain and humiliation, which gives to some scenes a sado-masochistic touch.

As a theatre director, Fabre is first of all an inventor of powerful images. Spectators will hardly forget them because they make a lasting imprint on the mind. Some of Fabre's images are so poignant that, according to some critical voices, they may be in danger of becoming too readable.[13] But here the dialectics and the difference between an image in the traditional sense of the term and the *durational theatre image* that Fabre creates, must be accounted for. The theatrical image (that is, the image on stage) belongs to a distinctly temporal art and this circumstance profoundly changes its structure. A brief thought-experiment may help to elucidate this. Sitting at the theatre watching a piece, it is easy to imagine that you have an impressive image before your eyes that is, indeed, quickly readable. Let us take an example from Fabre's seminal production *De macht der theaterlijke dwaasheden* (*The Power of Theatrical Madness*, 1984): two naked male performers with crowns dancing close together across the stage. Now you read – you read the king as incarnation of the individual subject; you notice

FIGURE 6.2 The Power of Theatrical Madness, *1984 (Patrick T. Sellitto).*

that the figure of the king is doubled and how this satirizes the pretended uniqueness of the 'king-subject'; you are reminded of the famous fairy tale about the naked emperor whose nakedness only the child dares to see; you read the homoerotic dimension. Now you have read the image and understood what it is about. What happens, however, is that the image *stays*, as Fabre deliberately decided to give time to the image and to let it go on. After a while, the ongoing duration of the real physical image on the stage literally corrodes its readability and the intellect gives way to something else as spectators start to realize that the image presented is obviously not only about the meaning just deciphered, but also about something which cannot be identified, but only experienced. *The meaning is not merely in the meaning*. The 'power of theatrical madness' relies in the timeline, in the durational aesthetics and the repetition this provokes, which is at work everywhere in Fabre's theatre. The durational aesthetics restores to the image the dimension of an apparition, the purity of the image as a given that overturns any act of understanding.

In durational performance, spectators have the rare chance to consciously perceive and experience the passing of time, taking up the position of a more or less patient observer. Thus, the long duration not only posits the real events on stage beyond or above any possible representation, but it also accentuates the actual theatre situation, the *communality* of players and viewers. The theatre as a coming together of all acting and observing participants, as a potential experience of passing real time together, is shifted to be the centre of attention. This communality is one of the most essential features of post-dramatic theatre. As I have argued elsewhere, 'Theatre means the collectively spent and used up lifetime in the collectively breathed air of that space in which the performing and the spectating take place.'[14] This specific form of sharing together a theatre space is completely different from traditional drama which, in principle, closes its fictive cosmos off from the audience, and even different from site-specific performance, where the focus lies in the fact that everyone, performers and audience alike, are *guests* of a specific location. In a durational performance, everyone inhabits the same time-space together, which creates a very specific experience.

Even if long duration has by now become an accepted element of the formal lingua franca of international theatre,[15] Fabre's approach remains quite exceptional. Already in some of his solo performances, Fabre was experimenting with duration as a key element in his work, such as in *Ilad of the Bic Art/The Bic Art Room* (1981) for which he enclosed himself for seventy-two hours in a gallery space. Also *This is Theatre as it was to be Expected and Foreseen* (1982) was based on a durational experience: the eight hours of a working day. This durational aspect culminated in Fabre's recent magnum opus *Mount Olympus: To Glorify the Cult of Tragedy* (2015), a production of twenty-four hours. It is for everyone involved (performers, technicians, collaborators and spectators) an exceptional experience. All the more when you take into account that the actors have a real sleep episode in the early hours of the morning, from which they are woken up after about twenty minutes – now in the role of delinquent, slumbering furies, they are driven back into action, into going after the scent of Orestes, Clytemnestra's murderer.

In *Mount Olympus*, as in earlier pieces by Fabre, durational aesthetics turn into an excess of time. We experience a transgression of limits, maybe an act of *hubris*, an excessive exertion of strength, of endurance and of devotion by the performers. This counts for the whole performance, but is certainly true for the last scene in which the whole cast, already completely exhausted, is engaged in a running scene, which has grown into a classic element of Fabre's work. While the performers are running on the spot, very fast and for an agonizingly long time, they are besmirched and bedaubed as in an action painting of Pollock. After sharing the space with these bodies for twenty-four hours, spectators can palpably feel the colossal effort of this seemingly simple task, reinforcing their position as witnesses to the boundless transgression that drives the entire performance of *Mount Olympus*.

Pain and risk

As a theatre director Fabre stands in the line from Artaud to Grotowski [see **Volume 5**] and the performance art which was driven by the conviction that only by inserting the 'real' body on stage, can the arts still reactivate the critical consciousness as well as the sensory experiences of human individuals. Aristotle already understood tragedy as an *attack* on the spectator: a means of achieving catharsis, through a passing fever of affect that makes the subject lose composure. Today one might say: with no violation of taboo, without risk of injury or insult, art cannot exist. In Fabre's theatrical practice, risk is a central artistic strategy. Already in his early solo performances he played at risk, deconstructing art as a gambling game.[16] His use of all kind of animals, such as parrots, frogs or cats, in several of his theatre productions is also risky. But the highest risk is undoubtedly connected to how Fabre rethinks human identity on stage, refiguring what we habitually call 'human' by digging deeply into the hollows of instinct, animality and social taboos.

Theatre that dedicates itself to the risk of transgression must necessarily aspire to touch something – painfully, embarrassingly, frighteningly and disturbingly – that has been forgotten or repressed, and which no longer reaches the surface of consciousness. Yet, time and again, moral reproach – which is, in fact, deeply amoral – often takes aim at precisely those artists who seek to go beyond the surface and stir up trouble in the forbidden recesses of culture. Ecstasy and transgression are motifs that place Jan Fabre in a fascinating affinity with the philosophy of Georges Bataille, who wrote extensively on how art can disclose what has been socially and culturally prohibited. In *The Tears of Eros*, Bataille elucidates the dynamics between prohibition and transgression as follows:

Prohibition gives to what it proscribes a meaning that in itself the prohibited action never had. A prohibited act invites transgression, without which the act would not have the wicked glow which is so seductive. In the transgression of the prohibition a spell is cast.[17]

To be sure, in an age when anything and everything can be discursified and made public, real taboos have become rare. All the same, they do exist; they are operative precisely in the realm of culture, as they re-emerge especially once they are or seem to be violated. As such, they recall the hubris and the desire to violate borders, which defines human beings. In Fabre's work, the violation of borders is often connected with sexuality, which is omnipresent, but never as a simple image of lust, let alone of pornographic imagination. Sexuality in Fabre's oeuvre rather epitomizes the desperation of being human: in an almost biblical manner, it becomes the place of black despair, a grotesque and tragi-comical search for a release or a salvation which remains forever out of reach. The clearest examples of this tension between religious and cultural oppression of sexuality and the longing towards a state of physical grace and freedom are to be found in *Orgy of Tolerance* (2009) and *Prometheus Landscape II* (2011). But the need for another body, a body free from dualities and moral codification, is a constant topic in Fabre's oeuvre. He thus dares to touch on the deepest questions of belief, salvation, the soul's revolt against its embodiment, and the body's refusal to be enchained by the mind.

FIGURE 6.3 Je suis sang, *2001 (Wonge Bergmann)*.

In Fabre's productions, the performer, even wearing clothes, is essentially naked. Bound up in the strictest, choreographic form, then again presenting its chaotic collapse, the endangered body faces us again and again. One may ridicule it, turn away in disgust or voice moral protest. However, it is also possible to experience mourning and then to shed 'tears of the body',[18] for and about its *animal* nature. This is perhaps the deeper reason for the constant presence of animals on Fabre's stage: to call to mind the animal nature of the human being – a dimension that we long for, but which remains closed off forever, like the gates to paradise. Together on stage, 'man and beast' recall a shared nature that civilization has progressively buried. Fabre, in this respect similar to the Socìetas Raffaello Sanzio and the work of Romeo Castellucci (see elsewhere in this volume), demonstrates an interest in animals because their presence offers the theatrical equivalent to a philosophical critique of a certain metaphysical 'humanism', which are caricatured in works of modern literature such as Franz Kafka and Heiner Müller. At the same time, the ongoing abuse of animals in the neoliberal age also gives a reason to mourn the souls inhabiting animal bodies, yearning for redemption from the deformation and disfigurement they experience.

Chaos and order

One of Fabre's working secrets is probably the absence of the fear of chaos. During the first phase of the conception of a work, he allows his mind and imagination constantly to be set on fire. He follows his wild imagination in his drawings that form an integral part of his artistic endeavour and he invites his performers to participate in this free-flowing research during the long and intense improvisation sessions with which every new creative process start. Only much later, the more structuralist Fabre enters the rehearsal stage with his unerring instinct for measure, symmetry and cold logic that shapes the actors' inventions to a strictly conceived order.

In this respect, Fabre's work shows a surprising similarity with the films of Stanley Kubrick, a director he highly admires and whose famous *2001: A Space Odyssey* (1968) he quotes directly in *Orgy of Tolerance* (2009). Both Kubrick and Fabre combine a deep sense for human affects which reign regardless of any moral inhibition and threaten man with self-destruction. At the same time, they also share an equally precise sense for some form of symbolic order, which is needed to tame the beast that the human being remains under a thin veil of civilization. There is a certain dualist, perhaps even manicheic mindset in these two artists who both thematize the unmediated clash of blind passion and strictest order, two foundational aspects of human existence. Both can be said to yield a profound artistic articulation of the basic experience and notions of our epoch. Moreover, both artists belong to the rare category of artists who are able to appeal to large audiences, while not giving into the temptation to compromise for the commercial demands that drive the entertainment business, at the expense of their artistic vision.

Beauty and *pharmakos*

For some time now, Fabre has sharpened his profile as the author of theatre texts. Like the trilogy *De keizer van het verlies* (*The Emperor of Loss*, 1996), *De koning van het plagiaat* (*The King of Plagiarism*, 2005), *De dienaar van de schoonheid* (*The Servant of Beauty*, 2010), they are mostly in the form of monologues and have been written for a specific actor or actress.[19] Highly self-reflective, they always question the role and function of art and the place of the artist. Fabre's texts have a ceremonial structure: often they sound like a litany repeating the same phrasings and motifs. Through the repetition – a strategy he also uses as a director – the texts have an almost intoxicating effect on the reader or spectator. Recurrent topics in his writings include loss and plagiarism, which have been of course amply discussed in the post-modern era. Besides these topics, there is one dominant theme that prevails: the quest for beauty. This is surprising because it is a classic gesture. However, this marriage of classic and radical post-modern aesthetics in Fabre is perhaps one of the few phenomena that gives some hope for a classic art of the future. The author portrays himself as the servant of beauty. Is beauty connected to a kind of masochist stance? Beauty appears personified as a severe dominatrix; the writer a servant. Beauty is his boss or patron. At the same time, this high quest for the sublime is often combined with a flavour of parody and the grotesque: in *The Servant of Beauty*, the main character (a puppeteer) is also constantly distracted by the all-too-human forms of his female puppets, which gives rise to crude and comical relief.

Beauty is an essential trope in Fabre's theatre, not only in his texts but also on his stage. Fabre likes to call his performers 'warriors of beauty'; he views their acts of often hardly protected self-humiliation as a kind of sacrifice. This is supposed to trigger what he calls 'catharsis', which he understands more as a physical than a mental process that involves both the performers and the spectators.[20] The term 'warrior of beauty' merits attention because it makes clear that, for Fabre, beauty is closely connected to something such as a fight, strife, even a war. In this respect, one would call him an unintentional Hegelian. It was Hegel who insisted that ideal beauty cannot be achieved by avoiding the negative – the pain, the wound, the violence, hardship, loss and, ultimately, death – but only by confronting it.[21]

Fabre throws light on the real body in order to present a critical counter-image to that all-too-contemporary body captured in the economy of seeming perfection. It is Jean Baudrillard who showed in theory what Fabre makes us understand physically and emotionally: paradoxically, the flipside of the civilization of idealized body images is the *denial* of the body.[22] The ideal of the perfect cosmetic body becomes readable as a protective shield against the becoming visible of the real body, which is made up of sweat, smells, urine, shit, trembling, weakness, fearful desires, illness, defects and abnormality.[23]

Like earlier founding fathers of the modern theatre Edward Gordon Craig and Stanisław Ignacy Witkiewicz, Fabre asks how in our world is beauty possible. It should be clear, however, that to Fabre, beauty is not the dull perfection of bodies functioning as the public relations agent of its owner. It is the Venus who only can ascend from the waves of danger and risk. Beauty without tragedy remains kitsch. And as Georges Bataille said: 'Eros is the tragic god'.[24] Craig related beauty to death and sorrow and made a beautiful remark that is also pertinent to Fabre's work: the one thing that remained with us from paradise and that is the wish to fly.[25] One of the most touching moments in Fabre's work appears in *Das Glas im Kopf wird vom Glas* (*The Glass in the Head Becomes Glass*, 1987), when the dancers in their heavy armour indicate in a wonderfully minimal gesture this hopeless desire: with their arms going up and down, they seem to express the desire to fly away from the heaviness of gravity.

Beauty cannot be simply positive – it even must prove indigestible for the conventional taste. For this reason, Fabre's aesthetics assigns a disturbing element to the image of beauty, like a poisonous green hue. Baroque still lifes come to mind, in which all kinds of disgusting creatures gnaw at blooming fruits and vegetables to signify, allegorically, *memento mori* and *vanitas*. There is a fascinating 'aesthetic of poisoning' at work,[26] which Fabre describes by referring to the Greek notion of *pharmakon*: 'the Greek word "pharmakon" means both a curing drug and a dangerous poison. That's the ambiguity of my work method and of my performances. To actors, dancers and audience alike, my theatre is an aesthetic of poison that just might cure'.[27]

The quest for beauty, together with the responsibility that goes hand-in-hand with this task, gives the artist in Fabre's view the aura of a hero. In so doing, he repeats (to all appearances unwittingly) a gesture of a number of artists in the dawn of modernity, who saw themselves as tragic heroes: as a Prometheus who steals the fire from the gods and brings it to mankind. Prometheus pays for his disobedience with inhuman suffering: he is chained for eternity to the chaucasian rock where day-by-day the vulture sent by Zeus hacks his entrails and feeds on his liver, which regenerates every night.[28]

From Hölderlin to Georg Trakl, a large number of radical artists founded (and perhaps stabilized) their persona through this type of identification, where mostly also the saviour Christ came into play. In Fabre's view, these heroes represent a paradoxical legitimate hubris. They dare to overstep the border of what is possible and allowed to the human being, even though they end up suffering for this transgression. They cannot do otherwise, because in the mythological imagination, these heroes are already, in their very being, a transgression: half-gods bred by divine fathers and human mothers, their essence is to exist as borderliners between humanity and deity. This makes them emblems of the artist. In his text *We Need Heroes Now* (2010), Fabre offers his personal description of how he envisages this convoluted figure of the martyr-hero-artist:

> Where is our hero? / Who will give his all for us / Even his life / To make his uniqueness count / To give his mortality / worth and meaning / and to escape from oblivion ... That triumphant hero/is a holy martyr / He doesn't conquer / He arrives / He is the bringer of the colour of freedom / And embodies the tragic beauty / of defeat / He will die / but he won't be dead.[29]

Theatre – a space of shared affectivity

Fabre sees himself – and, indeed, he objectively stands – in a tradition of radical theatre initiated by the 'Messias'[30] of modernity, Antonin Artaud, who coined for his Theatre of Cruelty the phrase of an 'affective athleticism'.[31] This athleticism should be exhibited by actors, a term that itself alludes to the *agon,* the competition between athletes in antiquity. It is relatively easy to draw the lines of influence running from Artaud's visionary view on theatre to Fabre's work. Most conspicuous among these is the conjunction of the Artaudian ekstasis (which involves extreme bodily experiences) and an equally extreme formalization of the theatre.[32]

It would be interesting to compare systematically all aspects of the theatrical visions of Fabre and Artaud. Such a comparison would be all the more revealing if it included Nietzsche's notions of the apollonian, the dionysian and the socratic, which he introduces in *The Birth of Tragedy*.[33] Such an enquiry may also reveal interesting differences in terms of artistic mentality. Fabre approaches theatre as a visual artist, though it must be acknowledged that this visual dimension is certainly important in Artaud's theatre as well. But if you remember the famous recording where his voice breaks, turning into sheer noise and sound,[34] you understand that it is above all a matter of the auditive dimensions of the chaotic breakdown of all meaning. By comparison, the special force of Fabre's theatre is a result of his visual energy, which he knows to mediate with sound, rhythm and language, and which results in performances with an enormous affective load.

In his aesthetics of affect, theatre becomes the space for *shared and reflected affectivity*, while the frame of dramatic representation breaks open. Like in the famous performance *The Artist is Present* (MOMA, 2010) of Fabre's friend Marina Abramović, for which she invited visitors to sit in a silent exchange of gaze with her, the spectator of Fabre's theatre is *addressed*: when the bodies on stage go to their limits, when taboos of sexuality are broken – then spectators cannot just turn their heads, while the piece itself also looks upon them. Fabre's so-called 'warriors of beauty' demonstrate the potential of the body, the myriad of possibilities in which it can transform to become something else. In this way, they appeal to an audience to affect their own physical and spiritual potentialities sleeping or slumbering in them. They gaze at the audience, not in silence, but in turmoil.

Fabre's theatre, which is so extremely physical in appearance, stems from a deep immersion in the physical being and it provokes the audience to take part in this endeavour. The bodily side of being transforms paradoxically into an unexpected spirituality. Fabre's use of the physicality of the body is not only meant to connect with and accept its inborn animality, the instincts and capacities of all its senses, but also to give rise to its spiritual powers. According to Jan Fabre, this spiritual being is the result of an inner conflict:

> I think man is the representation of two different kind of cults: the cult of immobility and the cult of movement … From that inner conflict the divine can be generated too. Sometimes, at the height of the conflict, you can feel the struggle coming to an end and a unification of spirit and body emerging. Then a spiritual being originates that converges with mind, matter and action.[35]

This is, perhaps, the sum of the Fabrian paradoxes: a spiritual physicality or physical spirituality. In this sense, his theatre can be described as a thoroughly materialist enterprise, but only without coupling his materialism to the messianic search for redemption that propelled Walter Benjamin's famous historical materialism.[36] In Fabre's work, this redemption remains absent, insofar as the bodies and creatures populating his pieces, but also the audiences attending his performances always fall back in the same cycle of rising up and stumbling down. From this perspective, what the director Fabre strives to create can be called – borrowing a notion from Heiner Müller – a *theatre of resurrection*.[37] Leading the mind to the edge of chaos, this theatre seems to confront us with the symbolic death of all meaning. *Angel of Death* (2003) and also other works have a strong apocalyptic tone, as they circle around a limit, a last moment where humans play at the edge of disappearance. But in the last moment – or, in a 'last minute rescue', so to speak – its resurrection takes place again and again through a momentaneous return of order and structure. Yet Fabre never has it the easy way: the resurrection is never guaranteed, never certain.

Post-dramatic tragedy

Even though, formally speaking, Fabre is an artist whose work is of a decidedly *post-dramatic* character,[38] he repeatedly returns to the great tragic plays of antiquity. And clearly his interest in the tragic tradition is growing rather than diminishing. After two studies on Prometheus, he realized a work which in many ways can be seen as something like a summa of his theatrical achievement and which I briefly referred to previously: *Mount Olympus: To*

Glorify the Cult of Tragedy (2015). For decades, and with remarkable consistency, Jan Fabre has advanced a theatrical practice as well as a discourse in which he ceaselessly searched for the possible forms a genuine tragic theatre could assume in the present day. Indeed, the director explicitly connected his work to ancient tragedy on several occasions long before his production *Mount Olympus*.[39]

This gesture is far from self-evident if you consider the critical voices you sometimes hear declaring that tragedy is dead. What such critics think of, however, is only the museum of tragic drama, which attempts to embalm a historical but outdated legacy. But Fabre is not interested at all in accurate restagings nor in easy re-interpretations of old dramas. However, he does disagree with the opinion that the core principles of tragedy have lost their credibility and force. In *Mount Olympus*, we do not find a narration of tragic fables employing the devices of representation. The intellectual contradictions of the tragedies are transformed into performative scenes, mostly monologues. The basic gestures of tragic theatre, read from a contemporary perspective, are presented in an excessive duration and with a radical mobilization of bodies: rite and choric dance, monologues of lamentation and bloody sacrifices, use of internal organs and sexuality, the tension between the collective and individuals. Tragedy comes alive here without the frame of dramatic storytelling.

It may be that in some future time we will understand how close the theatre of Fabre is to the heritage of the great Greek tragedies. After all, Attic tragedy was essentially not about the recounting of mythological narrations.

FIGURE 6.4 Mount Olympus, *2015 (Wonge Bergmann).*

At the heart of the ancient tragic theatre, which Fabre invokes, was the merciless exposition of the human body as a metaphorically naked sacrificial victim of the gods. It was about a visibility symbolized by the solitary appearance of the hero on the stage under the frightening gaze of the gods (and the audience), which makes the hero appear in all his vulnerability. The essence of the newly invented form of theatre was to point to the moment when the individual hero dared to step outside the collective. The basic theatrical experience of tragedy in its origin was this confrontation of the lonely voice of the hero with the chorus of the collective, not the dramatic story, which was generally known to the audience anyway.

In the secularized world of today, Jan Fabre strives to make the specific tragic experience accessible for the modern mind. What happens in *Mount Olympus* is the transformation of the tragic fables into physically crucial tests for the actual participating performers. It is the *tragedy of the body* which is enacted, and this formula is true for Fabre's work as a whole. It is the inner conflict between the skeleton and the flesh – the cult of immobility and of movement, the tension between form and energy – that is articulated throughout his oeuvre. Out of the rift between these tensions, there emerges a body as the site of pain and lust, which heroically oversteps the human limitations and enters into a scene of total breakdown – a body, in short, that balances between death and desire.

Jan Fabre's theatre succeeds in expressing the beauty and extreme fragility of human existence that is woven into the fabric of natural bodily being. Tragic theatre is not a gameplay about intellectual problems, but it is about a spiritual and physical need to step over boundaries, like Icarus whose tragic dream to reach the sun turned him into the martyr-hero of hubris. In Fabre's hands, any preconceived interpretations of ancient tragedy in terms of rationally 'thinkable' conflicts are devoured by a radical embodiment, only to reappear as a motif of physical existence. Consequently, the theatre of Jan Fabre remains in the great tradition of tragedy as a protest. As the German director Jürgen Fehling once said, 'there will be theatre as long as there will be the protest of the human being against the forever unjust Gods'. This protest is also an aesthetic endeavour, if we keep in mind Heiner Müller's tantalizing pun that 'it is the task of art to make reality impossible'.[40]

NOTES

Introduction to the Series

1   Simon Shepherd, *Direction* (Basingstoke: Palgrave Macmillan, 2012).

2   P.P. Howe, *The Repertory Theatre: A Record & a Criticism* (London: Martin Secker, 1910).

3   Alexander Dean, *Little Theatre Organization and Management: For Community, University and School* (New York: Appleton, 1926), 297–8.

4   Constance D'Arcy Mackay, *The Little Theatre in the United States* (New York: H. Holt, 1917).

5   William Lyon Phelps, *The Twentieth Century Theatre: Observations on the Contemporary English and American Stage* (New York: Macmillan, 1920); Hiram Kelly Moderwell, *Theatre of Today* (New York: Dodd, Mead & Co., 1914, 1923); Dean, *Little Theatre Organization and Management*.

Introduction to Volume 8

1   A historical overview of this lineage can be found in James Roose-Evans, *Experimental Theatre: From Stanislavsky to Peter Brook*, 4th edn, revised and updated (London: Routledge, 1989).

2   Mark Salber Phillips, *On Historical Distance* (New Haven, CT: Yale University Press, 2013), 203.

3   'In postdramatic forms of theatre,' Lehmann explains, 'staged text (*if* text is staged) is merely a component with equal rights in a gestic, musical, visual, etc., total composition' (*Postdramatic Theatre*, trans. Karen Jurs-Munby (Abingdon and New York: Routledge, 2006), 46).

4   It should be noted that, even though Lehmann introduces 'postdramatic theatre' as an overarching term for a new paradigm in theatre, he does offer a more refined categorization by elaborating what he calls a 'panorama of postdramatic theatre' (Lehmann, *Postdramatic Theatre*, 68–133). Remarkably enough, however, this chapter suffers from a reverse effect: rather than generalization, it is the accumulation of various subcategories that dazzles the reader and seemingly streamlines an inherently heterogeneous practice in an artificially delineated model of analysis. As one reviewer notes, 'his resulting construct has the potential to function as coercively as the terms of dramatic theatre to limit rather than expand how we perceive, define, and

critique contemporary theatre' (Jeanne Willcoxon, 'Postdramatic Theatre (review)', *Theatre Topics* 18, no. 2 (2008): 248).

5   See, for instance, Erika Fischer-Lichte, who writes that 'theatre is a communal institution, representing and establishing relationships which fulfill social functions. The drama, the production, and the location of the performance all contribute to these functions ... Theatre historians regularly acknowledge that theatre and society are closely related' (Erika Fischer-Lichte, *The Show and the Gaze of Theatre: A European Perspective* (Iowa City: University of Iowa Press, 1997), 25).

6   Methodological approaches to theatre historiography are, of course, a recurrent topic of discussion in theatre studies. Useful overviews can be found in Gary Jay Williams, ed., *Theatre Histories: An Introduction*, 2nd edn (Abingdon and New York: Routledge, 2006); 'Theater History and Historiography', in Janelle Reinelt and Joseph Roach (eds), *Critical Theory and Performance* (Ann Arbor: The University of Michigan Press, 2007), 191–257; Thomas Postlewait, *The Cambridge Introduction to Theatre Historiography* (Cambridge: Cambridge University Press, 2009); R.W. Vince, 'Theatre History as an Academic Discipline', in Thomas Postlewait and Bruce A. McConachie (eds), *Interpreting the Theatrical Past* (Iowa: University of Iowa Press, 1989), 1–18; Jacky Bratton, 'Theatre History Today', in *New Readings in Theatre History* (Cambridge: Cambridge University Press, 2003), 3–16; Rebecca Schneider, *Theatre & History* (Houndmills: Palgrave Macmillan, 2014).

7   For insightful discussions of the societal turmoil and various upheavals during the 1960s, see Martin Klimke and Joachim Scharloth, eds, *1968 in Europe: A History of Protest and Activism, 1956–1977* (Houndmills: Palgrave Macmillan, 2008); Ingo Cornils and Sarah Waters, eds, *Memories of 1968: International Perspectives* (Bern: Peter Lang, 2010); Daniel J. Sherman, Ruud Van Dijk, Jasmine Alinder and A. Aneesh, eds, *The Long 1968: Revisions and New Perspectives* (Bloomington and Indianapolis: Indiana University Press, 2013).

8   The influence of the Thatcher era on theatre is charted in D. Keith Peacock, *Thatcher's Theatre: British Theatre and Drama in the Eighties* (Westport, CT: Greenwood Press, 1999).

9   Peter Stein is one of the directors included in Volume 7 of this *Great European Stage Directors* series.

10   For more on twentieth-century political theatre, see Ingrid Gilcher-Holtey, Dorothea Kraus and Franziska Schößler, eds, *Politisches Theater nach 1968: Regie, Dramatik und Organisation* (Frankfurt and New York: Campus Verlag, 2006).

11   David Bradby and David Williams, *Director's Theatre* (New York: Macmillan Education, 1988), 15.

12   See Christopher Innes and Maria Shevtsova, 'Total Theatre: The Director as *auteur*', in *The Cambridge Introduction to Theatre Directing* (Cambridge: Cambridge University Press, 2013), 147–84.

13   Avra Sidiropolou, *Authoring Performance: The Director in Contemporary Theatre* (Houndmills: Palgrave Macmillan, 2011), 75.

14   See, for instance, Luk Van Den Dries and Thomas Crombez, 'Jan Fabre and tg STAN: Two Models of Postdramatic Theatre in the Avant-Garde Tradition', *Contemporary Theatre Review* 20, no. 4 (2010): 421–31.

15 Cf. Alison Oddey, *Devising Theatre: A Practical and Theoretical Handbook* (Abingdon and New York: Routledge, 1994); Deirdre Heddon and Jane Milling, eds, *Devising Performance: A Critical History* (Houndmills: Palgrave Macmillan, 2005).

16 Peter Boenisch, *Directing Scenes and Senses: The Thinking of Regie* (Manchester: Manchester University Press, 2015), 7; second italics added.

17 For a discussion of Lessing's view on dramaturgy and his legacy, as well as a broader historical overview of how the role of the dramaturgy has developed from the late eighteenth century onwards, see Mary Luckhurst, *Dramaturgy: A Revolution in the Theatre* (Cambridge: Cambridge University Press, 2006).

18 Katalin Trencsény and Bernadette Cochrane, 'Foreword – New Dramaturgy: A Post-Mimetic, Intercultural, Process-Conscious Paradigm', in *New Dramaturgy: International Perspectives on Theory and Practice* (London: Bloomsbury, 2014), xiii. For other recent volumes surveying recent developments in dramaturgy, see Katharina Pewny, Johan Callens and Jeroen Coppens, eds, *Dramaturgies in the New Millennium: Relationality, Performativity and Potentiality*, Schriftenreihe Forum Modernes Theater, 44 (Tübingen: Narr Verlag, 2014); Magda Romanska, ed., *The Routledge Companion to Dramaturgy* (Abingdon and New York: Routledge, 2015); Peter Eckersall, Helena Grehan and Edward Scheer, eds, *New Media Dramaturgy: Performance, Media and New-Materialism* (Houndmills: Palgrave Macmillan, 2017).

19 The lack of a consistent archivization of theatre works was a vital impetus for the research project *The Didascalic Imagination*, which we – together with a team of other researchers – have conducted at the University of Antwerp in collaboration with the Vrije Universiteit Brussels from 2013 until 2016. The project's aim was to investigate the changed function and form of director's notebooks in contemporary theatre. While such working documents provide rich resources to gain insight into the creative processes preceding the actual performances, there are hardly any sustained efforts to preserve them. See Frederik Le Roy, Edith Cassiers, Thomas Crombez and Luk Van Den Dries, 'Tracing Creation: The Director's Notebook as Genetic Document of the Postdramatic Creative Process', *Contemporary Theatre Review* 26, no. 4 (2016): 468–84.

20 For more on the objectives, mission and workings of the Pina Bausch Foundation, see Marc Wagenbach and Pina Bausch Foundation, eds, *Tanz erben: Pina lädt ein* (Bielefeld: transcript Verlag, 2014). See also Mariama Diagne's contribution to this volume.

21 ARCH stands for 'Archival Research and Cultural Heritage: The Theatre Archive of Socìetas Raffaello Sanzio'. More information can be found on the project's website: http://www.arch-srs.com/home (accessed 9 June 2017). For her chapter in this volume, Dr Eleni Papalexiou, who is one of the principal investigators of this project, draws heavily on the often unpublished resources they have collected during their primary research.

22 Jeanne Bovet and Yves Jubinville, 'Le répertoire: lieu de mémoire, lieu de création', *L'Annuaire Théâtral*, no. 53–54 (2013): 9.

23   The Tanztheater Wuppertal has currently about fifty original Bausch pieces in their repertoire, including famous works such as *Nelken* (1982), *Auf dem Gebrige hat man ein Geschrei gehört* (1984) or *Palermo Palermo* (1989). In 2015, Romeo Castellucci restaged his *Oresteia (an organic comedy?)*, exactly ten years after its 1995 premiere. In 2012, Jan Fabre returned to *This is theatre like it was to be expected and foreseen* (1982) as well as *The power of theatrical madness* (1984), two key works that launched him into the international theatre scene.

24   For a more elaborate discussion of the potential validity of the term 're-enactment' as a generic token for deliberate reinventions of performance pieces, see Timmy De Laet, 'Dancing Metamemories', *Performance Research* 17, no. 3 (2012): 102–8.

25   Raimund Hoghe, *Pina Bausch. Tanztheatergeschichten* (Frankfurt am Main: Suhrkamp Taschenbuch, 1986), 20.

26   Thomas Crombez, Jelle Koopmans, Frank Peeters, Luk Van Den Dries and Karel Vanhaesebrouck, *Theater. Een Westerse geschiedenis* (Leuven: Lannoo Campus, 2015), 308.

27   For a more extensive discussion of this scene from *Café Müller* as well as Bausch's use of repetition in general, see Ramsay Burt, 'Repetition: Brown, Bausch and De Keersmaeker', in *Judson Dance Theater: Performative Traces* (Abingdon and New York: Routledge, 2006), 138–61.

28   In his analysis of the piece, Emil Hrvatin elucidates how all twenty-four scenes are based on the principle of repetition. See Emil Hrvatin, *Jan Fabre: La discipline du chaos, le chaos de la discipline* (Éditions Armand Collin, Centre International de Bagnolet, 1994), 37. Also Stefan Hertmans has shown how repetition is a central strategy not only in Fabre's theatre performances but also in his visual art. See Stefan Hertmans, *Engel van de metamorfose: Over het werk van Jan Fabre* (Amsterdam: Meulenhoff, 2002), 47–54.

29   Hrvatin, *Jan Fabre*, 40.

30   Freddy Decreus, 'Over de esthetisering van geweld. Mythe en trauma in het theater van Castellucci', *Tetradion*, no. 25 (2016): 181.

31   Romeo Castellucci, 'Il pellegrino della materia', in Romeo Castellucci, Chiara Guidi and Claudia Castellucci (eds), *Epopea della polvere. Il teatro della Societas Raffaello Sanzio 1992–1999* (Milan: Ubulibri, 2001), 272.

32   Timmy De Laet and Edith Cassiers, 'The Regenerative Ruination of Romeo Castellucci', *Performance Research* 20, no. 3 (2015): 18.

33   Umberto Eco, *The Open Work*, trans. Anna Cancogni (Cambridge, MA: Harvard University Press, 1989).

34   Lehmann, *Postdramatic Theatre*, 87.

35   See, for instance, Claire Swyzen and Kurt Vanhoutte, eds, *Het statuut van de tekst in het postdramatische theater* (Brussels: University Press Antwerp, 2011).

36   Lehmann, *Postdramatic Theatre*, 148.

37   See Jacques Derrida, *Margins of Philosophy*, trans. Alan Bass (Chicago: The University of Chicago Press, 1982), 15.

38 Sigrid Bousset, 'In stilte achter glas', in *Mestkever van de verbeelding. Over Jan Fabre*, ed. Sigrid Bousset (Amsterdam: De Bezige Bij, 1994), 18.

39 Gabrielle Cody, 'Woman Man, Dog, Tree: Two Decades of Intimate and Monumental Bodies in Pina Bausch's Tanztheater', *TDR* 42, no. 2 (1998): 123.

40 Elinor Fuchs, *The Death of Character: Perspectives on Theater after Modernism* (Bloomington and Indianapolis: Indiana University Press, 1996).

41 Fuchs, *The Death of Character*, 92.

42 Hoghe, *Pina Bausch*, 37–38.

43 Luk Van Den Dries, *Corpus Jan Fabre. Observations of a Creative Process* (Ghent: Imschoot, Ghent, 2006), 17.

44 The call for auditions was issued online. Available at: https:// contemporaryperformance.com/2015/02/19/opportunities-auditions-for-romeo-castelluccis-oresteia/(accessed 14 June 2017).

Chapter 1

1 'Tanztheater' as a term had a different meaning in West and East Germany during the Cold War years, because it was applied to two distinct types of choreographic practices that differed in their aesthetics as well as their approach to dance technique. In East Germany, choreographers such as Tom Schilling continued to work with pointe shoes and the movement vocabulary of classical ballet, with a slight touch of modern dance. In West Germany, artists such as Pina Bausch, Reinhild Hoffmann, Gerhard Bohner and others refused to conform to the aesthetics and narrative structures of ballet, turning instead to pedestrian movement and finding inspiration in everyday life. For further definitions of 'Tanztheater' as a term, see Norbert Servos, 'V. Tanztheater. 1. Definition und theoretische Grundlagen', in *Musik in Geschichte und Gegenwart. Allgemeine Enzyklopädie der Musik*, ed. Finscher Ludwig, 2nd edn, vol. 9 (Kassel, Stuttgart: Bärenreiter-Verlag, J.-B.-Metzler, 1998), 355–9. For a compilation on several members of the German 'Tanztheater', see Susanne Schlicher, *TanzTheater. Traditionen und Freiheiten, Pina Bausch, Gerhard Bohner, Reinhild Hoffmann, Hans Kresnik, Susanne Linke* (Reinbek bei Hamburg: Rowohlt, 1987).

2 Royd Climenhaga's collection of articles on Bausch's time in Germany, the UK and the US tracing her early life and career until her passing, is a rich source for researchers. See *The Pina Bausch Sourcebook: The Making of Tanztheater*, ed. Royd Climenhaga (London and New York: Routledge, 2013). The following contributions in that volume are worth consulting: Deborah Jowitt, 'Please Do It Again, Do It Again, Again, Again [1984]' 137–41; Susan Allene Manning, 'An American Perspective on Tanztheater [1986]', 31–44; Marianne van Kerkhoven, 'The Weight of Time [1991]', 278–87; and Susan Kozel, 'Bausch and Phenomenology [1993/94]', 300–6.

3 The Pina Bausch Foundation was founded by her son, Salomon Bausch, who currently still serves as its director. The Foundation preserves Bausch's heritage

and also initiates artistic projects that help to keep the choreographer's legacy alive. See: www.pinabausch.org/en/home (accessed 2 March 2017).

4   Pina Bausch, 'Was mich bewegt' (What Moves Me), speech made on 11 November 2007. Available online: www.pinabausch.org/en/pina/what-moves-me (accessed 2 March 2017). The speech was prepared together with dramaturgs and authors that worked closely with Bausch, a procedure that reflects how also her choreographic work was often a montage of different scenes and images for which, as I will discuss in this chapter, the dancer's own input was essential. There are, in fact, two versions of the speech: next to 'Was mich bewegt', there is the longer speech 'Etwas finden, was keiner Frage bedarf' (To find something that does not require a question), held on 12 November 2007 at the 2007 Kyoto Prize Workshop in Arts and Philosophy, Inamori Foundation. Both speeches are reprinted in Stefan Koldehoff and Pina Bausch Foundation, eds, *O-Ton Pina Bausch: Interviews und Reden* (Wädenswil: nimbusbooks, 2016), 305, 317–33.

5   One oft-quoted phrase from the Kyoto Workshop speech is 'Dance, dance, otherwise we are lost'. It is rarely mentioned, however, that the expression is actually not Bausch's own. She herself is quoting here a young girl whom she met when visiting Romany families in Greece. Bausch recalls how, during the visit, some family members began to dance and to sing, while she was too shy to participate. She would remember the words the little girl said to get her to dance all of her life.

6   Jooss formed the Folkwang School out of his former school, Westfälische Akademie (Westphalian Academy). In 1933, Jooss left Germany overnight with the entire ensemble to protect Jewish dancers in his company from deportation. One year later, Jooss founded the Jooss-Leeder School of Dance at Dartington Hall, England. When he returned to Essen in 1949, he continued his work at the re-opened Folkwang School. Jooss also founded and directed an important dance ensemble, the Folkwang-Tanztheater-Experimentalstudio (which was later renamed the Folkwang Tanzstudio and subsequently the Folkwang Ballet), where members such as Pina Bausch, Jéan Cébron, Susanne Linke, Reinhild Hoffmann and many others, created, performed and experimented with new approaches to dance. This history is recounted in Patricia Stöckemann, *Etwas ganz Neues muß nun entstehen. Kurt Jooss und das Tanztheater* (Munich: Kieser Verlag, 2001).

7   For a discussion of the relationships between expressionist dance, modern dance and dance theatre, see Sabine Huschka, 'Pina Bausch, Mary Wigman, and the Aesthetic of "Being Moved"', in *New German Dance Studies*, ed. Susan Manning and Lucia Ruprecht (Chicago: University of Illinois Press, 2012), 182–99. For more on modern dance, see also Sabine Huschka, *Moderner Tanz. Stile, Konzepte, Utopien* (Reinbek: Rowohlt Verlag, 2002).

8   One of the key principles advanced by Laban was to use and shift the weight of the body while forming tension. Several modern dance artists still recall the importance of the relationship between effort and shape. Reinhild Hoffmann, for instance, who was a student of Jooss at the Folkwang School, pointed this out during an unrecorded conversation on 10 November 2015 at the Berlin State Ballet.

9   Stephan Brinkmann, *Bewegung Erinnern: Gedächtnisformen im Tanz* (Bielefeld: transcript Verlag, 2013), 21, 229–41.

10 Sabine Huschka, *Merce Cunningham und der Moderne Tanz. Körperkonzepte, Choreographie und Tanzästhetik* (Würzburg: Königshausen & Neumann, 2000), 95. See also Stöckemann, *Etwas ganz Neues*, 378.

11 There is actually no adequate English translation for the term 'Handlungsballett', which derives from the French 'ballet d'action' and refers to a genre in classical ballet that is often said to be inaugurated in 1760 by Jean Georges Noverre. In that year, Noverre wrote a manifest in which he proclaims that ballet has the same narrative potential to tell stories as theatrical drama.

12 A detailed analysis of the piece can be found in Suzanne K. Walther, *Dance of Death: Kurt Jooss and the Weimar Years* (Chur: Harwood Academic, 1994).

13 Corvino himself also danced for the Ballet Jooss during the Second World War in South America and had been trained in the Cecchetti dance technique, which was also taught by Antony Tudor. Corvino became director of the dance section at the Juilliard School in New York City in 1952 and served for nearly forty years. In 1959, he gave, next to Tudor and others, workshops at the Folkwang School in Essen. When Bausch became director of the Tanztheater Wuppertal, she held on to this line of classical ballet by asking Corvino to give daily classes for her company. According to company member Barbara Kaufmann, Corvino was not just 'giving' a warm-up, but 'teaching' a class (personal conversation with author on 15 January 2017). After Corvino's death in 2005, this tradition has been continued by former ensemble members as well as by Corvino's two daughters, Andra Corvino and Ernesta Corvino. The memories of their father are part of his biography written by Dawn Lillie, *Equipose: The Life and Work of Alfredo Corvino* (New York: Dance & Movement Press, 2009).

14 For an excellent analysis of Tudor's ballets, see Judith Chazin-Bennahum, *The Ballets of Antony Tudor: Studies in Psyche and Satire* (New York: Oxford University Press, 1994).

15 Chazin-Bennahum, *The Ballets of Antony Tudor*, 6. See also Alastair Macaulay, 'Under Analysis: The Psychology of Tudor's Ballets', *The New York Times*, 11 May 2008. Available online: www.nytimes.com/2008/05/11/arts/dance/11maca.html (accessed 12 March 2017).

16 'Etwas finden, was keiner Frage bedarf' (To find something that does not require a question), held on 12 November 2007 at the 2007 Kyoto Prize Workshop in Arts and Philosophy, Inamori Foundation.

17 Later during her career, she also directed the section of dance at the Folkwang University of the Arts.

18 According to playbills and photographs, Bausch has performed the role of the grandmother herself, in addition to ballet dancer Charlotte Butler, who left the ensemble after the first season.

19 Dominique Mercy, as cited in Nadine Meisner, 'Come Dance with Me [1992]', reprinted in Royd Climenhaga Word, ed., *The Pina Bausch Sourcebook*, 169.

20 *Wind von West*, which had its last staging in 1979, has been reconstructed by the Pina Bausch Foundation and the Tanztheater Wuppertal in 2013, together with students from the Folkwang School and the Juilliard School. The project was supported and also documented by the Tanzfonds Erbe (The German Dance Heritage Fund). On the Tanzfonds' website, one can find various interviews and videos documenting the rehearsal process, which was directed by former dancers of the Tanztheater Wuppertal. Some of them, including Jo Ann Endicott and John Griffin, had performed in the piece when it first premiered. For more on the reconstruction, see: http://tanzfonds.de/en/project/documentation-2013/wind-von-west-cantata/ (accessed 1 March 2017).

21 For more on the dream as a structural component of Bausch's choreographic work, see Royd Climenhaga Word's chapter in this volume.

22 There is a video recording of Bausch's *Le Sacre*, which was released in 2012 and shows a performance by the company in 1989, with a recorded version of the orchestra performing Stravinsky's score and conducted by Pierre Boulez. In Wuppertal, *Le Sacre* had always been staged with recorded music due to the fact that the orchestra pit was too small for the required number of musicians. Cf. Pina Bausch, 'Was mich bewegt', 11 November 2007, reprinted Koldehoff and Pina Bausch Foundation, eds, *O-Ton Pina Bausch*, 308.

23 Nijinsky developed the dance for the Chosen One together with his sister Bronislava Nijinska. She remembered the rehearsals as follows: 'I felt that my body must draw into itself, must absorb the fury of the hurricane. Strong, brusque, spontaneous movements seemed to fight the elements ... The Chosen Maiden danced as if possessed, as she must until her frenzied dance in the primitive sacrificial ritual kills her'. Bronislava Nijinska, *Early Memoirs*, translated and edited by Irina Nijinska and Jean Rawlinson (Durham, NC, and London: Duke University Press, 1992), 450.

24 The phrase 'Crime against Grace' is the title of Millicent Hodson's book in which she reports on the reconstruction of *Le Sacre* she created in 1987 together with dance historian Millicent Hodson and architect Kenneth Archer. See Millicent Hodson, *Nijinsky's Crime Against Grace: Reconstruction Score of the Original Choreography for Le Sacre du Printemps* (Stuyvesant, NY: Pendragon Press, 1996). Soon after its premiere, the Ballets Russes stopped performing *Le Sacre*, but the score and other pieces of historical evidence survived. The accuracy of Hodson and Archer's reading of these fragments has been contested, partly because, from the late 1990s onwards, dance scholars increasingly began to question the very possibility of reconstructing dance. See, for instance, Hanna Järvinen, '"They Never Dance": The Choreography of Le Sacre du Printemps, 1913', *AVANT* 4, no. 3 (2013): 69–108. Various choreographers have developed different tributes to Nijinsky's key avant-garde piece, including Pina Bausch who could not have seen Nijinsky's choreography, as it was only reconstructed in 1987.

25 Jo Ann Endicott, 'Inside Pina's *The Rite of Spring*', in *Le Sacre du Printemps*, [DVD], ed. L'Arche Éditeur and Pina Bausch Foundation, production of the

television broadcasting channel ZDF from 1978 at Tanztheater Wuppertal (Paris: L'Arche Éditeur, 2012), 68–69.

26   Endicott, 'Inside Pina's *The Rite of Spring*', 68.

27   Mariama Diagne, 'Atem Holen. Szenen vom Ende des Lebens im Tanztheater', in *Transmortale. Sterben, Tod und Trauer in der neueren Forschung*, ed. Moritz Buchner and Anna-Maria Gotz (Cologne, Weimar, Vienna: Böhlau Verlag, 2016), 213.

28   Ciane Fernandes, 'Appendix A: Interview with Dancer Ruth Amarante', in *Pina Bausch and the Wuppertal Dance Theater: The Aesthetics of Repetition and Transformation* (New York: Peter Lang Publishing, 2005), 117.

29   Endicott, 'Inside Pina's *The Rite of Spring*', 69.

30   Gitta Barthel in conversation with Gabriele Klein, 'Die Performanz des Rituals', in Gabriele Brandstetter and Gabriele Klein, eds, *Methoden der Tanzwissenschaft. Modellanalysen zu Pina Bauschs 'Le Sacre du Printemps/ Das Frühlingsopfer'*, 2nd edn (Bielefeld: transcript Verlag), 88.

31   *Dark Elegies* was originally created in 1937 in London, before Tudor emigrated to New York where the piece premiered in 1940. Comparing the movement material of this choreography to Bausch's early pieces, one might presume that Bausch did see performances of *Dark Elegies* in New York, either during her scholarship, or her later visit in 1972.

32   See Brandstetter and Klein, eds, *Methoden der Tanzwissenschaft*. Research on the piece benefits from a greater accessibility of sources, such as the video of Bausch's *Le Sacre* released in 2013.

33   Norbert Servos, *Pina Bausch: Dance Theatre* (Munich: Kieser Verlag, 2008), 7.

34   German dance critic and chronicler Horst Koegler cited this comment two years later in his article: 'Tanztheater Wuppertal [1979]', reprinted in Climenhaga, *The Pina Bausch Sourcebook*, 187.

35   Christina Thurner, unpublished paper presented at the conference *Dance Future II. Fokus PINA BAUSCH*, held at Kampnagel Internationale Kulturfabrik GmbH, 26–29 January 2017, Hamburg.

36   Narrative and weightlessness are typical elements of nineteenth-century Romantic classical ballets, such as *Giselle* (1841), *Swan Lake* (1877/1895) or *The Nutcracker* (1892), which often used the movement vocabulary of ballet to 'narrate' fairy tales.

37   Bausch experimented with the genre of theatrical revues quite early. In 1974, for example, she choreographed the revue *Zwei Krawatten* (Two Ties).

38   Pina Bausch, 'Man weiß gar nicht, wo die Phantasie einen hintreibt [2007]', interview with Jean-Marc Adolphe, reprinted in Koldehoff and Pina Bausch Foundation, eds, *O-Ton Pina Bausch*, 279.

39   Pina Bausch, 'Wenn ich mir ganz genau zuhöre, macht sich das Stück selber [1998]', interview with Roger Willemsen, (*Willemsens' Woche*), reprinted in Koldehoff and Pina Bausch Foundation, *O-Ton Pina Bausch*, 188.

40   Ibid., 189.

41   Ibid.

42 Pina Bausch, 'Tanz ist die einzig wirkliche Sprache [1990]', interview with Norbert Servos, reprinted in Koldehoff and Pina Bausch Foundation, *O-Ton Pina Bausch*, 138.

43 The question is cited in the notes that Raimund Hoghe, who worked as a dramaturg for Bausch from 1980 to 1990, took during rehearsals in Rome for *Viktor*. See Raimund Hoghe, 'Rom, Notizen. Beobachtungen während der Proben zu Viktor in Rom', in *Pina Bausch: Tanztheatergeschichten* (Frankfurt a.M.: Suhrkamp, 1986), 149. The English translation of the quote provided here is from Heidi Gilpin, 'Amputation, Dismembered Identities, and the Rhythms of Elimination: Reading Pina Bausch', in *Other Germanies: Questioning Identity in Women's Literature and Art*, ed. Karen Jankowsky (New York: State University of New York Press, 1997), 178.

44 Hoghe, *Pina Bausch. Tanztheatergeschichten*, 149; Gilpin, 'Amputation, Dismembered Identities, and the Rhythms of Elimination', 179.

45 Gilpin, 'Amputation, Dismembered Identities, and the Rhythms of Elimination', 179.

46 Bausch, 'Wenn ich mir ganz genau zuhöre', 188.

47 Ibid.

48 To be entirely accurate, it should be mentioned that Bausch and her cast of dancers and actors did read Shakespeare's *Macbeth* as well as Heiner Müller's 1971 reinterpretation of the play.

49 Glenn Loney, '"I pick my dancers as people" – Pina Bausch discusses her work with the Wuppertal Dance Theatre [1985]', reprinted in Climenhaga, *The Pina Bausch Sourcebook*, 89.

50 Actress Mechthild Grossmann is cited on this matter in Anne Linsel, 'Pina Bauschs Wildgruber', *k.west. Das Kulturmagazin des Westens. Magazin für Kunst, Kultur, Gesellschaft* 12 (2008). Available online: www.kulturwest. de/buehne/detailseite/artikel/pina-bauschs-wildgruber/(accessed 22 October 2017).

51 Servos, *Pina Bausch*, 60.

52 Moving in a diagonal across the stage is typically used in dance to highlight a dramatic or extraordinary development within the piece, but Bausch and Jooss only retain the formal structure of the movement without wanting to narrate something.

53 Pina Bausch, 'Eine gewisse Erregung dabei/Bin im Moment bei den Gefühlen [1976]', interview with Stephen Locke, reprinted in Koldehoff and Pina Bausch Foundation, eds, *O-Ton Pina Bausch*, 57.

54 Hedwig Müller and Claudia Rosiny, 'Ein Stückchen Tanztheater. Eine Szene von Pina Bausch', *Tanzdrama* 12, no. 3 (1990): 5.

55 See, for instance, Janet Adelman, '"Born of Woman": Fantasies of Maternal Power in *Macbeth*', in *Bloom's Modern Critical Interpretations: William Shakespeare's Macbeth* (new edition), ed. Harold Bloom (New York: Bloom's Literary Criticism, [1987] 2010), 33–59; Stephanie Chamberlain, 'Fantasizing Infanticide: Lady Macbeth and the Murdering Mother in Early Modern England', *College Literature* 32, no. 3 (2005): 72–91.

56 The title of the piece, *Danzón*, is a Spanish word that, as Norbert Servos explains, 'refers to a dancing fury, an obsession', pointing out that 'in Mexico it is used to describe a steadily accelerating dance, similar to a bolero'. Bausch's *Danzón* is a collage of various themes and motifs composed as dreamlike moments that evoke everyday situations in an exaggerate manner: two adults swinging on a sea saw, several undressed women enjoying a bath, or a man, wearing a huge diaper like a 'monster baby'. Servos, *Pina Bausch*, 153.

57 *Danzón* is, after *Fritz* (1974) and *Café Müller* (1978), the third and last piece in which Bausch appeared on stage as a dancer in her own works. During her lifetime, Bausch's part in *Café Müller* was also performed by company member Helena Pikone. After Bausch's death, the solo in *Danzón* was performed by a male dancer, Aleš Ćuček. According to Barbara Kaufmann, who has been a member of the Tanztheater Wuppertal since 1987, there was a similar sense of bodily doubleness when Ćuček performed the solo (personal conversation with the author, May 2014).

58 Pina Bausch, 'Etwas finden, was keiner Frage bedarf', 324.

59 José Gil 'The Paradoxical Body', in *Planes of Composition. Dance, Theory and the Global*, ed. Andre Lepecki and Jenn Joy (Calcutta, London: Seagull Books, 2009), 94.

60 Gil, 'The Paradoxical Body', 100. The icosahedron has, as Gil explains, 'the shape of an invisible polyhedron with 20 faces whose points of intersection mark the possible directions of the movements of a dancer (who remains at its center)' (100). Next to Laban's understanding of space, Gil's argument is based on the phenomenology of Maurice Merleau-Ponty and the philosophical concepts of 'multiplicities of fusion' and 'body without organs' (BwO), as theorized by Gilles Deleuze and Félix Guattari in *Anti-Oedipus: Capitalism and Schizophrenia I*, trans. Robert Hurley, Mark Seem and Helen R. Lane (Minneapolis: University of Minnesota Press, 1993) or in *A Thousand Plateaus: Capitalism and Schizophrenia*, trans. Brian Massumi (Minneapolis: University of Minnesota Press, 1993).

61 Erin Manning, *Always More than One: Individuation's Dance* (Durham, NC, and London: Duke University Press, 2013), 17.

62 Ibid.

63 Ibid., 19.

64 Pina Bausch and Kyomi Ichida, 'Dialogue during a rehearsal of *Le Sacre du Printemps* [1989]', in Pina Bausch, *Probe Sacre*, DVD and booklet (Paris: L'Arche Editeur, 2013), 49.

65 This rehearsal is also thoroughly analysed by dance scholar Gabriele Brandstetter, who maintains that the transmission of movement from one body to another can be understood as the passing on of one's own bodily 'signature'. Brandstetter draws on Jacques Derrida's 1972 essay 'Signature, Événement, Contexte' (Signature, Event, Context), in which he critically rethinks the relationship between speech and writing as well as the function of the signature therein. See Gabriele Brandstetter, 'Pina Bauschs *Das Frühlingsopfer*.

Signatur – Übertragung – Kontext', in Brandstetter and Brandstetter, eds, *Methoden der Tanzwissenschaft*, 95–124.

66 Alice Schwarzer, 'Ein Stück für Pina Bausch', interview with Mechthild Grossmann, *EMMA* 1 (2010): 50. It is worth pointing out that, while the German preposition 'von' in the phrase 'Ein Stück von Pina Bausch' would translate in English as 'by' rather than as 'of', it actually captures more accurately the meaning behind these seemingly random subtitles, since it indicates – as Grossmann rightly claims – how each piece of Bausch is a part *of* her own body as well as of her entire body *of* work.

67 Ibid.

68 Gil, 'The Paradoxical Body', 96.

69 Given the responsibilities Bausch granted to the dancers of her company in transmitting her work, it is not surprising that also their memories provide an important source of information on her pieces and working methods. This becomes particularly clear in Stephan Brinkmann's *Bewegung Erinnern: Gedächtnisformen im Tanz* (Bielefeld: transcript Verlag, 2012). As a former dancer at the Tanztheater Wuppertal, Brinkmann inserts his memories of rehearsals of *Le Sacre du Printemps* into a wider discourse on corporeal knowledge and physical memory, drawing on the philosophical writings of Henri Bergson and Maurice Merleau-Ponty, as well as on neuroscientific research on muscle memory.

70 The English translations of these works given here are the same as those mentioned on the website of the Pina Bausch Foundation. Literally translated, however, the titles would actually read as 'Kontakthof with Ladies and Gentlemen over 65' and 'Kontakthof with Teenagers over 14'. As it is impossible to find an adequate English term for 'Kontakthof', the titles retain the original German word (which actually does not exist in the German language). Its literal meaning would be a 'yard' or a 'garden of contact', thus pointing to a space where people encounter each other.

71 Together with former artistic director Ivan Liska, the director of the Bavarian State Ballet, Bettina Wagner-Bergelt, initiated the collaboration with the Tanztheater Wuppertal. Dance scholar Katja Schneider and her students followed the entire process by taking (not yet published) notes.

72 A notable exception is the performance of *Café Müller* by the Dutch theatre collective De Warme Winkel (The Warm Store). The title of their piece, *De Warme Winkel speelt de Warme Winkel* (The Warm Store plays the Warm Store, 2017) is misleading, since it mockingly announces that they will play themselves, while the second half of the work consists of a remarkably accurate reconstruction of Bausch's choreography, even though none of them are trained as professional dancers. The reconstruction is preceded by an astute discussion among the members of the collective on issues of appropriation and copying in the arts, which retroactively frames their redoing of *Café Müller* in larger debates related to originality and art history.

73 Labanotation is a system developed by Rudolf von Laban (1879–1958) to notate and analyse movement. In the 1910s, Laban worked together with Mary Wigman to start formulating several key parameters of movement, which he expanded in 1920s by collaborating with Kurt Jooss. His notational system consists of

abstract symbols for the direction, duration and quality of movement as well as for the body part executing it. During his exile in London, Laban began to apply his notation to bodily practices not related to dance, with the aim of optimizing the periodic movements done by factory workers during their shifts.

74 A recent publication demonstrates in detail the importance of Bausch being a dancer at first, but an archivist at last: *Inheriting Dance: An Invitation from Pina*, ed. Marc Wagenbach (Bielefeld: transcript Verlag, 2014). Inspired by Bausch's own method of archiving her dances, the lavishly illustrated book continues her work by collecting various essays, interviews and articles that provide an overview of the efforts that have been done after Pina Bausch passed away to keep her legacy alive. Some of the contributions also go deeper into the specific challenges that dance poses for archiving and historicizing a choreographic oeuvre such as Bausch's.

75 The exhibition *Pina Bausch and the Dance Theatre* was first presented at the Bundeskunsthalle in Bonn (from 4 March–24 July 2016) and then travelled to a second venue, the Martin Gropius Bau in Berlin (from 16 September 2016–9 January 2017). It was curated by Rein Wolfs (Director of the Bundeskunsthalle), Salomon Bausch (son of Pina Bausch and Chairman of the Board of Trustees of the Pina Bausch Foundation) and Miriam Leysner (dancer and dance scholar). For more information, see the extensive exhibition website: www.pina-bausch-ausstellung.de/en/index.html (accessed 18 October 2017). There is also a book that accompanied the exhibition, from which I have been drawing for the present chapter, as it contains various interviews with and texts from Pina Bausch. See Koldehoff and Pina Bausch Foundation, eds, *O-Ton Pina Bausch*.

76 The warm-ups were held by dancers Jo Ann Endicott, Cristiana Morganti, Pascal Merighi and Paul White. In addition to these activities, in which visitors could participate, the exhibition also included short choreographies created by Wuppertal dancers and inspired by the company's repertoire, while public lectures and talks gave audiences the opportunity to engage in the broader critical discourse on Bausch's oeuvre.

77 The actual rehearsal studio in Wuppertal was not open to the public, except for the few movie directors who were allowed to document parts of the rehearsal processes. See, for example, *Was tun Pina Bausch und ihre Tänzer in Wuppertal* (dir. Klaus Wildenhahn, 1982). The film gives an impression of creating and rehearsing the piece *Walzer* (1982).

78 José Gil cited in Manning, *Always More than One*, 13.

79 Pina Bausch, *Etwas finden*, 324.

Chapter 2

1 A search of the thirty-nine essays collected in Climenhaga, *The Pina Bausch Sourcebook* resulted in fifteen separate instances where Bausch's work was described as 'dream-like' or the structure was considered from the perspective of dreams.

2   Joan Ross Acocella, 'Reviews: New York City', *Dance Magazine* (March 1986): 22.

3   See in particular Sigmund Freud, *The Interpretation of Dreams* (New York: Basic Books, 2010). Freud's book was originally published in 1900 and translated into English by James Strachey in 1955.

4   States outlines his theory of dreams in *The Rhetoric of Dreams* and extends his analysis to the principles of narrativity in *Dreaming and Storytelling*.

5   Bert O. States, *The Rhetoric of Dreams* (Ithaca, NY: Cornell University Press, 1993), 57.

6   I use the term 'feeling structure' to indicate the kind of cognitive pathway States describes. My term and the way States eploys the concept are more fundamental patterns of experience than the 'structures of feeling' described by Raymond Williams as critical tropes used to analyse narrative structure, particularly in film.

7   Bert O. States, *Dreaming and Storytelling* (Ithaca, NY: Cornell University Press, 1993), 9–10.

8   Ibid., 92.

9   W.J.T. Mitchell, *Iconology: Image, Text, Ideology* (Chicago: University of Chicago Press, 1986), 9.

10   States, *The Rhetoric of Dreams*, 86.

11   States, *Dreaming and Storytelling*, 102.

12   Hedwig Müller and Norbert Servos, 'Expressionism? "Ausdruckstanz" and the New Dance Theatre in Germany', in *Festival International de Nouvelle Danse, Montreal, Souvenir Program*, trans. Michael Vensky-Stalling (1986), 13. This mode of performance corresponds to what Hans-Thies Lehmann would later theorize as 'postdramatic theatre'.

13   States, *The Rhetoric of Dreams*, 47.

14   See in particular his essays defining his concept of the Theatre and Cruelty in Antonin Artaud, *The Theater and Its Double* (New York: Grove Press, 1958), 84–100.

15   Theatre is usually thought of as existing in the dramatic mode where characters perform indicated action with spoken dialogue that creates the illusion of another time and place other than the one on stage. That theatrical convention was challenged with theatre in the epic mode that emphasized a use of the presence that stood alongside of the created action on stage to establish a commentary on the developed world. Artaud sought to return to the immediacy of the lyrical mode that defined more ritualistic theatrical practices, where events simply took place on stage without establishing an illusory structure or needing to stand alongside of that for conscious commentary. The work and legacy of Stanislavski is discussed in the first volume of this *Great Stage Directors* series, whereas Brecht is featured in the second volume.

16   Artaud, *The Theater and Its Double*, 85.

17 See Hans Ulrich Gumbrecht's distinction between 'meaning' and 'presence' in *Production of Presence: What Meaning Cannot Convey* (Stanford, CA: Stanford University Press, 2003).

18 Samuel Beckett, 'Dante ... Bruno. Vico. Joyce', in *Finnegans Wake: A Symposium - Exagmination Round His Incamination of Work in Progress* [... *&c.*] (Paris: Shakespeare & Co., 1929; facs. rep. edn, NY: New Directions, 1972), 1–22.

19 For more on the delineation of the subject through personal systems of categorizing similar experiences, see Paul Smith, *Discerning the Subject* (Minneapolis: University of Minnesota Press, 1988).

20 Anna Kisselgoff, 'Pina Bausch's "Palermo, Palermo" Explores a World beyond Logic', *New York Times* (30 September 1991): C13.

21 Quoted in Ann Daly, 'Tanztheater: The Thrill of the Lynch Mob or the Rage of Woman?', *The Drama Review: TDR* 30, no. 2 (1986): 50.

22 See also the chapter by Mariama Diagne in this volume.

23 States, *The Rhetoric of Dreams*, 87.

24 George Lakoff and Mark Johnson, *Metaphors We Live By* (Chicago: University of Chicago Press, 1980), 72.

25 States quotes Arthur Quinn's discussion of the 'real potentialities within our language, within ourselves' and goes further to quote Mary Warnock's seminal work *Imagination*: 'It now becomes clear (and indeed it was clear all along) that in talking about images we are talking not only about a class of *things which represent*, but about a species of thinking'. States, *The Rhetoric of Dreams*, 88.

26 M.H. Abrams, *A Glossary of Literary Terms*, 5th edn (Fort Worth: Holt, Rinehart and Winston, Inc., 1988), 66.

27 States, *The Rhetoric of Dreams*, 99. States is quoting from Kenneth Burke, *The Philosophy of Literary Form: Studies in Symbolic Action*. Rev. edn (New York: Random House, 1957).

28 Norbert Servos, *Pina Bausch Wuppertal Dance Theater or the Art of Training a Goldfish* (Cologne: Ballet-Bühnen Verlag, 1984), 146.

29 Ann Daly, 'Tanztheater', 54.

30 States, *The Rhetoric of Dreams*, 107.

31 Ibid., 108.

32 James Hillman, 'An Inquiry into Image', *Spring: An Annual of Archetypal Psychology and Jungian Thought* (1977), 80.

33 Mark Johnson, *The Body in the Mind: The Bodily Basis of Meaning, Imagination, and Reason* (Chicago: University of Chicago Press, 1987), 44, quoted in States, *Dreaming and Storytelling*, 136n9.

34 Johnson, *The Body in the Mind*, 29, quoted in States, *Dreaming and Storytelling*, 136n9. In the dream, image groupings of speaking to a group without wearing clothes, or showing up to school where you are told there is an exam that you are not prepared for, or the actor's nightmare of appearing on stage and not knowing your lines, all act as image schemata for feelings of insecurity we may encounter around a variety of much more complex experiences.

35 Abrams, *A Glossary of Literary Terms*, 65.

36 States, *The Rhetoric of Dreams*, 182.

37 Ibid., 145.

38 Joan Ross Acocella, 'Bausch's Inferno', *Art in America* (January 1992): 52.

39 Nadine Meisner, 'Come Dance with Me', *Dance and Dancers* (September/ October 1992): 15.

40 Ivor A. Richards, *Philosophy of Rhetoric* (New York and London: Oxford University Press, 1936).

41 Richards discusses the nature of the tenor and vehicle of metaphoric structure at length in the chapter on Metaphor in Richards, *Philosophy of Rhetoric*, 89–114.

42 Servos, *Pina Bausch Wuppertal Dance Theatre*, 21.

43 States, *Dreaming and Storytelling*, 68. States is quoting from Douglas R. Hofstadter, *Metamagical Themas: Questing for the Essence of Mind and Pattern* (New York: Bantam Books, 1986), 655.

44 Ibid., 69.

45 Ibid., 99.

46 Ibid.

47 See, for instance, Acocella, 52, described above.

48 Servos, *Pina Bausch Wuppertal Dance Theater*, 22.

49 Pina Bausch's *Die sieben Todsünden* was a reinterpretation of the music theatre piece *Die sieben Todsünden der Kleinburger* (*The Seven Deadly Sins of the Bourgeoisie*), created by Kurt Weill (music) and Bertolt Brecht (text) in 1933. Bausch showed the piece as a double-bill with *Fürchtet Euch nicht* (Don't be Afraid), in which she staged a range of songs from other Brecht-Weill productions.

50 Ibid., 42–43.

51 See, in particular, the work of Tadeusz Kantor or structures proposed, if not necessarily acted upon, by Artaud in his proposal for a Theater of Cruelty or Stanislas Ignacy Witkiewicz in his imaging of a Theatre of Pure Form. In dance, many of Mary Wigman's works derived from the same base in patterns of feeling.

52 Leonetta Bentivoglio, 'Dance of the Present, Art of the Future', *Ballett International* 8, no. 12 (1990): 19.

53 Servos, *Pina Bausch Wuppertal Dance Theater*, 22.

54 Ibid.

55 Barbara Confino, 'The Theater of Images: Pina Bausch and the Expressionist Temperament', *Cityweek* (18 July 1988): 42.

56 States, *The Rhetoric of Dreams*, 42.

57 *Was Tun Pina Bausch und Ihrer Tänzer in Wuppertal?* Videocassette. Dir. Klaus Wildenhahn. Inter Nationes, 1983. 60 minutes. The quotes mentioned in the following passage are taken from this video recording.

58 Oliver Sacks, *The Man Who Mistook His Wife for a Hat* (New York: Touchstone, 1988), 110–11, quoted in Marianne Van Kerkhoven, 'The Weight of Time', *Ballet International* 14, no. 2 (1991): 65.

59   Edmund Husserl coined the term *Empfindnisse*, derived from the German
     empfinden, which means to feel, perceive, have a sensation of (with the
     senses; to be aware or conscious or sensible of, sense with the mind). See
     Cassell's German Dictionary, rev. edn, ed. Harold T. Betteridge (New York:
     Macmillan Publishing Company, 1978). Husserl used the term to describe the
     completeness of a lived sensation as being a construction of past experience
     and more than simple sensory imput. Edmund Husserl, *Ideas: General
     Introduction to Pure Phenomenology*, rev. edn (Abingdon: Routledge, 2012).

60   Van Kerkhoven, 'The Weight of Time', 65.

61   States, *The Rhetoric of Dreams*, 176.

62   The quote of Sally Banes first appeared in *Eye International* (March 1986) and
     was reprinted in 'What the Critics Say about Tanztheater', *The Drama Review:
     TDR* 30, no. 2 (Summer 1986): 83.

63   States, *The Rhetoric of Dreams*, 144.

64   Van Kerkhoven, 'The Weight of Time', 64.

65   Barbara Confino, 'The Theatre of Images: Pina Bausch and the Expressionist
     Temperament', *Cityweek* (18 July 1988): 42.

66   Deborah Jowitt, 'Please Do it Again, Do it Again, Again … ', *Village Voice* (3
     July 1984): 93.

Chapter 3

1   Romeo Castellucci, 'Art is Fire', interview with Niki Orfanou, *Ef* 44, no. 3 (25
     June 2015): 5.

2   Marco De Marinis, 'Introduzione. Il teatro elementale di Romeo
     Castellucci', in *Toccare il reale*, ed. Piersandra Di Matteo (Naples:
     Cronopio, 2015), 24.

3   Antonin Artaud, *Le théâtre et son double* (Paris: Gallimard, 1938), 144.

4   Piersandra Di Matteo, 'A Stage Philosopher. A Portrait of Romeo Castellucci',
     Octave magazine (October 2015). Available online: www.operadeparis.fr/
     magazine/un-philosophe-de-la-scene (accessed 17 October 2015).

5   For more on the archetypical relation between watching and being watched,
     see: Eleni Papalexiou, 'The Dramaturgies of the Gaze: Strategies of Vision
     and Optical Revelations in the Theatre of Romeo Castellucci and the Socìetas
     Raffaello Sanzio', in *Theatre as Voyeurism: The Pleasures of Watching*, ed.
     George Rodosthenous (Houndmills: Palgrave Macmillan, 2015), 50–1.

6   *Archivio* and *ARCH: Archival Research & Cultural Heritage. The Theatre
     Archive of Socìetas Raffaello Sanzio* are two research projects which run in Italy,
     Greece and other European countries. They conduct primary research in the
     field of theatre genetics and cultural documentation, focusing on the work of
     Socìetas Raffaello Sanzio. See www.arch-srs.com (accessed 13 November 2017).

7   Romeo Castellucci, 'Romeo Castellucci Speaks to *Vimadonna* on the Value
     of Research', *Vimadonna*, interview by Ioanna Zymariti (5 February 2016).

Available online: www.tovima.gr/vimadonna/prosopa/article/?aid=774267 (accessed 5 February 2016).

8   Romeo Castellucci, interview by Eleni Papalexiou (Cesena, 15 July 2016).

9   In December 1979, for example, Romeo Castellucci participated together with his sister Claudia Castellucci and Paolo Guidi in the group exhibition *Pittura & Scenografia* (Painting & Scenography), at the Palazzo Capitano in Cesena. They presented the works *Spazzi Alterati; Residui dal Fondo* and *Una Finestra Aperta sul mondo* (Altered Spaces; Bottom Residues; An Open Window to the World).

10 Soc. Raffaello Sanzio, 'Come e dove si sono riconosciuti', unpublished typed document, 1986, in *ARCH-The Archive of Socìetas Raffaello Sanzio*, item 19_03_06.

11 The plays that were staged by the 'Explò – Esplorazione Teatro' include Beckett's *Happy Days* and *Krapp's Last Tape* (1978), Ibsen's *Rosmersholm* (1979), Ionesco's *The Killing Game* (1980) and Camus' *The Misunderstanding* (1980).

12 Chiara Guidi, cited in Federico Tiezzi, 'L'anima mentale e l'anima passionale', *WeStuff* 5 (1 September 1986): 69.

13 Amelio 'Memè' Perlini (1947–2017) was an Italian cinema and theatre director, known as a leading figure of the Italian avant-garde movement of the 1970s and 1980s. For a more detailed description of his profile, see Jane E. House, 'Perlini, Amelio (Memè)', in *The Oxford Companion to Theatre and Performance*, ed. Dennis Kennedy (Oxford: Oxford University Press, 2010), 460. His staging of Dallagiacoma's play *Ligabue Antonio: Commedia in 27 quadri* won the Premio Nazionale Riccione ATER for 1978–1979.

14 Angelo Dallagiacoma, interview by Giorgia Penzo, *Città Teatro* (5 August 2013).

15 Claudia Castellucci, 'La sindrome di Platone nel teatro delle operazioni', in Romeo Castellucci, Chiara Guidi and Claudia Castellucci, eds, *Epopea della polvere. Il teatro della Socìetas Raffaello Sanzio 1992–1999* (Milan: Ubulibri, 2001), 289.

16 Raffaello Sanzio, *Cenno*, in *ARCH*, 01_01_03.

17 Romeo Castellucci, interview by Eleni Papalexiou, (Cesena, 15 July 2016).

18 Ibid.

19 Società Raffaello Sanzio, 'Mitobiografia', in *XXXII Festival Internazionale del Teatro* (Venezia: La Biennale di Venezia, 1984): 188–90, also in *ARCH*, item 13_03_15.

20 Giuseppe Bartolucci, 'Raffaello Sanzio', *FlashArt. La prima Rivista d'arte in Europa* (February–March 1982): 4–5.

21 Comune di Ferrara, 'La Raffaello Sanzio, *Persia-Mondo 1a1*', printed leaflet in *ARCH*, item 03_01_09, 1981.

22 Paolo Guidi in the interview 'Questioni raffaellesche', *Il Patalogo 6, Annuario dello spettacolo 1983* (Milan: Ubulibri, 1983). Reprinted in *Società Raffaello*

Sanzio, Il teatro iconoclasta, ed. Tiziana Colusso (Ravenna: Edizioni Essegi, 1989), 92.

23   Società Raffaello Sanzio, 'Mitobiografia', 188–90.

24   Cf. Nico Garrone, 'Mondo-Persia 1a1 del gruppo Raffaello Sanzio', *La Reppublica* (13 January 1982); Franco Quadri, 'In teatro '82. 60 Festival di Polverigi', *Panorama* (9 August 1982): 15; Lorenzo Mango, 'Il pensiero marginale', *Lapis/Arte*, year 5, no. 5 (1984): 39.

25   The performance travelled to various cities of Emilia Romagna (Cesena, Forlimpopoli, Ravenna, Bologna), as well as to Florence, Rome, Turin and the Polverigi Festival.

26   Cf. related correspondence from 1981, *ARCH*, item 02_08_02_001, as well as Francesca Alinovi, 'Il teatro dell'aventura', in *Una generazione postmoderna*, ed. Renato Barilli, Fulvio Irace and Francesca Alinovi (Milan: Mazzotta, 1982), 33–6, 140.

27   Some of these reviews are included in the collection of articles by Pier Vittorio Tondelli, *Un weekend postmoderno. Cronache dagli anni ottanta* (Milan: Bompiani, 1990).

28   Oliviero Ponte Di Pino, *Il nuovo teatro italiano 1975–1988* (Firenze: La casa Usher, 1988), 17.

29   Eleni Papalexiou, Avra Xepapadakou and Valia Vraka, 'L'archive théâtrale de la Socìetas Raffaello Sanzio: un pèlerinage à la matière', in the Proceedings of the International Conference *Processus de création et archives du spectacle vivant: manque de traces ou risque d'inflation mémorielle?* (Rennes: Presses Universitaires de Rennes, forthcoming).

30   Chiara Guidi as cited in Tiezzi, 'L'anima mentale e l'anima passionale', 68.

31   Soc. Raffaello Sanzio, 'Popolo Zuppo. Spettacolo prodotto della Soc. Raffaello Sanzio', official poster, *ARCH*, 1982, item 06_03_01.

32   JKY, 'Popolo Zuppo', unpublished typed document, *ARCH*, 1982, item 06_01_01.

33   Soc. Raffaello Sanzio, 'Popolo Zuppo. Spettacolo prodotto della Soc. Raffaello Sanzio'.

34   Paolo Landi, 'Santarcangelo. Gli orizzonti in oscillazione del giovane teatro', *Il Manifesto* (14 September 1982).

35   Socìetas Raffaello Sanzio, 'Mitobiografia', 188–90.

36   Romeo Castellucci, interview by Eleni Papalexiou (Cesena, 15 July 2016).

37   Socìetas Raffaello Sanzio, '*Oratoria n. 2: Raptus*', in *Nuove Sensibilità Teatrali, Rassegna Di Spettacoli*, ed. Carlo Infante (Rome: Comuna di Roma. Assessorato alla Cultura-Spaziozero, Senzorbita, 1984), 23.

38   Socìetas Raffaello Sanzio, 'Mitobiografia', 188–90.

39   During the same period, Romeo Castellucci participated in several visual art exhibitions, such as *Mostra di Oggetti* (Exhibition of Objects) (Rome, 1983) and *Video Sound Art* (Cesena, 1984), where the visual installation, *Tappeto maior* (Major Carpet), was presented as a performance. He has also been engaged in four short films, among which the award-winning *Romolo und Remo* (1984). This film is the first of Romeo Castellucci's multiple attempts to approach the subject of fratricide, as he would take it up in the third act of his 1999

performance *Genesi* (Cain and Abel) as well as in the first episode C.#01 of his renowned *Tragedia Endogonidia* cycle (2002–4). His company Raffaello Sanzio also presented their two first oratorial interventions, *Oratorie*, based on texts by Claudia Castellucci, which inaugurate the triptych 'Psychedelic rebirth – Plow – Anti-nihilist Arcadia', a concept which will be further developed in their next performance, *I fuoriclasse della bontà* (The Champions of Goodness, 1983). *Oratoria n. 1: Rimpatriata Artistica* was presented on 21 March 1983, at the Lavatoio Contumanciale in Rome; The *Oratoria n. 2: Raptus* was presented on 25 February1984 at 'Spaziosero' in Rome and was also screened as a film on 9 May 1984, at Cinema Teatro Anteo, in Milan.

40 Romeo and Claudia Castellucci's sources were the thirteenth-century Catalan philosopher, poet and theologian Ramon Llull and the sixteenth-century Italian philosopher Giordano Bruno. See Gabriella Giannachi and Nick Kaye, *Staging the Post-Avant-Garde: Italian Experimental Performance after 1970* (Bern: Peter Lang, 2002), 139.

41 Tiezzi, 'L'anima mentale e l'anima passionale', 68.

42 Società Raffaello Sanzio, 'Mitobiografia', 188–90.

43 Claudia Manikòn, '*Santa Sofia. Teatro Khmer*. Drammaturgia', unpublished typed document, 1986, *ARCH*, item 19_01_07.

44 Claudia Manikòn, '*Santa Sofia. Teatro Khmer*', unpublished typed document, 1986, *ARCH*, item 19_01_02.

45 Claudia Madornal, '*I Miserabili*. Dall'Manifesto', in *Il teatro della Socìetas Raffaello Sanzio. Dal teatro iconoclasta alla super-icona,* ed. Castellucci and Castellucci (Milan: Ubulibri, 1992), 60.

46 Romeo Castellucci, interview by Eleni Papalexiou (Cesena, 15 July 2016).

47 Claudia Manikòn, '*Santa Sofia. Teatro Khmer*. Del manifesto consegnato in teatro', 1986, *ARCH*, item 19_01_01. Reprinted in Castellucci and Castellucci, *Il teatro della Socìetas Raffaello Sanzio*, 9–11.

48 Socìetas Raffaello Sanzio, 'Relazione artistica della Socìetas Raffaello Sanzio per la città di Cesena', unpublished typed document, 1993–1994, *ARCH*, item 5000_03_06.

49 This remarkably dialectic idea of iconoclasm as consisting of both destruction and creation is elucidated by Timmy De Laet and Edith Cassiers in 'The Regenerative Ruination of Romeo Castellucci', *Performance Research* 20 (3): 18–28. In this article, they take the notion of the ruin as an impetus to rethink the iconoclastic aesthetics of Romeo Castellucci's theatre.

50 Claudia Castellucci, 'La sindrome di Platone', 288.

51 Eleni Papalexiou, *Romeo Castellucci/Socìetas Raffaello Sanzio: When the Words Turn into Matter* (Athens: Plethron, 2009), 26–7.

52 Romeo Castellucci, '*L'Orestea* attraverso lo specchio', in Romeo Castellucci, Chiara Guidi and Claudia Castellucci, eds, *Epopea della polvere* (Milan: Ubulibri, 2001), 158.

53 Eleni Papalexiou, 'Ecce homo', *Theater der Zeit* 1 (January 2011): 67.

54 Cf. Annamaria Cascetta, 'Suggestioni conciliari nella drammatugia italiana', in *Il Concilio Vaticano II crocevia dell'umanesimo contemporaneo*, ed. Angelo Bianchi (Milan: Vita e pensiero, 2015), 241–7.

55　John 8: 7.

56　John 1: 29.

57　Papalexiou, 'The dramaturgies of the gaze', 63.

58　I Monaci delle colonne, 'L'imagine che non si può vedere due volte', in Out X Off Associazione Culturale, *Limitrofie*, 4 Milan (May 1986): 11; Romeo Castellucci, 'L'imagine che non si può vedere due volte', unpublished typed document, 1990, *ARCH*, items 20_03_01, 20_03_02 and 32_01_03.

59　Eleni Papalexiou, 'Homo Spectator', *Peak Performances*, Montclair State University, 9–12 June 2016, 2–3. First published as 'Homo Spectator', in *The Athens Festival Programme 2015* (Athens: The Athens Festival, 2015), 34–5. For an alternative reading of *Go down, Moses*, see Giorgos Pefanis, 'Dystopias, Heterotopias, Boundaries and other Theatrical Idioms of Space', *Parabasis, Journal of the Department of Theatre Studies University of Athens* 14, no. 2 (2016): 65–83.

60　For more on the notion of transgression in the *Tragedia Endogonidia*, see Thomas Crombez's chapter in this book as well as his text, 'La transgression dans la "Tragedia Endogonidia" de la Socìetas Raffaello Sanzio', in *OEdipe contemporain? Tragédie, tragique, politique*, ed. Paul Van Den Berghe, Christian Biet and Karel Vanhaesebrouck (Brussels: Les Impressions Nouvelles, 2007), 275–94.

61　Eleni Papalexiou, '*Nyx teleia*. Nella note profonda del mondo Greco antico', in *Toccare il reale*, ed. Piersandra Di Matteo (Naples: Cronopio, 2015), 36.

62　Arist. Metaph. 1024a. See also Johann Jakob Bachofen, *Il simbolismo funerario degli antichi*, ed. Mario Pezzella (Naples: Guida editori, 1989), 649–51.

63　Johann Jakob Bachofen, *Il Matriarcato. Ricerca sulla ginecocrazia del mondo antico nei suoi aspetti religiosi e guidici*, 2 vols, ed. Giulio Schiavoni (Turin: Einaudi, 1861/1988).

64　Romeo Castellucci, 'Superficies ad Dominum soli pertinet', in *Gilgamesh*, ed. Socìetas Raffaello Sanzio (Cesena: Casa del bello estremo, 1990), 21–22.

65　Romeo Castellucci, 'La riconquista della visione', in *Gilgamesh,* ed. Socìetas Raffaello Sanzio (Cesena: Casa del bello estremo, 1990), 23.

66　Romeo Castellucci, 'Epopteia', in *Gilgamesh*, ed. Socìetas Raffaello Sanzio (Cesena: Casa del bello estremo, 1990), 17.

67　The word 'epiphany' derives from the Greek verb φαίνω (phainō), which means to make something appear, become evident.

68　Papalexiou, '*Nyx Teleia*', 39–42.

69　Arist. fr. 15 = Synesius, *Dion* 8.42.

70　Paul Foucart, *Les Mystères d'Eleusis* (Paris: Picard, 1914), 496; George Emmanuel Mylonas, *Eleusis and the Eleusinian Mysteries* (Princeton: Princeton University Press, 1961), 261 ff.

71　Papalexiou, 'The Dramaturgies of the Gaze', 57.

72　Papalexiou, *Romeo Castellucci/Socìetas Raffaello Sanzio*, 116.

73　Castellucci, 'La riconquista della visione', 24.

74 Eleni Papalexiou, 'Conceiving the New Image of the World', *EF* 44 (25 June 2015), 6–9.

75 Romeo Castellucci, 'La quinta parete/Le cinquième mur', in *Le théâtre et ses publics. La création partagée*, ed. Nancy Delhalle (Besançon: Les Solitaires Intempestifs, 2013), 19.

76 *Rethinking la* Divina Commedia, ed. Eleni Papalexiou (Nafplion: University of Peloponnese-Dept. of Theatre Studies, forthcoming).

77 Arist. fr. 15 = Synesius, *Dion* 8.42.

78 Plato, *Phaedrus* 251, as cited in David Wiles, *Mask and Performance in Greek Tragedy: From Ancient Festival to Modern Experimentation* (Cambridge: Cambridge University Press, 2007), 233.

79 Ibid.

80 Romeo Castellucci, 'Asinina cogitatio', in *Masoch. I trionfi del teatro come potenza passiva, colpa e sconfitta*, published programme book (Cesena: Socìetas Raffaello Sanzio, 1993).

81 'And God said, Let there be light: and there was light. And God saw the light, that it was good: and God divided the light from the darkness. And God called the light Day, and the darkness he called Night'; Genesis 1.3–4.

82 Romeo Castellucci, 'Gather and Burn', trans. Joseph Cermatori (May 2014) 22.

83 Castellucci, 'L'*Orestea* attraverso lo specchio', 157.

84 Romeo Castellucci, 'Il pellegrino della materia', in *Epopea della polvere. Il teatro della Socìetas Raffaello Sanzio,* ed. Romeo Castellucci, Chiara Guidi and Claudia Castellucci (Milan: Ubulibri, 2001), 272.

85 Ibid.

86 Romeo Castellucci, interview with Eleni Papalexiou (Cesena, 19 July 2016).

87 Ibid.

88 Castellucci, 'Il pellegrino della materia', 272.

89 Ibid.

90 Papalexiou, *Romeo Castellucci/Socìetas Raffaello Sanzio*, 20.

91 Hans Blumenberg, *Arbeit am Mythos* (Frankfurt am Main: Suhrkamp, 1979), also translated in English by Robert M. Wallace as *Work on Myth* (Cambridge MA: MIT Press, 1985).

92 Romeo Castellucci, interviewed by Eleni Papalexiou, in *Romeo Castellucci/Socìetas Raffaello Sanzio*, 100.

93 Maurita Cardone, 'Romeo Castellucci and the Power of Speech. An interview with Italian director and author who is now in New York to stage his *Julius Caesar*', *La voce di New York* (1 October 2016). Available online: www.lavocedinewyork.com/en/arts/2016/10/01/romeo-castellucci-and-the-power-of-speech (accessed 2 October 2016).

94 Romeo Castellucci, interviewed by Eleni Papalexiou, in *Romeo Castellucci/Socìetas Raffaello Sanzio*, 100.

95 Jean-Pierre Vernant and Pierre Vidal-Naquet, *Mythe et tragédie en Grèce ancienne* (Paris: Maspéro, 1979), 25. The idea of the broken mirror is further

elaborated in Pierre Vidal-Naquet, *Le miroir brisé. Tragédie athénienne et politique* (Paris: Les belles lettres, 2002).

96   Romeo Castellucci, 'Représentation en tant que telle', *Puck. La Marionnette et les autres arts. Humain, non humain* 20 (2014): 17–20.

97   Romeo Castellucci, interview with Eleni Papalexiou, (Cesena, 19 July 2016).

98   Bruno Bettelheim, *The Empty Fortress: Infantile Autism and the Birth of the Self* (New York: The Free Press, 1967).

99   Romeo Castellucci, 'Amleto: Là dove la A risuona come alfa privativa', in *Epopea della polvere*, ed. Romeo Castellucci, Chiara Guidi and Claudia Castellucci (Milan: Ubulibri, 2001), 42.

100   The poem 'Jabberwocky' appeared in Carroll's novel *Through the Looking Glass* (1871), which was a sequel to *Alice's Adventures in Wonderland*. It was Artaud's psychiatrist Gaston Ferdière who advised Artaud to translate Carroll's poem as a part of his therapy. At the time, Artaud was staying at the Rodez asylum for treatment of his mental illness. Romeo Castellucci, interviewed by Eleni Papalexiou, (Cesena, 23 July 2015).

101   Vladimir Propp, *Edipo alla luce del folclore* (Turin: Einaudi, 1966).

102   Lewis Carroll, *Humpty Dumpty. L'Arve et l'Aume. Bindolo Rondolo*, ed. Carlo Pasi, trans. Antonin Artaud, Guido Almansi, Giuliana Poso and Stittori tradotti da scrittori (Einaudi: Turin, 1993). Information provided by Romeo Castellucci, interviewed by Eleni Papalexiou, (Cesena, 23 July 2015).

103   Castellucci, 'L'*Orestea* attraverso lo specchio', 157.

104   Claudia Castellucci, 'In assetto cosciente di solitudine assoluta', in *Epopea della polvere*, ed. Romeo Castellucci, Chiara Guidi, Claudia Castellucci *Epopea della polvere* (Milan: Ubulibri, 2001), 302.

105   Eleni Papalexiou and Avra Xepapadakou, 'Sur les traces de l'*Orestie (une comédie organique?)* de Romeo Castellucci: De sa conception (1995) à sa reprise (2015)', in the Proceedings of the International Conference on Theatre Genetics *Percursos de Genética Teatral* (Lisbon: Centro de Estudos de Teatro, Universidade de Lisboa, forthcoming).

106   Romeo Castellucci, 'In principio era l'immagine', in *La discesa di Inanna: Mito Sumero*, ed. Socìetas Raffaello Sanzio (Cesena: Casa del bello estremo, 1989), 8.

107   Papalexiou, 'Nyx teleia', 37.

108   Romeo Castellucci, 'Eubuleo', 16.

109   Ibid., 15.

110   Castellucci, 'L'*Orestea* attraverso lo specchio', 156.

111   For further reading, see Romeo Castellucci, 'Appunti di un clown', in Socìetas Raffaello Sanzio, *Orestea (una commedia organica?)*, programme booklet (Cesena: Socìetas Raffaello Sanzio, 1995), 4–14; Marco Belpoliti, 'Romeo Castellucci a Belpoliti, Cesena, 23 gennaio 1995', *Riga*, 8 (1995); 148–51, Anton Bierl, 'Romeo Castelluccis *Orestea*', in *Die Orestie des Aischylos auf der modernen Buhne* (Stuttgart: M&P, 1997), 90–110.

112   Antonin Artaud, 'L'arve et l'aume. Tentative anti-grammaticale contre Lewis Carroll', *L'Arbalète* 12 (1947): 159–84. 'Twas brillig, and the slithy toves / Did

gyre and gimble in the wabe; / All mimsy were the borogoves, / And the mome raths outgrabe.'

113 Antonin Artaud, *Selected Writings*, ed. Susan Sontag, trans. Helen Weaver (New York: Farrar, Strauss, Giroux, 1976), 451.

114 I borrow the term 'plagiat par anticipation' from Pierre Bayard, *Le plagiat par anticipation* (Paris: Les Editions de Minuit, 2009). Benoît Delaune also discusses Artaud's accusation of plagiarism against in `Un cas précis de "plagiat par anticipation": Antonin Artaud accuse Lewis Carroll', *Acta Fabula* 10, no. 2 (February 2009). Available online: www.fabula.org/acta/document4990.php (accessed 15 April 2017).

115 The phrases mentioned here are actually part of how Artaud translated only the title of 'Jabberwocky', and they continue as follows: 'Sofar Ami – TantarUpti / Momar Uni – SeptfarEsti / Gonpar Arak – Alak Eli'. Artaud, 'L'Arve et l'Aume', 159–84. The relationship between Carroll and Artaud in connection to the notion of descent has already been touched upon by Lucia Amara, 'Artaud figura', in *Toccare el reale*, ed. Piersandra Di Matteo (Naples: Cronopio, 2015), 54–8.

116 Gilles Deleuze, *La Logique du sens* (Paris: Les Éditions de Minuit, 1969), 101–14. Also translated into English by Mark Lester as *The Logic of Sense* (New York: Columbia University Press, 1990).

117 Ibid., 111–12.

118 For a further investigation on the elimination of language, which is central in a wide range of Castellucci's creations, from *Santa Sofia. Teatro Khmer* to the most recent *Democracy in America*, cf. Eleni Papalexiou, 'Pharmakòs or *Democracy in America*', *The Books' Journal* 78 (June 2017). Available online: http://booksjournal.gr/slideshow/item/2571-farmakos-h-democracy-in-america (accessed 10 August 2017).

119 Plato, *Gorgias* 493a, *Cratylus* 500c, *Phaedrus* 250c.

120 For a more extensive discussion of the anorexic body in Castellucci's *Julius Caesar*, see Eleni Papalexiou, 'The Body as Dramatic Material in the Theatre of Romeo Castellucci', in *Utopia and Critical Thinking in the Creative Process* (Besançon: Les Solitaires Intempestifs, 2012), 75–88.

121 The Long QT syndrome is a rare neurological disorder which consists in complete paralysis of all voluntary muscles except for those which control eye movement. Individuals with locked-in syndrome are conscious and awake, but have no ability to produce movement (apart from eye movement) or to speak (aphonia).

122 When Castellucci staged his *Orpheus and Eurydice* in Vienna, the role of Eurydice was 'played' by Karin Anna Giselbrecht. In Brussels, it was 'Els', a patient with LIS who preferred to stay anonymous.

123 Claudia Madornal, '*I Miserabili*. Dall'Manifesto', 59–64.

124 Cf. also 'Karin Anna Giselbrecht', text distributed to the audience of *Orfeo ed Euridice*, Halle E, Museumsquartier, Vienna, 11 May 2014.

125 Papalexiou, 'The Body as Dramatic Material in the Theatre of Romeo Castellucci', 84.

126 The presence of animals was never an easy matter for the director and his group. Although the animals were always treated with respect and while

all health and safety regulations were meticulously observed, the Socìetas Raffaello Sanzio was frequently attacked by animal rights organizations. In addition, due to stricter legislation for animals in certain countries, several performances had to be cancelled.

127 Cf. Romeo Castellucci, 'The Animal Being on Stage', *Performance Research* 5, no. 2 (2000): 23–8. In this text, Castellucci refers, among others, to the performance *La Discesa di Inanna* (1989), which is another example of his interest in including animals, as the actors cradled small goats in their arms, on their chest, breathing together as equal beings.

128 In the book *L'animal que donc je suis* (Paris: Galilée, 2006), the French philosopher Jacques Derrida argues against the tendency in Western philosophy to contrast man with the rest of the animal kingdom by defining the animal in a negative way in order to shed human's own 'animality'.

129 Romeo Castellucci, '*Gilgamesh*. Descrizione della rappresentazione', in *Il teatro della Socìetas Raffaello Sanzio*, ed. Castellucci and Castellucci (Milan: Ubulibri, 1992), 148.

130 Romeo Castellucci, Discussion with the audience of the Avignon Festival, 16 July 2008.

131 Romeo Castellucci, '*La discesa di Inanna*', in *Il teatro della Socìetas Raffaello Sanzio*, ed. Castellucci and Castellucci (Milan: Ubulibri, 1992), 112.

132 For an interesting example of how the inclusion of animals in Castellucci's work can lead to unpredictable situations that, in turn, unsettles the experience of spectators, see Enrique Pardo, 'Electricity in Hell: Notes on the Work of Romeo Castellucci and Praise for Italy', *Spring. A Journal for Archetype and Culture* 67 (2000): 161–74. Pardo recalls how during one performance of *Gilgamesh*, two dogs began to copulate on stage, which seemed to have caused a flurry of offended responses among spectators.

133 For more on the presence of animals on stage in Castellucci's work, see Thomas Crombez's chapter in this volume.

134 Introductory note by Romeo Castellucci in the text of Enrico Pitozzi and Annalisa Sacchi, 'La Minoration', in *Itinera* (Arles: Actes Sud, 2008), 195.

135 Castellucci, 'Il pellegrino della materia', 271.

136 Walter Benjamin, *Gesammelte Schriften*, vol. II-I (Frankfurt am Main: Suhrkamp, 1980), 219–20.

137 Socìetas Raffaello Sanzio, 'BR.#04, KunstenFESTIVALdesArts, Brussels, May 2003', in *The Theatre of Socìetas Raffaello Sanzio*, ed.Claudia Castellucci, Romeo Castellucci, Chiara Guidi, Joe Kelleher and Nicholas Ridout (Abingdon and New York: Routledge, 2007), 92.

138 For a more extensive discussion of how playing with gazes is central to Castellucci's work in various ways, see Papalexiou, 'The Dramaturgies of the Gaze'.

139 Shakespeare, *Hamlet*, 4.4.58

140 Castellucci, 'Asinina cogitatio', 5.

141 Romeo Castellucci, 'Représentation en tant que telle', *Puck. La Marionnette et les autres arts, Humain, non humain* 20 (2014): 17–20.

Chapter 4

1   This chapter draws on my book *Het antitheater van Antonin Artaud: Een onderzoek naar de veralgemeende artistieke transgressie, toegepast op het werk van Romeo Castellucci en de Socìetas Raffaello Sanzio* (Ghent: Academia Press, 2008). My approach is strongly informed by the series of interviews with Romeo Castellucci that I conducted together with Wouter Hillaert at several points during the production of the *Tragedia Endogonidia* (2002–4). The original French version of these interviews can be consulted in my book *Het antitheater van Antonin Artaud*, 291–316. All English translations of quotes from these interviews are my own.

2   Romeo Castellucci and Claudia Castellucci, *Les Pèlerins de la matière: Théorie et praxis du théâtre: Écrits de la Socìetas Raffaello Sanzio* (Besançon: Les Solitaires Intempestifs, 2001), 15–16. For an extensive discussion of the works created by Romeo Castellucci and the Socìetas Raffaello Sanzio during their first years, see the contribution by Eleni Papalexiou to this volume.

3   Claudia Castellucci and Romeo Castellucci, *Il teatro della Socìetas Raffaello Sanzio. Del teatro iconoclasta alla super-icona* (Milan: Ubulibri, 1992), 9–11.

4   Rosette Lamont, 'The Terrible but Unended Story of Norodom Sihanouk: King of Cambodia by Helene Cixous: Ariane Mnouchkine (Review)', *Performing Arts Journal* 10, no. 1 (1986): 46–50.

5   Romeo Castellucci's use of extreme bodies has been a much-discussed topic in the scholarly literature on his work. See, for example, Luk Van Den Dries, 'The Sublime Body', in *Bodycheck: Relocating the Body in Contemporary Art*, ed. Luk Van Den Dries et al. (Amsterdam: Rodopi, 2002), 70–95; Matthew Causey, 'Stealing from God: The Crisis of Creation in Socìetas Raffaello Sanzio's *Genesi* and Eduardo Kac's *Genesis*', in *Theatre and Performance in Digital Culture: From Simulation to Embeddedness* (New York: Routledge, 2006), 127–49; Rachel Fensham, 'The Rhetoric of Organs without Bodies. *Genesi: The Museum of Sleep*', in *To Watch Theatre: Essays on Genre and Corporeality* (Brussels: P.I.E. Peter Lang, 2009), 137–64. Romeo Castellucci discusses his view on corporeality in 'The Iconoclasm of the Stage and the Return of the Body: The Carnal Power of Theater', trans. Gloria Pastorino, *Theater* 37, no. 3 (2007): 37–45.

6   Thomas Crombez and Wouter Hillaert, 'Interview de Romeo Castellucci (Bruxelles, 2003)' in Crombez, *Het antitheater*, 291.

7   Tragedia Endogonidia di Romeo Castellucci: *Idioma Clima Crono I* (Cesena: SRS, 2002), 1.

8   Hans-Thies Lehmann, *Postdramatic Theatre*, trans. Karen Jürs-Munby (Abingdon: Routledge, 2006), 50. It should be noted that Lehmann does identify a new form of what he calls 'hypernaturalism' in postdramatic theatre, which nevertheless differs from traditional dramatic naturalism in that the depicted reality no longer needs to be repressed or elevated, but rather functions as a legitimate source for theatrical inspiration.

9   Lehmann, *Postdramatic Theatre*, 109–10, 164. In the German original, which is considerably longer than the English version, there are three references to

the work of the Socìetas. See Hans-Thies Lehmann, *Postdramatisches theater* (Frankfurt am Main: Verlag der Autoren, 1999), 198, 376, 388.

10 Lehmann, *Postdramatic Theatre*, 164.

11 Gerald Rabkin, 'The Play of Misreading: Text/Theatre/Deconstruction', *Performing Arts Journal* 7, no. 1 (1983): 44–60.

12 Lehmann, *Postdramatic Theatre*, 101.

13 Ibid., 21.

14 Ibid., 145.

15 Ibid., 148.

16 Thomas Crombez and Wouter Hillaert, 'Interview de Romeo Castellucci (Cesena, 2004)', in Crombez, *Het antitheater*, 309.

17 Lehmann, *Postdramatic Theatre*, 83, 87, 93.

18 In 1920, the first 'Institute for Theatre Studies' (Institut für Theaterwissenschaft) was founded at the University of Cologne, Germany.

19 For a more detailed history of the emergence of theatre studies, see Erika Fischer-Lichte, *The Transformative Power of Performance: A New Aesthetics*, trans. Saskya Iris Jain (Abingdon and New York: Routledge, 2008). While Fischer-Lichte focuses on Germany, the developments she charts can be extrapolated to the rest of Western Europe. The introduction to her book by Marvin Carlson, also places this history in relation to theatre studies in the USA.

20 See, among others, Marvin Carlson, *Theatre Semiotics: Signs of Life* (Bloomington: Indiana University Press, 1990); Erika Fischer-Lichte, *Semiotik des Theaters* (Tübingen: Gunter Narr Verlag, 1983); Anne Übersfeld, *Lire le théâtre* (Paris: Éditions Sociales, 1978).

21 Fischer-Lichte, *Semiotik des Theaters*, vol. 1, 10.

22 In a brief article, Stamatia Neofytou-Georgiou attempts to approach Romeo Castellucci's theatre from a semiotic perspective, but it is telling that her perspective leads to the rather unsatisfactory conclusion that his work 'will constitute a turning-point in the field of the semiotics of the history of the theatre'. See Stamatia Neofytou-Georgiou, 'The Semiotics of Images in Romeo Castellucci's Theatre', in *The Visual in Performance Practice: Interdisciplinary Perspectives*, ed. Adele Anderson, Filipa Malva and Chris Berchild (Oxford, UK: Inter-Disciplinary Press, 2012), 19.

23 See, for instance: Julia Kristeva, *Polylogue* (Paris: Seuil, 1977), 55–106; Yve-Alain Bois and Rosalind Krauss, *L'informe: Mode d'emploi* (Paris: Éditions du Centre Pompidou, 1996).

24 Tragedia Endogonidia di Romeo Castellucci: *Idioma Clima Crono I* (Cesena: SRS, 2002), 11.

25 Tragedia Endogonidia di Romeo Castellucci: *Idioma Clima Crono II* (Cesena: SRS, 2003), 2.

26 Tragedia Endogonidia di Romeo Castellucci: *Idioma Clima Crono III* (Cesena: SRS, 2003), 6.

27 Crombez and Hillaert, 'Interview de Romeo Castellucci' (Cesena, 2004)' in Crombez, *Het antitheater*, 309.

28 Lorraine Daston and Katherine Park, *Wonders and the Order of Nature: 1150–1750* (New York: Zone Books, 1998), 261.

29 See also Royd Climenhaga's contribution to this volume, in which he similarly relies on the dream as a structural analogy to describe how the image functions in the work of Pina Bausch, without claiming that what she shows on stage is a form of 'dream art'.

30 The oneiric is a popular term to describe surrealist theatre as well as the Theatre of the Absurd. See, for instance, Henri Béhar, *Étude sur le théâtre dada et surréaliste* (Paris: Gallimard, 1967); Gisèle Féal, *Ionesco: Un théâtre onirique* (Paris: Imago, 2001); Paul Vernois, *L'onirisme et l'insolite dans le théâtre français contemporain* (Paris: Klincksieck, 1974). In the contemporary performing arts, it is not only Castellucci's work that is reminiscent of the dream, but also that of Robert Wilson and others. Add to that the filmmakers whose work is described as oneiric, such as Luis Buñuel, Salvador *Dalí* and Jean Cocteau, or from post-war cinema, David Lynch, Alexandro Jodorowsky and Hans-Jürgen Syberberg. Both *Endgame* by Samuel Beckett (1957) and Jodorowsky's *El Topo* (1970) may be termed oneiric on account of their dramatic structure, but this conceals the profound differences between those works.

31 Umberto Eco, *The Open Work*, trans. A. Cancogni (Cambridge MA: Harvard University Press, 1989)

32 Thomas Crombez, Sara Colson and Hendrik Tratsaert, 'Interviews de Romeo Castellucci (Anvers, 2005)' in Crombez, *Het antitheater*, 312–13.

33 In terms of language, it is interesting to note that infant derives from the Latin 'in-fans', which means 'non-speaking'. As such, the presence of the child signals a prelinguistic state of being, which is a topic Eleni Papalexiou discusses further in her contribution to this volume.

34 The actual image used in the programmes and during the productions comes from a previous version of the phonographs, that is, the gold-anodized aluminium plaques placed on board the 1972 Pioneer 10 and 1973 Pioneer 11 spacecraft. Since Castellucci continuously refers to the image as coming from the Voyager Golden Record, I will also do so, even though it is factually incorrect.

35 Crombez and Hillaert, 'Interview de Romeo Castellucci (Cesena, 2004)' in Crombez, *Het antitheater*, 306.

36 Claudia Castellucci, Romeo Castellucci and Chiara Guidi, *Epopea della polvere: Il teatro della Socìetas Raffaello Sanzio 1992–1999* (Milan: Ubulibri, 2001).

37 See, for instance, Castellucci, 'The Iconoclasm of the Stage and the Return of the Body', 41, 44; Nicholas Ridout, 'Welcome to the Vibratorium', *The Senses and Society* 3, no. 2 (2008): 221–32; Freddy Decreus, 'The Nomadic Theatre of the Socìetas Raffaello Sanzio: A Case of Postdramatic Reworking of (the Classical) Tragedy', in *Companion to Classical Receptions*, ed. Lorna Hardwick and Christopher Stray (London: Blackwell, 2007), 274–86.

38 Antonin Artaud, *The Theatre and its Double* in *Collected Works IV*, trans. V. Corti (London: Calder and Boyars, 1974), 25.

39 Jerzy Grotowski, *Towards a Poor Theatre*, ed. E. Barba (New York: Routledge, 2002 [1968]), 23–24.

40 Maaike Bleeker et al., 'Interview with Romeo Castellucci' in *Bodycheck*, Luk Van Den Dries et al., 225.

41 'Vous délirez, Monsieur Artaud, vous êtes fou. Non. Je ne délire. Je ne pas délire pas. Je ne suis pas fou', in Antonin Artaud, *Œuvres complètes XIII*, ed. Paule Thévenin (Paris: Gallimard, 1974), 103.

42 Jacques Derrida, 'La parole soufflée' and 'Le théâtre de la cruauté et la clôture de la représentation', in *L'Écriture et la Différence* (Paris: Seuil, 1967), 253–92 and 341–68.

43 Castellucci and Castellucci, *Les Pèlerins de la matière*, 191.

44 Ibid., 152. Castellucci's view on Artaud is in line with the readings of Gilles Deleuze and Paule Thévenin in resp. *Logique du sens* (Paris: Minuit, 1969), 101–14 and 'Note to "L'Arve et l'Aume"', in Artaud, *Œuvres complètes IX*. See also Eleni Papalexiou's chapter in this volume.

45 Castellucci and Castellucci, *Les Pèlerins de la matière*, 152.

46 Claudia Castellucci and Romeo Castellucci, *Il theatro della Socìetas Raffaello Sanzio: Dal teatro iconoclasta alla super-icona* (Cesena: Casa del Bello Estremo Milan: Ubulibri, 1992).

47 See also Timmy De Laet and Edith Cassiers, 'The Regenerative Ruination of Romeo Castellucci', *Performance Research* 20, no. 3 (2015) 18–28.

48 See Crombez and Hillaert, 'Interview de Romeo Castellucci (Cesena, 2004)', in Crombez, *Het antitheater*, 302.

49 Jean Duvignaud, *Les ombres collectives: Sociologie du théâtre* (Paris: Presses Universitaires de France, 1973), 398.

50 Crombez and Hillaert, 'Interview de Romeo Castellucci (Cesena, 2004)', in Crombez, *Het antitheater*, 305.

51 Lehmann, *Postdramatic Theatre*, 89–90.

52 Castellucci and Castellucci, *Les Pèlerins de la matière*, 16.

53 André Breton, *Œuvres complètes I* (Paris: Gallimard, 1988), 330.

54 Breton, *Œuvres complètes I*, 338.

55 Romeo Castellucci, 'Interview with Romeo Castellucci conducted by Rachel Halliburton (London International Festival of Theatre)', 16 March 2004. Available at: www.theatrevoice.com/audio/lift-2004-romeo-castellucci-the-controversial-italian-direc/ (accessed 5 June 2017); 'Trois interviews'; Claudia Castellucci and Chiara Guidi, 'Ethics of Voice: Claudia Castellucci and Chiara Guidi in Conversation with Joe Kelleher', *Performance Research* 9, no. 4 (2004): 112–13; Crombez, Colson and Tratsaert, 'Interview de Romeo Castellucci (Anvers, 2005)', in Crombez, *Het antitheater*, 316.

56 Claudia Schmölders, 'Das Buch als Pathosformel: Zur Gefühlsgeschichte der Bibliothek', *Merkur* 676 (2005): 696.

57 Aby Warburg. *Der Bilderatlas Mnemosyne. Gesammelte Schriften II*.1, ed. Martin Warnke (Berlin: Akademie Verlag, 2003).

58 Crombez, Colson and Tratsaert, 'Interview de Romeo Castellucci (Antwerp, 2005)', in Crombez, *Het antitheater*, 316.

59   Georges Bataille, *Œuvres complètes I* (Paris: Gallimard, 1970), 393; Breton, *Œuvres complètes I*, 785.

60   Castellucci and Castellucci, *Les Pèlerins de la matière*, 122.

61   Crombez and Hillaert, 'Interview de Romeo Castellucci (Bruxelles, 2003)', in Crombez, *Het antitheater*, 291.

62   'L'art n'est point de la communication, c'est plûtot une révélation. La révélation est dans une relation renversée à la communication', in Crombez, *Het antitheater*, 315.

63   Crombez, Colson and Tratsaert, 'Interview de Romeo Castellucci (Antwerp, 2005)', in Crombez, *Het antitheater*, 314.

Chapter 5

1   In Jan Fabre, *Nachtboek 1978–1984* (Antwerp: De Bezige Bij, 2011), Fabre recounts extensively how he was drawn to performance art and began to experiment with 'real time/real action'. See also the following interview: Jan Fabre, 'S'entraîner à disparaître. Entretien', *Communications* 1, no. 92 (2013): 263–75.

2   Two key texts that historicize the emergence of performance art and survey its development are Roselee Goldberg, *Performance Art: From Futurism to the Present*, 3rd edn (London: Thames and Hudson, 2011); Marvin Carlson, *Performance: A Critical Introduction*, 2nd edn (Abingdon and New York: Routledge, 2004). For more on how performance art challenges conventional modes of spectatorship, see: Frazen Ward, *No Innocent Bystanders Performance Art and Audience* (Hanover, NH: Dartmouth College Press, 2012).

3   Characteristically, the title of the action says precisely what it does: *Route of tram 2 followed with the nose in the trails.*

4   *Doctor Fabre will cure you* is also the title of Pierre Coulibeuf's 2013 cinematographic reconstruction of a range of performances Fabre created during the early stages of his career. For this movie, Fabre re-performed several actions and interventions on several locations in the city of Antwerp.

5   See also Kurt Van Belleghem: 'Hier leeft en werkt Jan Fabre', in *Mythische sporen in de hedendaagse kunst*, ed. Claire Van Damme and Franciska Vandepitte (Ghent: Academia Press, 1996), 124.

6   For more on the blue 'bic' drawings of Fabre, see Yuko Hasegawa, 'Fabre, the Non-Existing Knight of the Twenty-first century: The Most Western but at the Same Time Most Non-western Personality', in *Homo Faber*, ed. Giacinto De Pietrantonio and Jan Fabre (Bruges: Mercatorfonds, 2006), 96–121; Jo Coucke, 'Jan Fabre's Blue Blood', in *Jan Fabre: The Years of the Hour Blue. Drawings and Sculptures, 1977–1992*, ed. Joke De Vos Jan Fabre (Milan: Silvana Editoriale, 2012), 105–9.

7   Emil Hrvatin, 'Het Dispositief van Fabres Performances', in *Homo Faber*, ed. Giacinto De Pietrantonio and Jan Fabre (Bruges: Mercatorfonds, 2006), 174, own translation.

8   Roselee Goldberg, *Performance: Live Art since the 60s* (London: Thames & Hudson, 1998), 65.

9   For more on the influence of performance art on the work of Jan Fabre, see Luk Van Den Dries, 'The Flemish Theatre in the Eighties. Precipitations of an History of Influence', *Documenta* 2, no. 3 (2009): 108–29.

10 Toon Brouwers, *Antwerpen theaterstad. Aspecten van het theaterleven in Antwerpen in de tweede helft van de twintigste eeuw* (Tielt: Lannoo, 2015), 70.

11 Fabre, *Nachtboek 1978–1984*, 21.

12 Ibid., 64.

13 The image of the writer is inspired by Salvador Dalí's painting *The Temptation of St Anthony* (1946). In Fabre's early oeuvre, there are many references to the Spanish surrealist, among others in his performance installation *Ilad of the Bic Art/The Bic Art Room.*

14 Jan Fabre, *Théâtre écrit avec un 'k' est un matou flamand/Theatre with a K is a Tomcat* (Paris: L'Arche, 2009); *C'est du theatre comme c'etait a esperer et a prevoir/This is Theatre as is was to be Expected and Foreseen* (Paris: L'Arche, 2009); *Le pouvoir des folies theatrales/The Power of Theatrical Madness* (Paris: L'Arche, 2009).

15 Bart Verschaffel, 'De dieren zullen het theater redden! De eerste theatervoorstellingen van Jan Fabre (1980–1984)', *Etcetera* 126 (2011): 53.

16 In 1995, for example, Fabre created an installation titled *Tea Bags Room.*

17 Verschaffel, 'De dieren', 57.

18 Kaaitheater was founded in 1977 as a festival for avant-garde theatre and changes into an arts centre with its own year-long programme from 1987. Today, the Kaaitheater is still one of the most exciting institutions in Belgium, hosting both upcoming and established artists.

19 Fabre, *Nachtboek 1978–1984*, 159.

20 See David Hopkins, '"Art" and "Life" and … Death', in *Neo-Avant-Garde*, ed. David Hopkins (Amsterdam and New York: Rodopi, 2006), 33.

21 Marcel Duchamp, interview by Richard Hamilton in London and George Heard Hamilton in New York, *Audio Arts Magazine* 2, no. 4 (1976).

22 Jan Fabre, 'Het is theater zoals te verwachten en te voorzien was', *Aktualiteiten BASTT* 10 (1983): 16.

23 Fabre, *Nachtboek 1978–1984*, 160.

24 Hans-Thies Lehmann cited in Gert Mattenklott, 'Ich bin durchtränkt mit meiner Widerspiegelung. Versuch über Jan Fabre', in *Jan Fabre. Texte zum Werk*, ed. Eckhard Schneider (Hanover: Kunstverein Hannover, 1992), 21.

25 In 2011, the Kunsthistorisches Museum in Vienna hosted another large retrospective exhibition, *The Years of the Hour Blue.*

26 Jan Fabre, *De keizer van het verlies* in *Geschiedenis van de tranen en andere teksten* (Antwerp: Meulenhoff/ Manteau, 2005), 38.

27 Jan Fabre, *De dienaar van de schoonheid* (Antwerp: Meulenhoff/ Manteau, 2010), 36.

28 For more on the connection between Fabre and Artaud, see Luk Van Den Dries, *Het geopende lichaam* (Antwerp: De Bezige Bij, 2014), 13–26.

29 Alexander Schwan, 'Calligraphies du corps: la danse comme fantasme incarné de l'écriture', in *Jan Fabre. Esthetique du paradoxe*, ed. Marianne Beauviche, Luk Van Den Dries and Lydie Toran (Avignon: L'Harmattan, 2013), 70.

30 Michel Foucault, *Discipline and Punish: The Birth of the Prison* (London: Allen Lane, 1977).

31 Emil Hrvatin, *Herhaling, waanzin, discipline. Het theaterwerk van Jan Fabre* (Amsterdam: International Theatre and Film Books, 1994), 90.

32 'Jan Fabre' in Hugo de Greef and Jan Hoet, *Gesprekken met Jan Fabre* (Leuven: Kritak, 1993), 109.

33 Heidi Gilpin, 'Symmetry and Abandonment', in *Jan Fabre: Texts on his Theatre-work*, ed. Sigrid Bousset (Brussels: Kaaitheater, 1993), 170–71.

34 Gilpin, 'Symmetry and Abandonment', 174.

35 Gert Mattenklott, 'Identity or Similarity? A Motif in Jan Fabre's Drama', in *Jan Fabre: Texts on his Theatre-work*, ed. Sigrid Bousset (Brussels: Kaaitheater, 1993), 59.

36 Hans-Thies Lehmann, 'When rage coagulates into form … ', in *Jan Fabre. Texts on his Theatre-work*, ed. Sigrid Bousset (Brussels: Kaaitheater, 1993), 139.

37 Christine Ramat, 'L'esthétique grotesque de Jan Fabre', in *Jan Fabre: Esthétique du paradoxe*, ed. Marianne Beauviche, Luk Van Den Dries and Lydie Toran (L'Harmattan, 2013) 139–40.

38 Geneviève Drouhet, 'Je suis sang. Transgression des interdits et profanation', *Alternatives Théâtrales*, no. 85–86 (2005): 91.

39 Eleni Varopoulou, 'L'âme et le corps: le baroque insolite de Jan Fabre', *Alternatives Théâtrales*, no. 85–86 (2005): 96.

40 This acting method is called 'From Act to Acting' and is taught by Fabre's Teaching Group through workshops and classes.

41 Jan Fabre in Van Den Dries, *Corpus Jan Fabre*, 339.

42 Stefan Hertmans, *Engel van de metamorfose. Over het werk van Jan Fabre* (Amsterdam: Meulenhoff, 2002), 115.

43 Ibid., 114.

44 Fabre created individual pieces for Els Deceukelier, Marc Moon Van Overmeir, Renée Copraij, Dirk Roofthooft, Wim Vandekeybus, Marc Vanrunxt, Annamirl Van der Pluym, Ivana Jozic, Lisbeth Gruwez, Annabelle Chambon, Cedric Charron and Tony Rizzi.

45 For example, many Wagnerian arias return in *The Power of Theatrical Madness* and Fabre also made drawings for an imaginary staging of *Der Ring des Nibelungen* and a film-performance titled *Lancelot* (2004). After *Tannhäuser*, he would also create *Tragedy for a Friendship* (2013), a music-theatre piece based on the thirteen operas of Wagner and the tempestuous friendship between Wagner and Nietzsche.

46 Swords are another recurrent motif in Fabre's oeuvre. Among the pieces they appear in are *The Power of Theatrical Madness, The Dance Sections, Je suis sang* and *Tragedy of a Friendship*.

47 Jan Fabre in Van Den Dries, *Corpus Jan Fabre*, 319.

48 Ibid., 320.

49 Jan Fabre in Van Den Dries, *Het geopende lichaam*, 272–73.

50 Already in 2009, Jan Fabre and his dramaturg Miet Martens had the first conversations about the massive project *Mount Olympus* with Hans-Thies Lehmann, who has written several standard works on Greek tragedy. Lehmann has also cooperated as a guest dramaturg in this production, together with classicist Freddy Decreus and theatre scholar Luk Van den Dries.

51 Edith Cassiers et al., 'Redrawing Bodily Boundaries: A Look into the Creation Process of Jan Fabre', in *Aesthetics and Ideology in Contemporary Literature and Drama*, ed. Madelena Gonzalez and Rene Agostini (Newcastle-upon-Tyne: Cambridge Scholars Publishing, 2015), 297–320.

52 Edith Cassiers et al., 'Physiological Performing Exercises by Jan Fabre: An Additional Training Method for Performers', *Theatre, Dance and Performance Training* 6, no. 3 (2015): 273–90.

Chapter 6

1 It was the Slowenian artist and critic Emil Hrvatin who was the first to publish a full book-length study on Fabre: *Ponavljanje, Norost, Disciplina: celostna umetnina Fabre* (Ljubljana: Moderna galerija Ljubljana, 1993), which appeared in 1994 in French under the title *La Discipline du chaos, le chaos de la discipline* (Seine Saint-Denis: Armand Collin). Also in 1993 Sigrid Bousset edited a collection of essays on Fabres work: *Jan Fabre: Texts on his Theatre-Work* (Brussels: Kaaitheater). Arnd Wesemann edited in 1994 a book in the series *Regie im Theater, Jan Fabre: Regie im Theater* (Frankfurt/M: Fischer-Taschenbuchverlag). Ever since, the academic and critical literature on Fabre has grown exponentially, not to mention all the commentaries and introductions to his work as a visual artist in catalogues and art books.

2 Jan Fabre, *Der Palast um vier Uhr Morgens, ... A.G.* (1989).

3 The irruption of the real is a typical postdramatic strategy, see Hans-Thies Lehmann, *Postdramatic Theatre*, trans. Karen Jürs-Munby (Abingdon and New York: Routledge, 2006), 99–104.

4 Also Erika Fischer-Lichte has written on liminality as a collision between aesthetic and ethical frameworks in performance and theatre. See Fischer-Lichte, *The Transformative Power of Performance. A New Aesthetics*, trans. Saskya Iris Jain (Abingdon and New York: Routledge, 2008),170–77.

5 See Bertolt Brecht, 'Theatre as Sport', in *Brecht on Theatre*, ed. Marc Silberman, Steve Giles and Tom Kuhn, 3rd edn (London: Bloomsbury Methuen Drama, 2015), 20–21.

6 For instance, *Art as a Gamble/Gamble as Art* (1981), in which he provocatively questions the relation between critic and artist, or *Money*

Performance (1979) in which he burns real money. For further discussion of these early performances, see the chapter by Luk Van den Dries in this volume.

7   One of the central techniques Fabre developed in his early visual art was blue ballpoint drawing, for which he used 'Bic' ballpoint pens and covered existing artworks and later also large blank surfaces with blue lines. Fabre's solo-exhibitions with his blue 'Bic' drawings date back to the late 1970s. See also the chapter by Luk Van den Dries in this volume.

8   Stefan Hertmans, *Engel van de metamorfose. Over het werk van Jan Fabre* (Amsterdam: Meulenhoff, 2002), 97.

9   Fabre created the following solo performances for and with Els Deceukelier: *She Was and She Is, Even* (1991), *Falsification As She Is, Unfalsified* (1992), *A Dead Normal Woman* (1995) and *Etant données* (2004).

10   *Theatre written with a K is a Tomcat* (1980), *This is Theatre as it was to be Expected and Foreseen* (1982), *The Power of Theatrical Madness* (1984).

11   Emil Hrvatin, *La Discipline du chaos, le chaos de la discipline* (Seine Saint-Denis: Armand Collin, 1994). In his analysis, Hrvatin refers to Fabre's choreographic works, such as *The Dance Sections* (1987), *The Sound of One Hand Clapping* (1990).

12   This new stage in Fabre's career is most clearly marked by the production *As Long as the World Needs a Warrior's Soul* (2000).

13   For example, Jan Fabre's large-scale production *Mount Olympus* (2015), which I discuss later in this chapter, was criticized for being too 'readible' by one Flemish reviewer. For the English translation of the review, see Sébastien Hendrickx, 'Regime Art', *Etcetera: Tijdschrift voor Podiumkunsten*, 22 September 2016. Available online: www.e-tcetera.be/jan-fabretroubleyn-mount-olympus-0 (accessed 21 April 2017).

14   Lehmann, *Postdramatic Theatre*, 17.

15   Examples of durational performances can be found in the work of Robert Wilson, Peter Brook, Marina Abramović and Forced Entertainment.

16   *Art as a Gamble/Gamble as Art* (1981). Fabre also planned another version of the same performance, playing Russian roulette, but this action was forbidden.

17   Georges Bataille, *The Tears of Eros*, trans. Peter Connor (San Francisco: City Lights Books, 1989), 67.

18   See, for example, Fabre's performances *The Crying Body* (2004) and *History of Tears* (2005).

19   This trilogy has been written for Dirk Roofthooft. Previous monologues have been written for Els Deceukelier and Marc Moon Overmeir.

20   'Jan Fabre' in Luk Van den Dries, *Corpus Jan Fabre: Observations of a Creative Process* (Ghent: Inschoot, 2006), 319.

21   See Georg W.F. Hegel, *Phenomenology of Spirit*, trans. A.V. Miller (Oxford: Oxford University Press, 1977), 19.

22   See Jean Baudrillard, 'The Body, or the Mass Grave of Signs', in *Symbolic Exchange and Death*, trans. Iain Hamilton Grant, rev. edn (London: Sage, 2017), 122–45.

23 Hans-Thies Lehmann, 'Wenn Wut zur Form gerinnt', in *Jan Fabre: Texts on his Theatre-work*, ed. Sigrid Bousset (Brussels/Frankfurt a.M.: Kaaitheater/Theater amTurm, 1993), 90–103.

24 Bataille, *The Tears of Eros*, 66.

25 Edward Gordon Craig, 'The Artists of the Theatre of the Future', in *On the Art of the Theatre*, ed. Franc Chamberlain (Abingdon and New York: Routledge, 2009), 23.

26 Lehmann, 'Wenn Wut zur Form gerinnt', 90–103.

27 Jan Fabre in Van den Dries, *Corpus Jan Fabre*, 320.

28 Fabre dedicated twice a performance to the tragic fate of Prometheus: *Prometheus Landscape* (1988), and *Prometheus Landscape II* (2011).

29 Jan Fabre, *We Need Heroes Now* (2010), unpublished manuscript. The text was part of the performance *Prometheus Landscape II* (2011).

30 Luk Van den Dries, *Het geopende lichaam* (Antwerp: De Bezige Bij, 2014), 15.

31 Antonin Artaud, *Collected Works*, vol. 4, trans. Victor Corti (London: John Calder, 1999), 100.

32 Artaud's appeal to cruelty and physicality goes hand-in-hand with an extreme codification as in a sign language. See his famous essay on Balinese theatre: Artaud, *Collected Works*, vol. IV, 38–50.

33 Friedrich Nietzsche, *The Birth of Tragedy out of the Spirit of Music*, trans. Walter Kaufman (New York: Vintage, 1967).

34 Antonin Artaud, *Pour en finir avec je jugement de dieu* (recording for French radio, ORTF, 1947).

35 Jan Fabre in Van den Dries, *Corpus Jan Fabre*, 322.

36 Walter Benjamin, 'On the Concept of History', in *Selected Writings*, vol. 4, ed. Howard Eiland and Michael W. Jennings, trans. Edmund Jephcott et al. (Cambridge: Harvard University Press, 2003), 398–400.

37 Heiner Müller, 'Brief an Erich Wonder', in *Raum-Szenen/Szenen-Raum*, ed. Erich Wonder (Stuttgart: Hatje Verlag), 1986.

38 Lehmann, *Postdramatic Theatre*, 98–100, 114.

39 Jan Fabre in Van den Dries, *Corpus Jan Fabre*, 319.

40 Heiner Müller, 'Mülheim Address (1989)', in *Explosion of a Memory: Writings*, ed. Carl Weber (New York: PAJ Publications, 1989), 89–92. The text originally appeared in *Theater Heute* 10 (1979).

BIBLIOGRAPHY

General

Boenisch, Peter. *Directing Scenes and Senses: The Thinking of Regie*. Manchester: Manchester University Press, 2015.

Bousset, Sigrid. 'In stilte achter glas'. In *Mestkever van de verbeelding. Over Jan Fabre*, edited by Sigrid Bousset, 17–30. Amsterdam: De Bezige Bij, 1994.

Bovet, Jeanne and Yves Jubinville. 'Le répertoire: lieu de mémoire, lieu de création'. *L'Annuaire théâtral*, no. 53–54 (2013): 9–12.

Bradby, David and David Williams. *Director's Theatre*. New York: Macmillan Education, 1988.

Bratton, Jacky. 'Theatre History Today'. In *New Readings in Theatre History*, 3–16. Cambridge: Cambridge University Press, 2003.

Burt, Ramsay. 'Repetition: Brown, Bausch and De Keersmaeker'. In *Judson Dance Theater: Performative Traces*, 138–61. Abingdon and New York: Routledge, 2006.

Castellucci, Romeo, Chiara Guidi and Claudia Castellucci. *Epopea della polvere. Il teatro della Societas Raffaello Sanzio 1992–1999*. Milan: Ubulibri, 2001.

Cody, Gabrielle. 'Woman Man, Dog, Tree: Two Decades of Intimate and Monumental Bodies in Pina Bausch's Tanztheater'. *TDR* 42, no. 2 (1998): 115–38.

Cornils, Ingo and Sarah Waters, eds. *Memories of 1968: International Perspectives*. Bern: Peter Lang, 2010.

Crombez, Thomas, Jelle Koopmans, Frank Peeters, Luk Van Den Dries and Karel Vanhaesebrouck. *Theater. Een Westerse geschiedenis*. Leuven: Lannoo Campus, 2015.

Decreus, Freddy. 'Over de esthetisering van geweld. Mythe en trauma in het theater van Castellucci'. *Tetradion*, no. 25 (2016): 179–202.

De Laet, Timmy. 'Dancing Metamemories'. *Performance Research* 17, no. 3 (2012): 102–8.

De Laet, Timmy and Edith Cassiers. 'The Regenerative Ruination of Romeo Castellucci'. *Performance Research* 20, no. 3 (2015): 18–28.

Derrida, Jacques. *Margins of Philosophy*. Translated by Alan Bass. Chicago: The University of Chicago Press, 1982.

Eckersall, Peter, Helena Grehan and Edward Scheer, eds. *New Media Dramaturgy: Performance, Media and New-Materialism*. London: Palgrave Macmillan, 2017.

Eco, Umberto. *The Open Work*. Translated by Anna Cancogni. Cambridge, MA: Harvard University Press, 1989.

Fischer-Lichte, Erika. *The Show and the Gaze of Theatre: A European Perspective.* Iowa City: University of Iowa Press, 1997.

Fuchs, Elinor. *The Death of Character: Perspectives on Theater after Modernism.* Bloomington and Indianapolis: Indiana University Press, 1996.

Gilcher-Holtey, Ingrid, Dorothea Kraus and Franziska Schößler, eds. *Politisches Theater nach 1968: Regie, Dramatik und Organisation.* Frankfurt and New York: Campus Verlag, 2006.

Heddon, Deirdre and Jane Milling, eds. *Devising Performance: A Critical History.* Houndmills: Palgrave Macmillan, 2005.

Hertmans, Stefan. *Engel van de metamorfose: Over het werk van Jan Fabre.* Amsterdam: Meulenhoff, 2002.

Hoghe, Raimund. *Pina Bausch. Tanztheatergeschichten.* Frankfurt am Main: Suhrkamp Taschenbuch, 1986.

Hrvatin, Emil. *Jan Fabre: La discipline du chaos, le chaos de la discipline.* Éditions Armand Collin. Paris: Centre International de Bagnolet, 1994.

Innes, Christopher and Maria Shevtsova. 'Total Theatre: The Director as *auteur*'. In *The Cambridge Introduction to Theatre Directing*, 147–84. Cambridge: Cambridge University Press, 2013.

Klimke, Martin and Joachim Scharloth. *1968 in Europe: A History of Protest and Activism, 1956–1977.* New York: Palgrave, 2008.

Lehmann, Hans-Thies. *Postdramatic Theatre.* Translated by Karen Jürs-Munby. Abingdon and New York: Routledge, 2006.

Le Roy, Frederik, Edith Cassiers, Thomas Crombez and Luk Van Den Dries. 'Tracing Creation: The Director's Notebook as Genetic Document of the Postdramatic Creative Process'. *Contemporary Theatre Review* 26, no. 4 (2016): 468–84.

Luckhurst, Mary. *Dramaturgy: A Revolution in the Theatre.* Cambridge: Cambridge University Press, 2006.

Oddey, Alison. *Devising Theatre: A Practical and Theoretical Handbook.* Abingdon and New York: Routledge, 1994.

Peacock, D. Keith. *Thatcher's Theatre: British Theatre and Drama in the Eighties.* Westport, CT: Greenwood Press, 1999.

Pewny, Katharina, Johan Callens and Jeroen Coppens, eds. *Dramaturgies in the New Millennium: Relationality, Performativity and Potentiality, Schriftenreihe Forum Modernes Theater*, 44. Tübingen: Narr Verlag, 2014.

Postlewait, Thomas. *The Cambridge Introduction to Theatre Historiography.* Cambridge: Cambridge University Press, 2009.

Reinelt, Janelle and Joseph Roach, eds. *Critical Theory and Performance.* Revised and enlarged edn. Ann Arbor: The University of Michigan Press, 2007.

Romanska, Magda, ed. *The Routledge Companion to Dramaturgy.* Abingdon and New York: Routledge, 2015.

Roose-Evans, James. *Experimental Theatre: From Stanislavsky to Peter Brook*, 4th edn, revised and updated. Abingdon and New York: Routledge, 1989.

Schneider, Rebecca. *Theatre & History.* Houndmills: Palgrave Macmillan, 2014.

Sherman, Daniel J., Ruud Van Dijk and Jasmine Alinder, eds. *The Long 1968: Revisions and New Perspectives.* Bloomington: Indiana University Press, 2013.

Sidiropolou, Avra. *Authoring Performance: The Director in Contemporary Theatre.* Houndmills: Palgrave Macmillan, 2011.

Swyzen, Claire and Kurt Vanhoutte, eds. *Het statuut van de tekst in het post dramatische theater.* Brussels: University Press Antwerp, 2011.

Trencsény, Katalin and Bernadette Cochrane. 'Foreword – New Dramaturgy: A Post-Mimetic, Intercultural, Process-Conscious Paradigm'. In *New Dramaturgy: International Perspectives on Theory and Practice*, xi–xx. London: Methuen Drama, 2014.

Van Den Dries, Luk. *Corpus Jan Fabre. Observations of a Creative Process*. Ghent: Imschoot, 2006.

Van Den Dries, Luk and Thomas Crombez. 'Jan Fabre and tg STAN: Two Models of Postdramatic Theatre in the Avant-Garde Tradition'. *Contemporary Theatre Review* 20, no. 4 (2010): 421–31.

Vince, R.W. 'Theatre History as an Academic Discipline'. In *Interpreting the Theatrical Past*, edited by Thomas Postlewait and Bruce A. McConachie, 1–18. Iowa: University of Iowa Press, 1989.

Wagenbach, Marc and Pina Bausch Foundation, eds. *Tanz erben: Pina lädt ein.* Bielefeld: transcript Verlag, 2014.

Willcoxon, Jeanne. 'Postdramatic Theatre (review)'. *Theatre Topics* 18, no. 2 (2008): 248–9.

Williams, Gary Jay, ed. *Theatre Histories: An Introduction*, 2nd edn. Abingdon and New York: Routledge, 2006.

Pina Bausch

Abrams, M.H. *A Glossary of Literary Terms*, 5th edn. Fort Worth: Holt, Rinehart and Winston, Inc., 1988.

Acocella, Joan. 'Bausch's Inferno'. *Art in America*, January 1992: 50–3.

Acocella, Joan. 'Reviews: New York City'. *Dance Magazine*, March 1986: 20–4 and 40–3.

Adelman, Janet. '"Born of Woman": Fantasies of Maternal Power in *Macbeth*'. In *Bloom's Modern Critical Interpretations: William Shakespeare's Macbeth* (New Edition), edited by Harold Bloom, 33–59. New York: Bloom's Literary Criticism, 2010.

Artaud, Antonin. *The Theatre and Its Double*. Translated by M.C. Richards. New York: Grove Press, 1958.

Banes, Sally. 'What the Critics Say about Tanztheater'. *TDR: The Drama Review* 30, no. 2 (Summer 1986): 80–4.

Bausch, Pina. 'Eine gewisse Erregung dabei/Bin im Moment bei den Gefühlen', interview with Stephen Locke [1979]. Reprinted in Koldehoff and Pina Bausch Foundation, eds, *O-Ton Pina Bausch*, 45–60.

Bausch, Pina. 'Etwas finden, was keiner Frage bedarf' (speech given at the Kyoto Prize Workshop in Arts and Philosophy, 12 November 2007). Reprinted in Koldehoff and Pina Bausch Foundation, eds, *O-Ton Pina Bausch*, 317–33.

Bausch, Pina. 'Ich bin das Publikum', interview with Ingrid Seyfarth [1987]. Reprinted in Koldehoff and Pina Bausch Foundation, eds, *O-Ton Pina Bausch*, 123–8.

Bausch, Pina. 'Man weiß gar nicht, wo die Phantasie einen hintreibt', interview with Jean-Marc Adolphe [2007]. Reprinted in Koldehoff and Pina Bausch Foundation, eds, *O-Ton Pina Bausch*, 273–95.

Bausch, Pina. 'Tanz ist die einzig wirkliche Sprache', interview with Norbert Servos [1990]. Reprinted in Koldehoff and Pina Bausch Foundation, eds, *O-Ton Pina Bausch*, 137–42.

Bausch, Pina. 'Was mich bewegt', speech at the Kyoto Prize festivities, 12 November 2007. Reprinted in Koldehoff and Pina Bausch Foundation, eds, *O-Ton Pina Bausch*, 295–315.

Bausch, Pina. 'Wenn ich mir ganz genau zuhöre, macht sich das Stück selber', interview with Roger Willemsen, *Willemsens' Woche* [1998]. Reprinted in Koldehoff and Pina Bausch Foundation, eds. *O-Ton Pina Bausch*, 185–96.

Bausch, Pina and Kyomi Ichida. 'Dialogue during a rehearsal of "Le Sacre du Printemps"' [1989]. In *Probe Sacre*, edited by Pina Bausch, [Film], DVD and booklet. Paris: L'Arche Editeur, 2013.

Baxmann, Inge. 'Dance Theatre: Rebellion of the Body, Theatre of Images and an Inquiry into the Sense of the Senses'. *Ballett International* 13, no. 10 (January 1990): 55–60.

Beckett, Samuel. 'Dante ... Bruno. Vico. Joyce'. In *Finnegans Wake: A Symposium – Exagmination Round His Incamination of Work in Progress [... &c.]*, 1–22. Paris: Shakespeare & Co., 1929; facs. rep. edn, New York: New Directions, 1972.

Betteridge, Harold. *Cassell's German Dictionary*, rev. edn. New York: Macmillan Publishing Company, 1978.

Bentivoglio, Leonetta. 'Dance of the Present, Art of the Future'. *Ballett International* 8, no. 12 (December 1985): 24–8.

Bentivoglio, Leonetta and Francesco Carbone. *Pina Bausch oder Die Kunst über Nelken zu tanzen*. Frankfurt am Main: Suhrkamp, 2007.

Brandstetter, Gabriele and Gabriele Klein, eds. *Methoden der Tanzwissenschaft. Modellanalysen zu Pina Bauschs 'Le Sacre du Printemps/Das Frühlingsopfer'*, 2nd edn. Bielefeld: transcript Verlag, 2015.

Brandstetter, Gabriele. 'Pina Bauschs *Das Frühlingsopfer*. Signatur – Übertragung – Kontext' [2007]. In *Methoden der Tanzwissenschaft. Modellanalysen zu Pina Bauschs 'Le Sacre du Printemps/Das Frühlingsopfer'*, edited by Gabriele Brandstetter and Gabriele Klein, 2nd edn. Bielefeld: transcript Verlag, 2015.

Brinkmann, Stephan. *Bewegung Erinnern, Bewegung Erinnern. Gedächtnisformen im Tanz*. Bielefeld: transcript Verlag, 2013.

Bronislava, Nijinska. *Early Memoirs*. Translated and edited by Irina Nijinska and Jean Rawlinson. Durham, NC, and London: Duke University Press, [1981] 1992.

Burke, Kenneth. *The Philosophy of Literary Form: Studies in Symbolic Action*, rev. edn. New York: Random House, 1957.

Chamberlain, Stephanie. 'Fantasizing Infanticide: Lady Macbeth and the Murdering Mother in Early Modern England'. *College Literature* 32, no. 3 (2005): 72–91.

Chazin-Bennahum, Judith. *The Ballets of Antony Tudor: Studies in Psyche and Satire*. New York: Oxford University Press, 1994.

Climenhaga, Royd. *Pina Bausch: Performance Practitioner Series*. New York: Routledge, 2009.

Climenhaga, Royd, ed. *The Pina Bausch Sourcebook. The Making of Tanztheater*. London and New York: Routledge, 2013.

Confino, Barbara. 'The Theater of Images: Pina Bausch and the Expressionist Temperament'. *Cityweek*, 18 July 1988: 41–2.

Daly, Ann. 'Tanztheater: The Thrill of the Lynch Mob or the Rage of Woman?' *TDR: The Drama Review* 30, no. 2 (1986): 46–56.

Dawn, Lillie. *Equipose: The Life and Work of Alfredo Corvino*. New York: Dance & Movement Press, 2009.

Deleuze, Gilles and Félix Guattari. *Anti-Oedipus: Capitalism and Schizophrenia I*. Translated by Robert Hurley, Mark Seem and Helen R. Lane. Minneapolis: University of Minnesota Press, 1993.

Deleuze, Gilles and Félix Guattari. *A Thousand Plateaus. Capitalism and Schizophrenia*. Translated by Brian Massumi. Minneapolis: University of Minnesota Press, 1993.

Derrida, Jacques. 'Signatur, Événement, Contexte.' In *Marges de la philosophie*, 365–93. Paris: Les éditions de Minuit, 1972.

Diagne, Mariama. 'Atem Holen. Szenen vom Ende des Lebens im Tanztheater'. In *transmortale. Sterben, Tod und Trauer in der neueren Forschung*, edited by Moritz Buchner and Anna-Maria Götz, 198–219. Cologne, Weimar, Vienna: Böhlau Verlag, 2016.

Endicott, Jo Ann. 'Inside Pina's *The Rite of Spring*'. In *Le Sacre du Printemps*, edited by L'Arche Éditeur and Pina Bausch Foundation, [DVD], production of the television broadcasting channel ZDF from 1978 at Tanztheater Wuppertal, 68–9. Paris: L'Arche Éditeur, 2012.

Fernandes, Ciane. 'Appendix A: *Interview with Dancer Ruth Amarante*'. In *Pina Bausch and the Wuppertal Dance Theater: The Aesthetics of Repetition and Transformation*, edited by Ciane Fernandes, 111–17. New York: Peter Lang Publishing, 2005.

Fischer-Lichte, Erika. *The Transformative Power of Performance: A New Aesthetics*. Translated by Saskya Iris Jain. New York and Abingdon: Routledge, 2008.

Freud, Sigmund. *The Interpretation of Dreams*. Translated by James Strachey. New York: Basic Books, [1955] 2010.

Gil, José. 'The Paradoxical Body'. In *Planes of Composition: Dance, Theory and the Global*, edited by André Lepecki and Jenn Joy, 85–106. Calcutta and London: Seagull Books, 2009.

Gilpin, Heidi. 'Amputation, Dismembered Identites, and the Rhythms of Elimination: Reading Pina Bausch'. In *Other Germanies: Questioning Identity in Women's Literature and Art*, edited by Karen Jankowsky, 165–90. New York: State University of New York Press, 1997.

Gumbrecht, Hans Ulrich. *Production of Presence: What Meaning Cannot Convey*. Stanford, CA: Stanford University Press, 2003.

Hillman, James. 'An Inquiry into Image'. *Spring: An Annual of Archetypal Psychology and Jungian Thought* (1977): 62–88.

Hodson, Millicent. *Nijinsky's Crime against Grace: Reconstruction Score of the Original Choreography for Le Sacre du Printemps*. Stuyvesant, NY: Pendragon Press, 1996.

Hoghe, Raimund. *Bandoneon: Working with Pina Bausch*. Translated by Penny Black. London: Oberon Books, 2016.

Hoghe, Raimund. *Pina Bausch: Tanztheatergeschichten*. Frankfurt a.M.: Suhrkamp, 1986.

Huschka, Sabine. *Merce Cunningham und der Moderne Tanz. Körperkonzepte, Choreographie und Tanzästhetik*. Würzburg: Königshausen & Neumann, 2000.

Huschka, Sabine. *Moderner Tanz. Stile, Konzepte, Utopien*. Reinbek: Rowohlt Verlag, 2002.

Huschka, Sabine. 'Pina Bausch, Mary Wigman, and the Aesthetic of "Being Moved"'. In *New German Dance Studies*, edited by Susan Manning and Lucia Ruprecht, 182–99. Chicago: University of Illinois Press, 2012.

Husserl, Edmund. *Ideas: General Introduction to Pure Phenomenology*, rev. edn. Abingdon: Routledge, 2012.

Järvinen, Hanna. '"They Never Dance": The Choreography of Le Sacre du Printemps, 1913'. *AVANT* 4, no. 3 (2013): 69–108.

Jeschke, Claudia. *Tanz als Bewegungstext. Analysen zum Verhältnis von Tanztheater und Gesellschaftstanz (1910–1965)*, with contribution by Cary Rick. Tübingen: Niemeyer, 1999.

Johnson, Mark. *The Body in the Mind: The Bodily Basis of Meaning, Imagination, and Reason*. Chicago: University of Chicago Press, 1987.

Jowitt, Deborah. 'Please Do It Again, Do It Again, Again … '. *Village Voice*, 3 July 1984: 93–4.

Kisselgoff, Anna. 'Pina Bausch's "Palermo, Palermo" Explores a World beyond Logic'. *New York Times*, 30 September 1991: C13–14.

Klein, Gabriele. 'Die Performanz des Rituals'. In *Methoden der Tanzwissenschaft. Modellanalysen zu Pina Bauschs 'Le Sacre du Printemps/Das Frühlingsopfer'*, edited by Gabriele Brandstetter and Gabriele Klein, 2nd edn, 75–81. Bielefeld: transcript Verlag, 2015.

Koegler, Horst. 'Tanztheater Wuppertal' [1979]. In *The Pina Bausch Sourcebook*, edited by Royd Climenhaga, 182–7. London and New York: Routledge, 2013.

Kott, Jan. *Shakespeare heute*. Munich: R.Piper Verlag, 1970.

Kozel, Susan. 'Bausch and Phenomenology' [1993–4]. In *The Pina Bausch Sourcebook*, edited by Royd Climenhaga, 182–7. London and New York: Routledge, 2013.

Lakoff, George and Mark Johnson. *Metaphors We Live By*. Chicago: University of Chicago Press, 1980.

Lehmann, Hans-Thies. *Postdramatic Theatre*. Translated by Karen Jürs-Munby. New York and Abingdon: Routledge, 2006.

Loney, Glenn Loney. '"I Pick My Dancers As People" – Pina Bausch Discusses Her Work with the Wuppertal Dance Theatre' [1985]. Reprinted in *The Pina Bausch Sourcebook*, edited by Royd Climenhaga, 88–98. London and New York: Routledge, 2013.

Linsel, Anne. 'Pina Bauschs Wildgruber'. *k.west. Das Kulturmagazin des Westens. Magazin für Kunst, Kultur, Gesellschaft* 12 (2008).

Macaulay, Alastair. 'Under Analysis: The Psychology of Tudor's Ballets'. *The New York Times*, 11 May 2008.

Manning, Susan. 'An American Perspective on Tanztheater' [1986]. In *The Pina Bausch Sourcebook: The Making of Tanztheater*, edited by Royd Climenhaga, 31–44. London and New York: Routledge, 2013.

Manning, Erin. *Always More than One: Individuation's Dance*. Durham, NC and London: Duke University Press, 2013.

Manning, Susan and Lucia Ruprecht, eds. *New German Dance Studies*. Chicago: University of Illinois Press, 2002.

Meisner, Nadine. 'Come Dance With Me' [1992]. In *The Pina Bausch Source Book: The Making of Tanztheater*, edited by Royd Climenhaga, 167–76. London and New York: Routledge, 2013.

Mitchell, W.J.T. *Iconology: Image, Text, Ideology*. Chicago: University of Chicago Press, 1986.

Müller, Hedwig and Claudia Rosiny. 'Ein Stückchen Tanztheater. Eine Szene von Pina Bausch'. *Tanzdrama* 12, no. 3 (1990): 4–10.

Müller, Hedwig and Norbert Servos. 'Expressionism? "Ausdruckstanz" and the New Dance Theatre in Germany'. In *Festival International de Nouvelle Danse, Montreal, Souvenir Program*, translated by Michael Vensky-Stalling, 10–15, 1986.

Müller, Heiner. 'Blut ist im Schuh, oder das Rätsel der Freiheit' [1982]. In *Tanz-Legenden: Essays zu Pina Bauschs Tanztheater*, edited by Ulrike Hanraths and Hubert Winkels, 117–23. Frankfurt: Tende, 1984.

Richards, Ivor A. *Philosophy of Rhetoric*. New York and London: Oxford University Press, 1936.

Schlicher, Susanne. *TanzTheater. Traditionen und Freiheiten, Pina Bausch, Gerhard Bohner, Reinhild Hoffmann, Hans Kresnik, Susanne Linke*. Reinbek bei Hamburg: Rowohlt, 1987.

Schwarzer, Alice. 'Ein Stück für Pina Bausch', interview with Mechthild Grossmann. *EMMA 1* (2010): 44–50.

Servos, Norbert. *Pina Bausch: Dance Theatre*. Munich: Kieser Verlag, 2008.

Servos, Norbert. *Pina Bausch Wuppertal Dance Theater or the Art of Training a Goldfish*. Cologne: Ballett-Bühnen-Verlag, 1984.

Servos, Norbert. 'V. Tanztheater. 1. Definition und theoretische Grundlagen', 355–9, in 'Tanz', article by several authors. In *Musik in Geschichte und Gegenwart. Allgemeine Enzyklopädie der Musik*, edited by Finscher Ludwig, 2nd edn, vol. 9. Kassel, Stuttgart: Bärenreiter-Verlag, J.-B.-Metzler, 1998.

Smith, Paul. *Discerning the Subject*. Minneapolis: University of Minnesota Press, 1988.

States, Bert O. *Dreaming and Storytelling*. Ithaca, NY: Cornell University Press, 1993.

States, Bert O. 'Performance as Metaphor'. *Theatre Journal* 48, no. 1 (1996): 1–26.

States, Bert O. *The Rhetoric of Dreams*. Ithaca, NY: Cornell University Press, 1988.

Stöckemann, Patricia. *Etwas ganz Neues muß nun entstehen. Kurt Jooss und das Tanztheater*. Munich: Kieser Verlag, 2001.

Van Kerkhoven, Marianne. 'Dance, Theatre, and their Hazy Boundaries'. *Ballett International* 16, no. 1 (1993): 11–15.

Van Kerkhoven, Marianne. 'The Weight of Time'. *Ballett International* 14, no. 2 (February 1991): 63–8.

Wagenbach, Marc, ed. *Inheriting Dance: An Invitation from Pina*. Bielefeld: Transcript Verlag, 2014.

Walther, Suzanne K. *Dance of Death: Kurt Jooss and the Weimar Years*. Chur: Harwood Academic, 1994.

Was Tun Pina Bausch und Ihrer Tänzer in Wuppertal? Videocassette. Dir. Klaus Wildenhahn. Inter Nationes, 1983.

Romeo Castellucci

Alinovi, Francesca. 'Il teatro dell'aventura'. In *Una generazione postmoderna*, edited by Renato Barilli, Fulvio Irace and Francesca Alinovi, 33–6. Milan: Mazzotta, 1982.

Amara, Lucia. 'Artaud figgura in *Epopea della polvere*'. In *Toccare il reale*, edited by Piersandra Di Matteo, 54–8. Napoli: Cronopio, 2015.

Artaud, Antonin. *Œuvres complètes XIII*. Edited by Paule Thévenin. Paris: Gallimard, 1974.

Artaud, Antonin. 'L'arve et l'aume. Tentative anti-grammaticale contre Lewis Carroll'. *L'Arbalète* 12 (1947): 159–84.

Artaud, Antonin. *Le théâtre et son double*. Paris: Gallimard, 1938.

Artaud, Antonin. *Selected Writings*. Edited by Susan Sontag and translated by Helen Weaver. New York: Farrar, Strauss, Giroux, 1976.

Bachofen, Johann Jakob. *Il Matriarcato. Ricerca sulla ginecocrazia del mondo antico nei suoi aspetti religiosi e giuridici*, 2 vols. Edited by Giulio Schiavoni. Turin: Einaudi, 1861/1988.

Bachofen, Johann Jakob. *Il simbolismo funerario degli antichi*. Edited by Mario Pezzella. Naples: Guida editori, 1989.

Bartolucci, Giuseppe. 'Raffaello Sanzio'. *FlashArt. La prima Rivista d'arte in Europa* (February–March 1982): 4–5.

Bataille, Georges. *Œuvres complètes I*. Paris: Gallimard, 1970.

Béhar, Henri. *Étude sur le théâtre dada et surréaliste*. Paris: Gallimard, 1967.

Belpoliti, Marco. 'Romeo Castellucci a Belpoliti, Cesena, 23 gennaio 1995'. *Riga 8* (1995): 148–51.

Benjamin, Walter. *Gesammelte Schriften*, vol. I–II. Frankfurt am Main: Suhrkamp, 1980.

Bettelheim, Bruno. *The Empty Fortress: Infantile Autism and the Birth of the Self*. New York: The Free Press, 1967.

Bierl, Anton. 'Romeo Castelluccis Orestea'. In *Die Orestie des Aischylos auf der modernen Buhne*, 90–110. Stuttgart: M&P, 1997.

Blumenberg, Hans. *Arbeit am Mythos*. Frankfurt am Main: Suhrkamp, 1979.

Bois, Yve-Alain and Rosalind Krauss. *L'informe: Mode d'emploi*. Paris: Éditions du Centre Pompidou, 1996.

Breton, André. *Œuvres complètes I*. Paris: Gallimard, 1988.

Carlson, Marvin. *Theatre Semiotics: Signs of Life*. Bloomington: Indiana University Press, 1990.

Carroll, Lewis. *Humpty Dumpty. L'Arve et l'Aume. Bindolo Rondolo*. Edited by Carlo Pasi and translated by Antonin Artaud, Guido Almansi and Giuliana Poso. Stittori tradotti da scrittori. Turin: Einaudi, 1993.

Cascetta, Annamaria. 'Suggestioni conciliari nella drammatugia italiana'. In *Il Concilio Vaticano II crocevia dell'umanesimo contemporaneo*, edited by Angelo Bianchi, 241–7. Milan: Vita e pensiero, 2015.

Castellucci, Claudia. 'In assetto cosciente di solitudine assoluta'. In *Epopea della polvere*, edited by Romeo Castellucci, Chiara Guidi and Claudia Castellucci, 301–2. Milan: Ubulibri, 2001.

Castellucci, Claudia. 'La sindrome di Platone nel teatro delle operazioni'. In *Epopea della polvere. Il teatro della Socìetas Raffaello Sanzio 1992–1999*, edited by Romeo Castellucci, Chiara Guidi and Claudia Castellucci, 288–93. Milan: Ubulibri, 2001.

Castellucci, Claudia and Romeo Castellucci. *Il teatro della Socìetas Raffaello Sanzio. Dal teatro iconoclasta alla super-icona*. Milan: Ubulibri, 1992.

Castellucci, Claudia and Chiara Guidi. 'Ethics of Voice: Claudia Castellucci and Chiara Guidi in Conversation with Joe Kelleher'. *Performance Research* 9, no. 4 (2004): 112–13.

Castellucci, Claudia, Romeo Castellucci and Chiara Guidi. *Epopea della polvere: Il teatro della Socìetas Raffaello Sanzio 1992–1999*. Milan: Ubulibri, 2001.

Castellucci, Claudia, Romeo Castellucci, Chiara Guidi, Joe Kelleher and Nicholas Ridout. *The Theatre of Socìetas Raffaello Sanzio*. Abingdon and New York: Routledge, 2007.

Castellucci, Romeo. 'The Animal Being on Stage'. *Performance Research* 5, no. 2 (2000): 23–8.

Castellucci, Romeo. 'Appunti di un clown'. In *Orestea (una commedia organica?)*, edited by Socìetas Raffaello Sanzio, 4–14. Programme book. Cesena: Socìetas Raffaello Sanzio, 1995.

Castellucci, Romeo. 'Art is Fire', interview with Niki Orfanou. *Ef* 44, no. 3 (June 2015): 4–5.

Castellucci, Romeo. 'Asinina cogitatio'. In Masoch. *I trion del teatro come porenza passiva, colpa e scon tta*. Published programme book. Cesena: Societas Raffaello Sanzio, 1993.

Castellucci, Romeo. 'Gather and Burn', translated by Joseph Cermatori. *PAJ* 107 (2014): 22–5.

Castellucci, Romeo. 'In principio era l'immagine'. In *La discesa di Inanna: Mito Sumero*, edited by Socìetas Raffaello Sanzio, 5–11. Cesena: Casa del bello estremo, 1989.

Castellucci, Romeo. 'La quinta parete/Le cinquième mur'. In *Le théâtre et ses publics. La création partagée*, edited by Nancy Delhalle, 17–28. Besançon: Les Solitaires Intempestifs, 2013.

Castellucci, Romeo. 'Représentation en tant que telle'. *Puck. La Marionnette et les autres arts. Humain, non humain* 20 (2014): 17–20.

Castellucci, Romeo. 'Romeo Castellucci speaks to *Vimadonna* on the value of research'. *Vimadonna*, interview by Ioanna Zymariti, 5 February 2016. Available online: http://www.tovima.gr/vimadonna/prosopa/article/?aid=774267.

Castellucci, Romeo. 'Superficies ad Dominum soli pertinet'. In *Gilgamesh*, edited by Socìetas Raffaello Sanzio, 21–2. Cesena: Casa del bello estremo, 1990.

Castellucci, Romeo. 'Epopteia'. In *Socìetas Raffaello Sanzio, Gilgamesh*, 17–18. Cesena: Casa del bello estramo, 1990.

Castellucci, Romeo. 'La riconquista della visione'. In *Socìetas Raffaello Sanzio, Gilgamesh*, 23–5. Cesena: Casa del bello estramo, 1990.

Castellucci, Romeo. 'La discesa di Inanna'. In *Il teatro della Socìetas Raffaello Sanzio*, edited by Claudia Castellucci and Romeo Castellucci, 108–12. Milan: Ubulibri, 1992.

Castellucci, Romeo. '*Gilgamesh*. Descrizione della rappresentazione'. In *Il teatro della Socìetas Raffaello Sanzio*, edited by Claudia Castellucci and Romeo Castellucci, 145–62. Milan: Ubulibri, 1992.

Castellucci, Romeo. 'Asinina cogitatio'. In *Masoch. I trionfi del teatro come potenza passiva, colpa e sconfitta*, 2–16. Published programme book. Cesena: Socìetas Raffaello Sanzio, 1993.

Castellucci, Romeo. 'Amleto: Là dove la A risuona come alfa privativa'. In *Epopea della polvere*, edited by Romeo Castellucci, Chiara Guidi and Claudia Castellucci, 42–54. Milan: Ubulibri, 2001.

Castellucci, Romeo. 'L'Orestea attraverso lo specchio'. In *Epopea della polvere*, edited by Romeo Castellucci, Chiara Guidi and Claudia Castellucci, 156–9. Milan: Ubulibri, 2001.

Castellucci, Romeo. 'Il pellegrino della materia'. In *Epopea della polvere*, edited by Romeo Castellucci, Chiara Guidi and Claudia Castellucci, 270–7. Milan: Ubulibri, 2001.

Castellucci, Romeo. Introductory note to Pitozzi and Sacchi, 'La Minoration'. In *Itinera*, 195. Arles: Actes Sud, 2008.

Castellucci, Romeo and Claudia Castellucci. *Les Pèlerins de la matière: Théorie et praxis du théâtre: Écrits de la Socìetas Raffaello Sanzio*. Besançon: Les Solitaires Intempestifs, 2001.

Causey, Matthew. 'Stealing from God: The Crisis of Creation in Socìetas Raffaello Sanzio's *Genesi* and Eduardo Kac's *Genesis*'. In *Theatre and Performance in Digital Culture: From Simulation to Embeddedness*, 127–49. New York: Routledge, 2006.

Crombez, Thomas. *Het antitheater van Antonin Artaud: Een onderzoek naar de veralgemeende artistieke transgressie, toegepast op het werk van Romeo Castellucci en de Socìetas Raffaello Sanzio*. Ghent: Academia Press, 2008.

Crombez, Thomas. 'La transgression dans la "Tragedia Endogonidia" de la Socìetas Raffaello Sanzio'. In *Œdipe contemporain? Tragédie, Tragique, Politique*, edited by Paul Van Den Berghe, Christian Biet and Karel Vanhaesebrouck, 275–94. Brussels: Les Impressions Nouvelles, 2007.

Daston, Lorraine and Katherine Park. *Wonders and the Order of Nature: 1150–1750*. New York: Zone Books, 1998.

Decreus, Freddy. 'The Nomadic Theatre of the Socìetas Raffaello Sanzio: A Case of Postdramatic Reworking of (the Classical) Tragedy'. In *A Companion to Classical Receptions*, edited by Lorna Hardwick and Christopher Stray, 274–86. London: Blackwell, 2007.

De Laet, Timmy and Edith Cassiers. 'The Regenerative Ruination of Romeo Castellucci'. *Performance Research* 20, no. 3 (2015): 18–28.

Delaune, Benoît. 'Un cas précis de "plagiat par anticipation": Antonin Artaud accuses Lewis Carroll'. *Acta Fabula* 10, no. 2 (February 2009). Available online: www.fabula.org/acta/ document4990.php (accessed 15 April 2017).

Derrida, Jacques. *L'animal que donc je suis*. Paris: Galilée, 2006.

Deleuze, Gilles. *La Logique du sens*. Paris: Les éditions de Minuit, 1969.

Dallagiacoma, Angelo. 'Interview with Giorgia Penzo'. *Città Teatro*, 5 August 2013. Available online: https://www.facebook.com/notes/citt%C3%A0-teatro/ torna-a-riccione-dopo-35-anni-il-testo-di-angelo-dallagiacoma-che-nel-1978-vinse/632293860128588/

De Marinis, Marco. 'Introduzione. Il teatro elementale di Romeo Castellucci'. In *Toccare il reale*, edited by Piersandra Di Matteo, 21–7. Naples: Cronopio, 2015.

Derrida, Jacques. "La parole soufflée" and "Le théâtre de la cruauté et la clôture de la représentation". In *L'Écriture et la Différence*, 253–92 and 341–68. Paris: Seuil, 1979.

Di Matteo, Piersandra. 'A Stage Philosopher. A Portrait of Romeo Castellucci'. *Octave magazine*, October 2015. Available online: https://www.operadeparis.fr/ en/magazine/a-stage-philosopher

Duvignaud, Jean. *Les ombres collectives: Sociologie du théâtre*. Paris: Presses Universitaires de France, 1973.

Eco, Umberto. *The Open Work*. Translated by A. Cancogni. Cambridge, MA: Harvard University Press, 1989.

Féal, Gisèle. *Ionesco: Un théâtre onirique*. Paris: Imago, 2001.

Federico, Tiezzi. 'L'anima mentale e l'anima passionale'. *WeStuff* 5 (1 September 1986): 68.

Fensham, Rachel. 'The Rhetoric of Organs without Bodies. *Genesi: The Museum of Sleep*'. In *To Watch Theatre: Essays on Genre and Corporeality*, 137–64. Brussels: P.I.E. Peter Lang, 2009.

Fischer-Lichte, Erika. *Semiotik des Theaters*. Tübingen: Narr, 1983.

Fischer-Lichte, Erika. *The Transformative Power of Performance: A New Aesthetics*. Translated by Saskya Iris Jain. Abingdon: Routledge, 2008.

Foucart, Paul. *Les Mystères d'Eleusis*. Paris: Picard, 1914.

Garrone, Nico. 'Mondo-Persia 1a1 del gruppo Raffaello Sanzio'. *La Reppublica*, 13 January 1982: 4.

Giannachi, Gabriella and Nick Kaye. *Staging the Post-Avant-Garde: Italian Experimental Performance after 1970*. Bern: Peter Lang, 2002.

Grotowski, Jerzy. *Towards a Poor Theatre*. Edited by E. Barba. New York: Routledge, [1968] 2002.

House, Jane E. 'Perlini, Amelio (Memè)'. In *The Oxford Companion to Theatre & Performance*, edited by Dennis Kennedy, 460. Oxford: Oxford University Press, 2010.

I Monaci delle colonne. 'L'imagine che non si può vedere due volte'. In Out X Off Associazione Culturale, *Limitrofie* 4 (May 1986): 11.

Kristeva, Julia. *Polylogue*. Paris: Seuil, 1977.

Lamont, Rosette. 'The Terrible but Unended Story of Norodom Sihanouk: King of Cambodia by Helene Cixous: Ariane Mnouchkine (Review)'. *Performing Arts Journal* 10, no. 1 (1986): 46–50.

Landi, Paolo. 'Santarcangelo. Gli orizzonti in oscillazione del giovane teatro'. *Il Manifesto*, 14 September 1982.

Lehmann, Hans-Thies. *Postdramatic Theatre*. Translated by Karen Jürs-Munby. Abingdon: Routledge, 2006.

Manikòn, Claudia. 'Santa So a. Teatro Khmer. Del manifesto consegnato in teatro' [1986]. Reprinted in *Il teatro della Socìetas Raffaello Sanzio*, edited by Claudia Castellucci and Romeo Castellucci, 9–11. Milan: Ubulibri, 1992.

Madornal, Claudia. '*I Miserabili*. Dall'Manifesto'. In *Il teatro della Societas Raffaello Sanzio. Dal teatro iconoclasta alla super-icona*, edited by Claudia Castellucci and Romeo Castellucci, 59–64. Milan: Ubulibri, 1992.

Mango, Lorenzo. 'Il pensiero marginale'. *Lapis/Arte* 5 (1984): 58–5.

Mylonas, George Emmanuel. *Eleusis and the Eleusinian Mysteries*. Princeton, NJ: Princeton University Press, 1961.

Neofytou-Georgiou, Stamatia. 'The Semiotics of Images in Romeo Castellucci's Theatre'. In *The Visual in Performance Practice: Interdisciplinary Perspectives*, edited by Adele Anderson, Filipa Malva and Chris Berchild, 15–22. Oxford: Inter-Disciplinary Press, 2012.

Papalexiou, Eleni. 'The Body as Dramatic Material in the Theatre of Romeo Castellucci'. In *Utopia and Critical Thinking in the Creative Process*, 75–88. Besançon: Les Solitaires Intempestifs, 2012.

Papalexiou, Eleni. 'Conceiving the New Image of the World'. *EF* 44 (25 June 2015): 6–9.

Papalexiou, Eleni. 'The Dramaturgies of the Gaze: Strategies of Vision and Optical Revelations in the Theatre of Romeo Castellucci and the Socìetas Raffaello

Sanzio'. In *Theatre as Voyeurism: The Pleasures of Watching*, edited by George Rodosthenous, 50–68. London: Palgrave Macmillan, 2015.

Papalexiou, Eleni. 'Ecce homo'. *Theater der Zeit*, 1 January 2011: 67.

Papalexiou, Eleni. 'Homo Spectator'. In *The Athens Festival Programme 2015*, 34–5. Athens: The Athens Festival, 2015.

Papalexiou, Eleni. '*Nyx teleia*. Nella note profonda del mondo Greco antico'. In *Toccare il reale*, edited by Piersandra Di Matteo, 31–4. Naples: Cronopio, 2015.

Papalexiou, Eleni. 'Pharmakòs or *Democracy in America*'. *The Books' Journal* 78 (June 2017). Available online: http://booksjournal.gr/slideshow/item/2571-farmakos-h-democracy-in-america

Papalexiou, Eleni. *Rethinking la Divina Commedia*. Nafplion: University of Peloponnese-Dept. of Theatre Studies, forthcoming.

Papalexiou, Eleni and Avra Xepapadakou. 'Sur les traces de l'Orestie (une comédie organique?) de Romeo Castellucci: De sa conception (1995) à sa reprise (2015)'. In *Proceedings of the International Conference on Theatre Genetics Percursos de Genetica Teatral*. Lisbon: Centro de Estudos de Teatro, Universidade de Lisboa, forthcoming.

Papalexiou, Eleni, Avra Xepapadakou and Valia Vraka. 'L'archive théâtrale de la Socìetas Raffaello Sanzio: un pèlerinage à la matière'. In *Proceedings of the International Conference Processus de création et archives du spectacle vivant: manque de traces ou risque d'inflation mémorielle?* Rennes: Presses Universitaires de Rennes, forthcoming.

Papalexiou, Eleni. *Romeo Castellucci/Socìetas Raffaello Sanzio: When the Words Turn into Matter*. Athens: Plethron, 2009.

Pardo, Enrique. 'Electricity in Hell. Notes on the Work of Romeo Castellucci and Praise for Italy'. *Spring. A Journal for Archetype and Culture* 67 (2000): 161–74.

Pefanis, Giorgos. 'Dystopias, Heterotopias, Boundaries and other Theatrical Idioms of Space'. *Parabasis, Journal of the Department of Theatre Studies University of Athens* 14, no. 2 (2016): 65–83.

Ponte Di Pino, Oliviero. *Il nuovo teatro italiano 1975–1988*. Firenze: La casa Usher, 1988.

Propp, Vladimir. *Edipo alla luce del folclore*. Turin: Einaudi, 1966.

Quadri, Franco. 'In teatro '82. 60 Festival di Polverigi'. *Panorama*, 9 August 1982: 15.

Rabkin, Gerald. 'The Play of Misreading: Text/Theatre/Deconstruction'. *Performing Arts Journal* 20, no. 1 (1983): 55–60.

Ridout, Nicholas. 'Welcome to the Vibratorium'. *The Senses and Society* 3, no. 2 (2008): 221–32.

Schmölders, Claudia. 'Das Buch als Pathosformel: Zur Gefühlsgeschichte der Bibliothek'. *Merkur* 676 (2005): 692–703.

Socìetas Raffaello Sanzio. 'Mitobiografia'. In *XXXII Festival Internazionale del Teatro*, 188–90. Venezia: La Biennale di Venezia, 1984.

Socìetas Raffaello Sanzio. 'BR.#04, KunstenFESTIVALdesArts, Brussels, May 2003'. In *The Theatre of Societas Raffaello Sanzio*, edited by Claudia Castellucci, Romeo Castellucci, Chiara Guidi, Joe Kelleher and Nicholas Ridout, 90–2. Abingdon and New York: Routledge, 2007.

Socìetas Raffaello Sanzio. 'Oratoria n. 2: Raptus'. In *Nuove Sensibilità Teatrali, Rassegna di spettacoli*, edited by Carlo Infante. Rome: Comuna di Roma. Assessorato alla Cultura-Spaziozero, Senzorbita, 1984.

Tondelli, Pier Vittorio. *Un weekend postmoderno. Cronache dagli anni ottanta*. Milan: Bompiani, 1990.

Übersfeld, Anne. *Lire le théâtre*. Paris: Éditions Sociales, 1978.

Van Den Dries, Luk. 'The Sublime Body'. In *Bodycheck: Relocating the Body in Contemporary Art*, edited by Luk Van Den Dries et al., 70–95. Amsterdam: Rodopi, 2002.

Vernois, Paul. *L'onirisme et l'insolite dans le théâtre français contemporain*. Paris: Klincksieck, 1974.

Vernant, Jean-Pierre and Pierre Vidal-Naquet. *Mythe et tragédie en Grèce ancienne*. Paris: Maspéro, 1979.

Vidal-Naquet, Pierre. *Le Miroir brisé. Tragédie athénienne et politique*. Paris: Les belles lettres, 2002.

Warburg, Aby. *Der Bilderatlas Mnemosyne. Gesammelte Schriften II.1*. Edited by Martin Warnke. Berlin: Akademie Verlag, 2003.

Wiles, David. *Mask and Performance in Greek Tragedy. From Ancient Festival to Modern Experimentation*. Cambridge: Cambridge University Press, 2007.

Jan Fabre

Artaud, Antonin. *Collected Works*, vol. IV. Translated by Victor Corti. London: John Calder, 1999.

Artaud, Antonin. *Pour en finir avec je jugement de dieu*. Recording for French radio, ORTF, 1947.

Bataille, Georges. *The Tears of Eros*. Translated by Peter Connor. San Francisco: City Lights Books, 1989.

Baudrillard, Jean. 'The Body, or the Mass Grave of Signs'. In *Symbolic Exchange and Death*, translated by Iain Hamilton Grant, rev. edn, 122–45. London: SAGE, 2017.

Benjamin, Walter. 'On the Concept of History'. In *Selected Writings*, vol. 4, edited by Howard Eiland and Michael W. Jennings, translated by Edmund Jephcott et al, 389–400. Cambridge MA: Harvard University Press, 2003.

Brecht, Bertolt. 'Theatre as Sport'. In *Brecht on Theatre*, edited by Marc Silberman, Steve Giles and Tom Kuhn, 3rd edn, 20–1. London: Bloomsbury Methuen Drama, 2015.

Brouwers, Toon. *Antwerpen theaterstad. Aspecten van het theaterleven in Antwerpen in de tweede helft van de twintigste eeuw*. Tielt: Lannoo, 2015.

Carlson, Marvin. *Performance: A Critical Introduction*, 2nd edn. Abingdon and New York: Routledge, 2004.

Cassiers, Edith et al. 'Physiological Performing Exercises by Jan Fabre: An Additional Training Method for Performers'. *Theatre, Dance and Performance Training* 6, no. 3 (2015): 273–90.

Cassiers, Edith et al. 'Redrawing Bodily Boundaries. A Look into the Creation Process of Jan Fabre'. In *Aesthetics and Ideology in Contemporary Literature and Drama*, edited by Madelena Gonzalez and René Agostini, 297–320. Newcastle-upon-Tyne: Cambridge Scholars Publishing, 2015.

Coucke, Jo. 'Jan Fabre's Blue Blood'. In *Jan Fabre. The Years of the Hour Blue: Drawings and Sculptures, 1977–1992*, edited by Joke De Vos and Jan Fabre, 105–9. Milan: Silvana Editoriale, 2012.

Craig, Edward Gordon. 'The Artists of the Theatre of the Future'. In *On the Art of the Theatre*, edited by Franc Chamberlain, 1–26. Abingdon and New York: Routledge, 2009.

de Greef, Hugo and Jan Hoet. *Gesprekken met Jan Fabre*. Leuven: Kritak, 1993.

Drouhet, Geneviève. 'Je suis sang. Transgression des interdits et profanation'. *Alternatives Théâtrales*, no. 85–86 (2005): 90–1.

Duchamp, Marcel. 'Interview by Richard Hamilton in London and George Heard Hamilton in New York'. *Audio Arts Magazine* 2, no. 4 (1976).

Fabre, Jan. *C'est du théâtre comme c'était à espérer et à prévoir/This is Theatre as it was to be Expected and Foreseen*. Paris: L'Arche, 2009.

Fabre, Jan. *De keizer van het verlies in Geschiedenis van de tranen en andere teksten*. Antwerp: Meulenhoff/Manteau, 2005.

Fabre, Jan. 'Het is theater zoals te verwachten en te voorzien was'. *Aktualiteiten BASTT* 10 (1983).

Fabre, Jan. *Le pouvoir des folies théâtrales/The Power of Theatrical Madness*. Paris: L'Arche, 2009.

Fabre, Jan. *Nachtboek 1978–1984*. Antwerp: De Bezige Bij, 2011.

Fabre, Jan. *Théâtre écrit avec un 'k' est un matou flamand/Theatre with a K is a Tomcat*. Paris: L'Arche, 2009.

Fabre, Jan. 'S'entraîner à disparaître. Entretien'. *Communications* 1, no. 92 (2013): 263–75.

Fabre, Jan. *De dienaar van de schoonheid*. Antwerpen: Meulenhoff/ Manteau, 2010.

Fischer-Lichte, Erika. *The Transformative Power of Performance: A New Aesthetics*. Translated by Saskya Iris Jain. Abingdon and New York: Routledge, 2008.

Foucault, Michel. *Discipline and Punish: The Birth of the Prison*. London: Allen Lane, 1977.

Gilpin, Heidi. 'Symmetry and Abandonment'. In *Jan Fabre: Texts on his Theatrework*, edited by Sigrid Bousset, 163–76. Brussels: Kaaitheater, 1993.

Goldberg, Roselee. *Performance Art: From Futurism to the Present*, 3rd edn. London: Thames and Hudson, 2011.

Goldberg, Roselee. *Performance: Live Art since the 60s*. London: Thames and Hudson, 1998.

Hasegawa, Yuko. 'Fabre, the Non-Existing Knight of the 21st Century: The Most Western but at the Same Time Most Non-western Personality'. In *Homo Faber*, edited by Giacinto De Pietrantonio and Jan Fabre, 96–121. Bruges: Mercatorfonds, 2006.

Hegel, Georg W.F. *Phenomenology of Spirit*. Translated by A.V. Miller. Oxford: Oxford University Press, 1977.

Hendrickx, Sébastien. 'Regime Art'. *Etcetera: Tijdschrift voor Podiumkunsten*, September 2016.

Hertmans, Stefan. *Engel van de metamorfose. Over het werk van Jan Fabre*. Amsterdam: Meulenhoff, 2002.

Hopkins, David. '"Art" and "Life" and … Death'. In *Neo-Avant-Garde*, edited by David Hopkins, 19–36. Amsterdam and New York: Rodopi, 2006.

Hrvatin, Emil. *Herhaling, waanzin, discipline. Het theaterwerk van Jan Fabre*. Amsterdam: International Theatre and Film Books, 1994.

Hrvatin, Emil. 'Het dispositief van Fabres performances'. In *Homo Faber*, edited by Giacinto De Pietrantonio and Jan Fabre, 173–7. Bruges: Mercatorfonds, 2006.

Hrvatin, Emil. *La Discipline du chaos, le chaos de la discipline*. Seine Saint-Denis: Armand Collin, 1994.

Hrvatin, Emil. *Ponavljanje, Norost, Disciplina: Celostna Umetnina Fabre*. Ljubljana: Moderna galerija Ljubljana, 1993.

Lehmann, Hans-Thies. *Postdramatic Theatre*. Translated by Karen Jürs-Munby. Abingdon and New York: Routledge, 2006.

Lehmann, Hans-Thies. '*Wenn Wut zur Form gerinnt*' (When Rage Coagulates into Form …). In *Jan Fabre: Texts on His Theatre-work*, edited by Sigrid Bousset, 90–103 and 133–42. Brussels: Kaaitheater, 1993.

Mattenklott, Gert. 'Ich bin durchtränkt mit meiner Widerspiegelung. Versuch über Jan Fabre'. In *Jan Fabre. Texte zum Werk*, edited by Eckhard Schneider, 17–22. Hanover: Kunstverein Hannover, 1992.

Mattenklott, Gert. 'Identity or Similarity? A Motif in Jan Fabre's Drama'. In *Jan Fabre: Texts on his Theatre-work*, edited by Sigrid Bousset, 57–65. Brussels: Kaaitheater, 1993.

Müller, Heiner. 'Brief an Erich Wonder'. In *Raum-Szenen/Szenen-Raum*, edited by Erich Wonder, 72–3. Stuttgart: Hatje Verlag, 1986.

Müller, Heiner. 'Mülheim Address'. In *Explosion of a Memory: Writings*, edited by Carl Weber, 89–92. New York: PAJ Publications, 1989.

Nietzsche, Friedrich. *The Birth of Tragedy out of the Spirit of Music*. Translated by Walter Kaufman. New York: Vintage, 1967.

Ramat, Christine. 'L'esthétique grotesque de Jan Fabre'. In *Jan Fabre: Esthétique du paradoxe*, edited by Marianne Beauviche, Luk Van Den Dries and Lydie Toran, 129–42. Avignon: L'Harmattan, 2013.

Schwan, Alexander. 'Calligraphies du corps: la danse comme fantasme incarné de l'écriture'. In *Jan Fabre. Esthétique du paradoxe*, edited by Marianne Beauviche, Luk Van Den Dries and Lydie Toran, 69–77. Avignon: L'Harmattan, 2013.

Van Bellegem, Kurt. 'Hier woont en werkt Jan Fabre'. In *Mythische sporen in de hedendaagse kunst*, edited by Claire Van Damme and Franciska Vandepitte, 123–38. Ghent: Academia Press, 1996.

Van den Dries, Luk. *Corpus Jan Fabre. Observations of a Creative Process*. Ghent: Imschoot, 2006.

Van den Dries, Luk. 'The Flemish Theatre in the Eighties: Precipitations of an History of Influence'. *Documenta* 2, no. 3 (2009): 108–29.

Van den Dries, Luk. *Het geopende lichaam*. Antwerp: De Bezige Bij, 2014.

Varopoulou, Eleni. 'L'âme et le corps: le baroque insolite de Jan Fabre'. *Alternatives Théâtrales*, no. 85–86 (2005): 96.

Verschaffel, Bart. 'De dieren zullen het theater redden! De eerste theatervoorstellingen van Jan Fabre (1980–1984)'. *Etcetera* 126 (2011).

Ward, Frazen. *No Innocent Bystanders Performance Art and Audience*. Hanover, NH: Dartmouth College Press, 2012, 52–7.

Wesemann, Arnd. *Regie im Theater, Jan Fabre: Regie im Theater*. Frankfurt/M: Fischer-Taschenbuchverlag, 1994.

INDEX

Note: Page references with letter 'n' followed by locators denote note numbers.